MULTICULTURAL E[

JAMES A. BANKS, Series Editor

(continued)

Culturally and Socially Responsible Assessment

Theory, Research, and Practice

Catherine Taylor
with Susan B. Nolen

TEACHERS COLLEGE PRESS

TEACHERS COLLEGE | COLUMBIA UNIVERSITY
NEW YORK AND LONDON

Published by Teachers College Press® 1234 Amsterdam Avenue, New York, NY 10027

Copyright © 2022 by Teachers College, Columbia University

Front cover photo by insta_photos, Shutterstock.

Library of Congress Cataloging-in-Publication Data is available at loc.gov

ISBN 978-0-8077-6688-0 (paper)
ISBN 978–0-8077–6689-7 (hardcover)
ISBN 978–0-8077-8099-2 (ebook)

Printed on acid-free paper
Manufactured in the United States of America

Contents

Series Foreword

In this informative, engaging, and illuminating book, Taylor and Nolen describe and illustrate ways in which teacher-made and standardized tests and assessments contribute to racial, gender, and social class stratification and inequality. Taylor writes, "The dominance of standardized testing has supported the marginalization and oppression of students from diverse cultural and social backgrounds for a century" (p. 51). Assessment practices that contribute to the marginalization of students from diverse groups include standardized tests that focus on White middle-class culture and exclude other cultures, as well as teachers' implicit biases about and low expectations for students of color. These practices often result in tracking and ability groups that stigmatize marginalized students, special education classes that enroll high percentages of males and students of color, and bias in assessment tools and processes. This edifying, copiously researched, and practical book describes how test-makers and classroom teachers can create culturally responsive and valid assessments that provide equal learning and measurement opportunities for students from diverse racial, ethnic, cultural, and linguistic groups.

Taylor and Nolen describe how teacher opinions about the academic abilities and knowledge of students and the performance of students on standardized tests influence their academic life in significant ways. They cite research that indicates the complex and nuanced relationship of communities of practice, assessment, grades, and school dropouts. The accelerated dropout rates among African American males is related to low grades, weak scores on standardized assessments, and the academic problems they experience beginning in primary school (Howard, 2014). Many students of color and low-income students are denied admission to schools, colleges, and universities because they perform poorly on standardized tests that contain items and vocabulary from White middle-class culture that they have not had opportunities to learn. During the 1960s, some African American youths who later became eminent scholars and researchers were denied admission to prestigious colleges and universities because of their poor performance on standardized tests such as the Miller Analogies Test, which contained vocabulary and cultural allusions they had never encountered growing up in rural communities in the South or urban communities in northern cities.

The authors cite research that illustrates how implicit bias among teachers has a powerful influence on the academic trajectories and experiences of students from diverse racial, ethnic, and cultural groups. When Kenneth B. Clark, the eminent African American psychologist, was in the 9th grade, his White guidance counselor told him that he should attend a vocational rather than an academic high school. Clark's mother angrily rejected the counselor's advice and insisted that Clark attend an academic high school (Clark, 1993). Michelle Obama had an experience similar to Clark's when she was a student at Whitney M. Young High School in Chicago. When Obama (2018) expressed an interest in attending Princeton University, a college counselor told her that she wasn't "Princeton material." Obama had a successful academic experience at Princeton and later graduated from Harvard Law School. Obama did not internalize the counselor's advice and was determined to defy and resist it.

It is important to implement culturally responsive and sustaining assessment in U.S. schools in order to structure testing and evaluations that provide equal educational opportunities for the increasing population of students from diverse racial, ethnic, cultural, and linguistic groups in U.S. schools. American classrooms are experiencing the largest influx of immigrant students since the beginning of the 20th century. Approximately 12.6 million new immigrants—documented and undocumented—settled in the United States in the years from 2000 to 2016 (Zong et al., 2018). Less than 10% came from nations in Europe. Most came from Mexico, nations in South Asia, East Asia, Latin America, the Caribbean, and Central America. Although African immigrants make up a small part of the U.S. immigrant population (2,060 in 2015), they increased by 41% from 2000 to 2013 (Anderson, 2017). In 2018, the largest number of immigrants to the United States came from China (149,000 people), India (129,000), Mexico (120,000), and the Philippines (46,000). Since 2009, in most years more Asian immigrants have come to the United States than Hispanic immigrants (Budiman, 2020). The influence of an increasingly diverse population on U.S. schools, colleges, and universities is and will continue to be enormous.

The increasing diversity of the school population reflects the growing racial and ethnic diversity of the U.S. population. The 2020 Census indicates that the White population remained the largest race or ethnic group in the United States, although it was the only population that decreased (for the first time in U.S. history) by 8.6% from 2010 to 2020. The multiracial population increased 276% (from 9 million in 2010 to 33.8 million in 2020). The Hispanic population increased by 23%; the Asian by 36%; and the Black by 6%. Almost one in four Americans now identify as either Hispanic or Asian (Tavernise & Beveloff, 2021; U.S. Census, 2021).

Schools in the United States are more diverse today than they have been since the early 1900s, when a multitude of immigrants entered the United States from Southern, Central, and Eastern Europe (C. A. M. Banks,

2005). In 2017, the National Center for Education Statistics estimated that students from ethnic minority groups made up more than 52% of the students in prekindergarten through 12th grade in U.S. public schools, an increase from 39.2% in 2001. Latinxs made up 25% of the children in the United States in 2017; African Americans were 15%, Asian and Pacific Island children were 6%, and American Indians were 1% (Annie E. Casey Foundation, 2019).

Language and religious diversity are also increasing in the U.S. student population. A Center for Migration Studies publication estimated that 21.6% of Americans aged 5 and older (65.5 million) spoke a language other than English at home in 2016 (Camarota & Ziegler, 2017). This percentage has doubled since 1990, and almost tripled since 1980. The significant number of immigrants from nations such as India and China has also greatly increased religious diversity in the United States. Harvard professor Diana L. Eck (2001) called the United States the "most religiously diverse nation on earth" (p. 4). Islam is now the fastest growing religion in the United States, as well as in several European nations such as France, the United Kingdom, and the Netherlands (Banks, 2009; O'Brien, 2016).

The major purpose of the Multicultural Education Series is to provide preservice educators, practicing educators, graduate students, scholars, and policymakers with an interrelated and comprehensive set of books that summarizes and analyzes important research, theory, and practice related to the education of ethnic, racial, cultural, and linguistic groups in the United States and the education of mainstream students about diversity. The dimensions of multicultural education, developed by Banks and described in the *Handbook of Research on Multicultural Education* (Banks, 2004), *The Routledge International Companion to Multicultural Education* (Banks, 2009), and in the *Encyclopedia of Diversity in Education* (Banks, 2012), provide the conceptual framework for the development of the publications in the series. The dimensions are content integration, the knowledge construction process, prejudice reduction, equity pedagogy, and an empowering institutional culture and social structure. The books in the Multicultural Education Series provide research, theoretical, and practical knowledge about the behaviors and learning characteristics of students of color (Conchas & Vigil, 2012; Lee, 2007), language minority students (Gándara & Hopkins, 2010; Valdés, 2001; Valdés al., 2011), low-income students (Cookson, 2013; Gorski, 2018), multiracial youth (Joseph & Briscoe-Smith, 2021; Mahiri, 2017), and other minoritized population groups, such as students who speak different varieties of English (Charity Hudley & Mallinson, 2011), and LGBTQ+ youth (Mayo, 2022).

This trenchant, meticulously researched, and useful book describes how, for nearly a century, the "teach, test, and move on" mentality has dominated testing and assessment in U.S. schools. As stated in this book's preface, this "factory model of schooling, supported (and driven) by standardized testing, has validated the dominant culture and ignored or implicitly devalued" the cultures and experiences of students from diverse racial, ethnic, cultural, and linguistic groups. This book, using robust theoretical insights and empirical findings, describes how test developers and teachers can transform assessment in the nation's schools and classrooms and make it culturally responsive so that it will facilitate equitable learning and achievement for students from diverse groups. The theoretical parts of this book are enriched by the practical suggestions for action that are contained in its well-conceptualized and designed appendices. I hope this book will attain the significant influence and readership among test developers and classroom teachers that it richly deserves.

—James A. Banks

REFERENCES

Anderson, M. (2017, February 14). *African immigrant population in the U.S. steadily climbs.* Pew Research Center. https://www.pewresearch.org/fact-tank/2017/02/14/african-immigrant-population-in-u-s-steadily-climbs/

Annie E. Casey Foundation. (2019). *2019 kids count data book: State trends in child well-being.* https://www.aecf.org/resources/2019-kids-count-data-book

Banks, C. A. M. (2005). *Improving multicultural education: Lessons from the intergroup education movement.* Teachers College Press.

Banks, J. A. (2004). Multicultural education: Historical development, dimensions, and practice. In J. A. Banks & C. A. M. Banks (Eds.), *Handbook of research on multicultural education* (pp. 3–29). Jossey-Bass.

Banks, J. A. (Ed.). (2009). *The Routledge international companion to multicultural education.* Routledge.

Banks, J. A. (2012). Multicultural education: Dimensions of. In J. A. Banks (Ed.), *Encyclopedia of diversity in education* (Vol. 3, pp. 1538–1547). SAGE.

Budiman, A. (2020, August 20). *Key findings about U.S. immigrants.* Pew Research Center. https://www.pewresearch.org/fact-tank/2020/08/20/key-findings-about-u-s-immigrants/

Camarota, S. A., & Ziegler, K. (2017, October 24). *65.5 million U.S. residents spoke a foreign language at home in 2016.* Center for Immigration Studies. https://cis.org/Report/655-Million-US-Residents-Spoke-Foreign-Language-Home-2016

Charity Hudley, A. H., & Mallinson, C. (2011). *Understanding language variation in U. S. schools.* Teachers College Press.

Clark, K. B. (1993). Racial progress and retreat: A personal memoir. In H. Hill & J. E. Jones Jr. (Eds.), *Race in America: The struggle for equality* (pp. 3–18). University of Wisconsin Press.

Conchas, G. Q., & Vigil, J. D. (2012). *Streetsmart schoolsmart: Urban poverty and the education of adolescent boys.* Teachers College Press.

Cookson, P. W., Jr. (2013). *Class rules: Exposing inequality in American high schools.* Teachers College Press.

Eck, D. L. (2001). *A new religious America: How a "Christian country" has become the world's most religiously diverse nation.* HarperSanFrancisco.

Gándara, P., & Hopkins, M. (Eds.). (2010). *Forbidden language: English language learners and restrictive language policies.* Teachers College Press.

Gorski, P. C. (2018). *Reaching and teaching students in poverty: Strategies for erasing the opportunity gap* (2nd ed.). Teachers College Press.

Howard, T. C. (2014). *Black male(d): Peril and promise in the education of African American males.* Teachers College Press.

Joseph, R. L., & Briscoe-Smith, A. (2021). *Generation mixed goes to school: Radically listening to multiracial kids.* Teachers College Press.

Lee, C. D. (2007). *Culture, literacy, and learning: Taking bloom in the midst of the whirlwind.* Teachers College Press.

Mahiri, J. (2017). *Deconstructing race: Multicultural education beyond the color-bind.* Teachers College Press.

Mayo, C. (2022). *LGBTQ youth and education: Policies and practices* (2nd ed.). Teachers College Press.

National Center for Education Statistics. (2017). *Enrollment and percentage distribution of enrollment in public elementary and secondary schools, by race/ethnicity and region: Selected years, fall 1995 through fall 2025.* https://nces.ed.gov/programs/digest/d15/tables/dt15_203.50.asp

Obama, M. (2018). *Becoming.* Crown.

O'Brien, P. (2016). *The Muslim question in Europe: Political controversies and public philosophies.* Temple University Press.

Steele, D. M. (2012). Identity-safe environments, creating. In J. A. Banks (Ed.), *Encyclopedia of diversity in education* (Vol. 2, pp. 1125–1128). SAGE.

Steele, D. M., & Cohn-Vargas, B. (2013). *Identity safe classrooms: Places to belong and learn.* Corwin.

Tavernise, S., & Beveloff, R. (2021, August 13). Census shows sharply growing numbers of Hispanic, Asian, and multicultural Americans. *The New York Times.* https://www.nytimes.com/2021/08/12/us/us-census-population-growth-diversity.html

U.S. Census. (2021). *Ethnicity measures reveal U. S. population is much more multiracial.* https://www.census.gov/library/stories/2021/08/improved-race-ethnicity-measures-reveal-united-states-population-much-more-multiracial.html

Valdés, G. (2001). *Learning and not learning English: Latino students in American schools.* Teachers College Press.

Valdés, G., Capitelli, S., & Alvarez, L. (2011). *Latino children learning English: Steps in the journey.* Teachers College Press.

Zong, J., Batalova, J., & Hallock, J. (2018, February 11). *Frequently requested statistics on immigrants and immigration in the United States.* Migration Policy Institute. https://www.migrationpolicy.org/article/frequently-requested-statistics-immigrants-and-immigration-united-states#Demographic

Preface

In this book, I bring my research and the research of others to bear on a problem that affects the work of all educators—the degree to which traditional methods of assessment, in the classroom and at district and state levels, undermine the capacity of schools to serve students with diverse cultural and social backgrounds and identities.

Effective classroom assessment is student centered. It helps students understand what they are to learn so they can take the next steps in their learning. For example, writers' workshops use feedback and opportunities for revision to help students become more effective writers. Culturally and socially responsible classroom assessment goes a step further by making sure the assessment practices honor students for who they are and integrate what they bring to the learning experience. If education is to serve all students, transformation to effective, culturally and socially responsible classroom assessment practices must begin in classrooms and schools.

I once thought that standardized testing programs could help improve education for all students. However, between destructive testing policies and entrenched testing methodologies, where generating scores is more important than providing useful information, I no longer think it is possible for large-scale tests to serve the best interests of the public—much less the interests of children and their teachers.

Standardized testing dominates our thinking about the purpose of schooling, what counts as knowledge, and how teachers assess and grade in the classroom. The factory model of schooling, supported (and driven) by standardized testing, has validated the dominant culture and ignored or implicitly devalued the lived experiences, literacy, language, culture, values, and knowledge of students with diverse social and cultural identities. For too long, the primary function of educational assessment has been to label and track students—to reward those who possess the experiences, knowledge, and values of the dominant culture and to marginalize those who don't.

Standardized testing emerged from the eugenics movement of the 19th century as an effort to discriminate between people who have the knowledge and skills valued by the dominant culture and those who do not. Early intelligence tests tested concepts and vocabulary likely to be known by people who have traveled, who know the difference between working-class and professional-class jobs, who have been exposed to literary texts written by Western authors, who live in homes where academic vocabulary is the norm. Early standardized achievement tests, built on the same models as intelligence tests, were designed to generate normal curves by including concepts and skills beyond students' grade levels—knowledge and skills that could only have been learned outside of school. Norm-referenced tests thereby reified a social order defined by people in power by privileging the knowledge and skills valued by middle- to upper middle-class White people.

For the better part of a century, classroom assessment practices have emulated standardized testing models. Teach, test, grade, move on. Rather than using assessment results to decide what to do next to help students learn, classroom assessments have served as punctuation marks along a trajectory of lessons, instructional units, and grading periods. Some students learn; some do not. Those who do not learn fall further and further behind.

Modern ideas about large-scale[1] achievement testing have moved beyond creating tests that discriminate to tests that are intended to find out if students have learned what educators and policymakers want them to learn (academic standards). Although the purpose of testing is supposed to have changed, methods of testing have not changed; nor have the consequences of large-scale testing programs. For the past 40 years, iterations of the Elementary and Secondary Education Act (e.g., No Child Left Behind) have led to a frenzied increase in testing that has further impacted classroom practices. Today, classroom instruction and assessment practices—particularly for students of color, low-income students, students with disabilities, English learners, and other marginalized students—are driven by efforts to raise large-scale test scores, at the expense of students' opportunities to learn how to use knowledge and skills in authentic ways. Despite overwhelming evidence that shows how classroom assessment can be used to support student learning, efforts to improve classroom-based assessment practices have been unsuccessful. If we are to ensure that assessment practices are appropriate for all students, change must begin in the classroom. Large-scale, standardized tests cannot provide fair and valid assessment of all students.

Susan Nolen and I acknowledge that, as White women, we have less direct, personal experience with the oppression that more than a century of standardized testing has caused for marginalized students. Yet, as teachers and as teacher educators, we have directly witnessed the effects of educational oppression on our own students and on students in schools where we place preservice teachers.

I began teaching in 1973 in an urban high school in the Midwest. Sixty percent of students at this high school were African American, and 40% were White. In those days, it was an apartheid school. Classes were divided into "Black classes" with one or two low-performing White students and "White classes" with one or two high-performing African American students. It didn't take long for me to realize that this school system failed to serve my students. The students were very bright; however, nearly all of the African American students were struggling readers and writers. The "teach, test, grade, move on" mentality was well entrenched in the system. Student learning was attributed to student ability rather than the structure of the system or the quality of teaching.

In this school district, high school students were required to do a writing assessment each year. When writing assessment day came along, my students looked at me with pain in their eyes. I just said, "You can do this. Give it a shot." Their writing may not have been good when it came to grammar, punctuation, and spelling, but their ideas were beautiful. Had there been writers workshops as there are today, with opportunities for feedback and revision, their work would have been very good, and they would have learned how to be better writers. I know there are thousands and thousands of students like them—dis-served by schools and oppressed by an educational system that was supposed to serve democracy.

As a teacher educator, my focus has been on helping teachers use assessment to support student learning. I have taught student-centered assessment practices intended to ensure fair and valid assessment of all students. As I did the research for this book, I came to understand how the more traditional assessment practices have contributed to cultural, social, and racial oppression. At this point in history, I no longer believe that knowing how to use student-centered assessment practices is sufficient to improve the educational trajectory for students with diverse cultural and social identities. Fair and valid assessment requires direct and purposeful action to make assessment relevant and responsive to the lived experiences of students.

In this book, we integrate our expertise in assessment, motivation, school cultures, and teacher education with the expertise of those who focus on issues of race, class, gender, culture, and other aspects of diversity in order to help educators understand what can be done to make assessment relevant to and supportive of students with diverse backgrounds.

I begin the book describing how validity theory can guide thinking about fair assessment of students with diverse cultural and social identities. I speak of validity, not as a technical term, but as a way to think about honest and appropriate assessment of student learning. The remaining chapters focus on the factors that can affect the validity of claims about student learning: sources of bias in assessment tools and processes, how principles of culturally relevant and culturally responsive pedagogy (Gay, 2010; Ladson-Billings, 1995a) can improve the appropriateness of assessments for diverse students, the role of student engagement in assessment performance, how communities of practice[2] (Lave & Wenger, 1991; Reeves & Gomm, 2015) influence teachers' assessment practices, and how local, state, and national education policies drive teaching and assessment practices. Throughout the book, I refer back to the concept of validity as it applies to bias, culturally responsive assessment, student engagement, and the contexts in which assessment takes place.

Hopefully, the ideas and research presented here can help educators see a way out of current assessment practices. Change is possible if educators work together to change the focus of assessment practices—moving away from systems dominated by narrowly defined academic standards and standardized tests to systems designed to support every student's learning and progress. Culturally and socially responsible assessment must help students achieve high expectations, understand how knowledge and skills learned in school are relevant to their own lives, and develop understanding of and appreciation for their own cultures and communities. To borrow from Howard and Rodriguez-Minkoff (2017), rethinking assessment at this point in history supports efforts to "move educational research, theory, and practice . . . in a distinctly different and transformative direction" (p. 4).

Acknowledgments

I am grateful to my friend and colleague, Susan Nolen, for taking my initial ideas for this book to a much better place. Susan read drafts of my chapters, and we wrote two chapters together. Her contributions to thinking about communities of practice and student engagement are referenced throughout the book.

I am grateful to those who challenge all of us to address issues of educational oppression based on race, class, culture, gender, sexual preference, disability, immigration status, and language proficiency. I am grateful to those who help us understand the power of multicultural education. I am especially grateful to the scholars who had a significant impact on my thinking as I wrote this book: Jamal Abedi, James Banks, Paul Black, Susan Brookhart, Linda Darling Hammond, Geneva Gay, Tyrone Howard, Gloria Ladson-Billings, Samuel Messick, Django Paris, Lorrie Shepard, Claude Steele, Richard Stiggins, and Dylan Wiliam, to name only a few.

I am grateful to my husband, Laurie, my daughters, Robin and Courtney, and my friends Betsy and David who have supported me through so much over the past few years and have cheered me on while writing this book.

Finally, I am grateful to all of my students at the high school where I began my teaching career. These students set the stage for my entire career as an educator.

I have learned a great deal while writing this book. I am grateful for the opportunity to write it.

CHAPTER 1

Theoretical Perspectives on Assessment in Diverse Classrooms

I frame the ideas in this book around the concept of validity—not as a technical term but as an idea about truth—how we can use assessment tools and practices to construct an accurate and honest narrative about students' achievement and how we can use assessment results to truly support student learning. In this chapter, I describe how validity theory can guide our thinking about fair assessment of students with diverse cultural and social identities[1] and how a focus on validity can change the way educators think about assessment in diverse educational contexts. I also describe the current status of classroom assessment practices and how they must change to ensure fair and valid assessment of student learning. Although the principles of fair and valid assessment described here are generally applied to large-scale tests, if we are to serve students with diverse cultural and social identities, high-quality assessment must be grounded in the classroom.

The remaining chapters focus on factors that can support or detract from the validity of scores on tests and other assessments, teachers' evaluations of students work, grades, and decisions about students. I provide research on sources of bias in assessment tools and processes and describe how applying principles of culturally responsive pedagogy (Gay, 2010; Ladson-Billings, 1995a) can improve the appropriateness of assessments for students with diverse identities. We describe the role of engagement in students' assessment performance, how lack of engagement can invalidate scores and grades, and how specific assessment practices can improve students' engagement in assessment events. We also present a situative perspective on assessments; how "communities of practice" (Lave & Wenger, 1991; Reeves & Gomm, 2015) influence teachers' assessment practices; and how local, state, and national education policies drive teaching and assessment practices. I end the book by providing strategies and resources educators can use to improve the validity of assessment practices for students with diverse cultural and social identities. Throughout the book, I refer back to the concept of validity as it applies to bias, student engagement, culturally responsible assessment, and the contexts in which assessment takes place.

DIVERSITY IN SCHOOLS

Schools in the United States, like schools in many other nations, are becoming increasingly diverse in terms of the racial, cultural, and personal identities of students. Given the degree of migration throughout the world, anthropologists (e.g., Vertovec, 2007) and linguists (e.g., Blommaert & Rampton, 2011) use the term *superdiversity* to describe the complex "socio-economic, cultural, religious, and linguistic diversity" emerging throughout the world (Arnaut et al., 2016, p. 2).

Recent U.S. Department of Education statistics show that more than 50% of public school students in U.S. public schools are students of color (National Center for Educational Statistics [NCES], 2020a). Fourteen percent of students receive special education services (Schaeffer, 2020), and at least 10% are classified as English language learners (NCES, 2020b). A 2016 survey of U.S. high school students by the Centers for Disease Control (CDC) found that approximately 8% identified themselves as gay, lesbian, or bisexual, and more than 2% were unsure of their sexual identity (Kann et al., 2016).

Students have multiple identities based on intersections of race, gender, home language, income, special needs, and other variables. This diversity has the potential to create rich instructional contexts for all students. It also presents challenges in making sure that assessments provide fair and unbiased opportunities for students to show what they know and can do in relation to learning goals. In recognition of how migration patterns have impacted schools and classrooms, Nortvedt et al. (2020) summarize the assessment challenge for teachers:

> At the classroom level, this increased complexity necessitates teacher knowledge and awareness of student backgrounds. Teachers must also be sensitive to how these factors might interact and how they might affect participation and learning and, thus, assessment situations and practices. (p. 9)

Given this complex context, we hope to help educators understand how to fairly and validly assess students with diverse cultural and social identities and how their assessment practices are influenced by socially constructed systems of meaning that must be negotiated as they work to create just and equitable educational contexts. One book cannot accomplish these lofty goals; however, we hope to encourage educators at all levels of the educational system to move away from using conventional assessment practices that provide little to no benefit to students and toward a situation where the primary purpose of classroom assessment is to support student learning.

WHAT IS ASSESSMENT?

The term *assessment* has many connotations in and outside of education. For this book, I define assessment as "systematically gathering, analyzing, and interpreting relevant information for a given purpose." In the literature about educational assessment and in everyday conversations, the term *assessment* may refer to a tool, a process, an event, or a judgment. *Assessment tools* are the assignments given to students (e.g., tests, homework, directions for projects, writing prompts). *Assessment processes* are the processes educators use to develop assessment tools, to evaluate students' work and progress, to provide feedback, and to aggregate scores and grades from various tasks into end-of-term or end-of-course reports. *Assessment events* are the formal and semiformal occasions when students engage with assessment tasks, such as taking a test, doing a self-evaluation, working on a group project, and so forth.

Assessment is not limited to testing, evaluation, or grading. Research has shown that teachers can spend from 33% to 50% of their workday engaged in assessment-related activities—establishing learning goals, developing or selecting a range of assessment tools, conducting informal observations of students during instruction, reviewing students' work, and generating subject area or course grades (Stiggins & Conklin, 1992). Teachers may use observational assessment to adjust instruction during a lesson, or they may use the results of a test or quiz to evaluate the success of their instruction. Assessment may involve giving feedback on an assignment before returning it to students for their revisions or interviewing students about their thinking as they completed assignments. In this book, I do not deal with assessment as judgment, largely because the term *judgment* carries with it a notion of finality. Learning never stops; therefore, any conclusions drawn about students are likely to be based on insufficient information and could result in harm (such as denying students an opportunity to take certain high school courses based on judgments about their capacity to learn).

VALIDITY THEORY AND FAIR ASSESSMENT

Educators hear the terms *validity* and *reliability* tossed about frequently with little attention to their meaning (e.g., "The test is reliable and valid") and often by people who have little understanding of what these terms mean. Here, I hope to explain how the principles of validity theory can help teachers improve assessments in general and improve the appropriateness of classroom assessment tools and processes for students with diverse cultural and social identities. Validity theory is focused on both the meaning and purpose of assessment *results*; in other words, do scores and grades mean what we say they mean, and can scores and grades be used for their intended purposes (Kane, 2006, 2012; Messick, 1989a, 1989b, 1990, 1994a, 1994b; Shepard, 2013; Taylor, 2014)?

In its most formal sense, validity theory is a theory about how we can evaluate whether the claims we make about student learning are trustworthy. For example, per current validity theory, a score of 80% on an assignment is a claim that students have learned 80% of what teachers wanted them to learn. A semester grade of F is a claim that students have failed to learn what teachers wanted them to learn over the course of a semester. The validity of claims such as these are questionable when a score of 80% is given to an assignment that meets all expectations but is 2 days late or when a grade of F is due to missing homework rather than failing performance in class on projects or tests. How valid are claims about student learning when scores and grades incorporate elements that may penalize students because of factors over which they have little control? For example, students who are homeless, who must work to help support the family or must care for younger siblings after school may achieve important learning goals but have difficulty getting support at home or turning in homework on time.

Validity theory has developed over many generations, beginning with philosophies of science in the 1600s through guidelines for the methods used to validate test scores, grades, and other forms of evaluation today (Kane, 2006; Messick, 1989b; Taylor 2014). A dictionary definition of *valid* will include words like "true," "logically sound," or "fact based." Validity theory guides common strategies for testing and validating theories in physics, arguments in law, and scores from large-scale tests.

Early discussions of validity in educational testing described the "validity of tests" as if validity was a property of assessment tools themselves. At one time, all that was needed to claim an achievement test score was valid was to have educators review test items, writing prompts, and task directions and agree that they were targeting academic standards. This misuse of the term *validity* is still common today—particularly among school administrators, policymakers, and representatives of testing companies.

The idea of validity as a property of assessment tools does not take into account how *students interpret* test items and directions for assignments; it does not take into account how their *responses are evaluated*. The validity of assessment *results* depends on whether

- students comprehend test items or directions for assignments and interpret items or task directions as intended;
- students engage with assessment tasks;
- factors in assessment tools prevent students from showing their knowledge and skills;
- students' work is evaluated for demonstration of the targeted knowledge and skills rather than features of the work unrelated to the learning goals (e.g., evaluating spelling when the learning goal is

conceptual understanding of an economic or geographic concept) or characteristics of students themselves (e.g., implicit biases based on race, gender, language proficiency, and so forth).

The principles of validity theory demand that, for any claim made about student learning (such a grade of C on a mathematics test), the assessor has evidence that items and tasks from the assessment tool actually draw out students' learning related to the targeted learning goals—evidence we can only get from looking at students' work, asking students to explain their choices, and, sometimes, talking directly to students about how they interpreted items, tasks, and directions for assignments (Messick, 1989a). In addition, any claims we make about the meaning of students' scores or grades require evidence about how students' work was evaluated. Students' scores on a classroom performance or project are a combination of the quality of their work and the quality of the judgment made by a teacher or other evaluator.

Bias is a central consideration for fair and valid assessment. Students' language proficiency and the clarity of teachers impact students' comprehension of test items and directions for assignments. Students' life experiences, prior knowledge, language proficiency, and cultural perspectives impact their comprehension and interpretation of reading passages, science or mathematics problems, test items, and directions for assignments. Even if an assessment tool *appears* to assess whether students have learned important concepts and/or skills, students' scores on tests and other assignments may not represent what they actually learned. Teachers' a priori expectations for students and teachers' personal biases can impact their evaluation of student work (Bennett et al., 1993; Copur-Gencturk et al., 2019; Ferguson, 2003). Since the 1980s, assessment specialists have come to believe that we cannot make claims about the validity of assessment results unless we focus on students' interpretations and responses and how students' work is evaluated by others (Brennan, 2013; Kane, 2006, 2012; Messick, 1989a, 1989b, 1990, 1994a, 1994b, 1995). In short, bias occurs when factors unrelated to the learning goals influence students' performances and/or teachers' evaluations of student work (Copur-Gencturk et al., 2019; Downing, 2002; Taylor & Lee, 2011, 2012).

Evaluating the validity of assessment results for their intended meanings and purposes requires knowing the intended meanings and purposes: what information assessments are intended to provide and how results are intended to be used. In a classroom where assessment tools are used only as punctuation marks along a trajectory of lessons, units, and grading periods and to generate points for a grade book, it is difficult to make valid claims about what students have learned. It is also difficult to use assessment results for any purpose other than to populate a gradebook. In a large-scale testing context, where tests generate scores that have little informational value, it is hard to make claims about score meaning. Only when educators clearly define learning goals and are certain that student performance represents their achievement of those goals can they make claims about the meaning of grades in school or scores on large-scale tests.

Learning Goals and Validity

Clarity about what teachers want students to learn (learning goals)—whether developed by a state, a teacher, or students themselves—is essential for making valid claims about student learning. Too often, teachers move through the lessons in a textbook or basal without thinking about learning goals. The primary goal of instruction is to complete the lessons. If teachers have clear ideas about their learning goals, they are more likely to select lessons that target the learning goals, teach to the learning goals, assess students' achievement of the learning goals, and provide feedback about students' progress toward achieving the learning goals. They also have a better chance of making sure that students understand test items, task directions, and feedback.

Once teachers are clear about learning goals, they can evaluate whether each and every assessment tool draws out valued knowledge and skills and is appropriate for students. They can observe students' work to evaluate whether assessment tools or processes benefit some students more than others. Teachers can use the principles of validity theory to help them determine whether their own assessments and published classroom assessments are appropriate for their students by asking themselves these validity-related questions:

1. Am I clear about what I want students to learn, and have I communicated that information to students?
2. Are the tasks I give to students (e.g., tests, projects, performances) asking students to demonstrate what I want them to learn?
3. Does student work suggest they are interpreting items, tasks or directions for assignments differently than I (or the publisher) had intended?
4. Are students clear about the expectations for their work so that they are able to show what they know and can do?[2]
5. Does an assessment tool ask students to demonstrate knowledge and skills I never actually taught?
6. Are the scoring rubrics related to the targeted learning standards (see Figure 1.1)?
7. Are there factors within the tasks or the assessment context that prevent students from showing me what they know and are able to do related to my learning goals (e.g., not giving ample time to complete an assignment, asking students to write a story about something they have never experienced)?

Figure 1.1. Scoring Rubric Factors That Affect the Validity of Scores

The alignment of scoring rubrics to targeted standards is a critically important validity issue. Students' scores are derived from scoring rubrics rather than the tasks themselves. Examples of misalignment include the following:

- *Missing the mark* (e.g., scoring only for accuracy of a final answer when the standard is focused on mathematical problem-solving strategies)
- *Inclusion of expectations or requirements students have not been taught* (e.g., telling students cite references for a paper without teaching them the expected style for citing references; expecting students to identify themes in an author's work without showing them how to look for themes; expecting students to "show their work" when solving problems without teaching students *how* to show their work—especially when solution processes can involve mental mathematics processes)
- *Inclusion of features students didn't know were expected* (e.g., scoring for effectiveness of a "visual aid" when visual aid was not included in the task directions)
- *Inclusion of factors unrelated to the targeted academic standard* (e.g., deducting points for spelling when the focus of a task is on reading comprehension)

8. Are there any factors in an item, task, or assignment that will prevent some of my students from comprehending the item or task directions (e.g., language complexity, unfamiliar vocabulary, unfamiliar context)?
9. Does an item or task ask students to engage in an activity that is culturally inappropriate such that they must violate their own cultural norms to respond?

Any of these factors can interfere with valid responses from and scores for students and detract from the validity of claims about students' learning. Answering these validity questions can help teachers focus on student learning of academic standards and classroom learning goals rather than on procedural aspects of assessment and grading. Alignment of instruction, assessment, and student performance with learning goals is the heart of validity.

Currently, each state and territory in the United States has its own academic standards (learning goals), typically developed by a state's educators through long adjudication processes. In some states, students, parents, business leaders, and community members also contribute to defining academic standards. State academic standards provide social consensus of what students are to know and be able to do as a result of instruction. Therefore, a fundamental responsibility for public school teachers is to ensure that instruction and assessment help students achieve state academic standards.

Trouble arises from two sources. First, there may be differences in how teachers interpret the meaning of academic standards. For example, a state's mathematics standards may include a standard for "mathematical problem solving." One teacher may focus on the word *solve* and give students worksheets of arithmetic tasks (e.g., multiplication of two-, three-, or four-digit numbers). Students' grades in this teacher's class will be based on *accuracy of computation results*. Another teacher may focus on the word *problem* and give students nonstandard (nontextbook) problems that require reasoning, a variety of problem-solving strategies, and several mathematical operations. Students' grades in the second teacher's class will be based on *how well students used their mathematical tools* (reasoning, problem solving, concepts, and operations) to develop a solution. Clearly, assessment *results* in these two classrooms will have different meanings even though both teachers believe they are teaching to the same academic standard. These two teachers will take different steps to make certain that students achieve. Clarity about the meaning and intent of academic standards is one area where communities of practice become critical in the success of students.

The second source of trouble occurs when policymakers enact laws and policies that define learning goals based on biased political agendas. For example, at the time of this writing, legislatures in several states[3] are attempting to ban the teaching of African American history or slavery in the United States. A lack of knowledge about African American history or slavery will likely impact students' understanding of other historical and current events such as the civil rights movement. When this is the case, grades from U.S. history classes are unlikely to allow for valid inferences about students' knowledge of U.S. history.

Educational stakeholders (parents/guardians, community members, policymakers, etc.) also interpret academic standards in many different ways. To provide useful narratives about students' learning, teachers must clearly articulate what students are supposed to learn, oftentimes by showing students, parents/guardians, colleagues, and school administrators the types of work students are expected to learn how to do. Meaning and purpose are related. Students, parents/guardians, and other stakeholders cannot act on assessment results unless they understand what the scores and grades mean.

In addition to state academic standards, teachers may expect students to learn many of the skills that are important to success in school and life beyond school such as diligence, timeliness, group-work skills, self-accountability, critical thinking skills, self-respect, and respect for others. Some educators believe that these important skills cannot be defined or assessed, yet even without clear definition, nonacademic expectations are incorporated into assessment and grading practices in classrooms every day (Brookhart et al., 2016; Guskey, 2002; McMillan, 2001; McMillan et al., 2002).

Many educators also want students to embrace knowledge and skills that will ultimately help them be productive and active citizens in our democracy (e.g., connecting content to local issues; civic participation). They may want students to develop understanding of the economic and social factors in our society that lead to racism, sexism, and other forms of discrimination.

Educators may want students to develop appreciation for skills, knowledge, and ways of thinking unique to the students' own cultures. These learning goals typically go beyond state academic standards but may be critical to students' abilities to navigate through their experiences in school and in life as adults.[4] If teachers want students to engage with their communities, develop an understanding of social justice, and achieve culturally sustaining learning goals, teachers (working with students) must define the goals, create opportunities for students to learn, and fairly assess students' learning related to these goals.[5]

Validity and Communication About Student Learning

Communication with students, parents/guardians, peers, and administrators about student achievement is an essential teaching responsibility. In order to support student learning, teachers must be able to present a clear narrative about what students have learned (in ways that are more useful than summary grades); teachers and students must be able to tell others what students were expected to learn and describe students' progress toward achieving the goals. A grade on a progress report or a report about missing assignments provides no information that parents/guardians and students can use to improve achievement in school.

At the end of the day, valid assessment provides an accurate and useful narrative about students' learning. Teachers can explain to students, parents/guardians, colleagues, and school administrators what a course grade means in terms of what students have actually learned and how well students have achieved specific learning goals. Unless teachers are clear about what they want students to learn, they will have difficulty with all these assessment-related activities. Without clarity about learning goals, teachers cannot do the following:

- Ensure that learning opportunities, assessment tools and processes, and grading practices are appropriate for students from diverse cultural and social backgrounds
- Help students evaluate their own learning and set personal learning goals for themselves
- Use the information they have about students to communicate a coherent and useful narrative about students' learning

THE STATE OF CLASSROOM ASSESSMENT PRACTICES

In considering the validity of classroom assessment for students from diverse cultural and social backgrounds, it is important to look at the overall picture of classroom assessment. Many of the factors that make assessment and grading unfair to students in general are exacerbated when students come to school with backgrounds, languages, and experiences different from that of their teachers or of the professionals who develop instructional and assessment materials.

Although teachers routinely assess students and provide grades or written reports about students' progress, we have long known that most teachers have little to no training on how to use assessment practices to gather valid information and to communicate with students and others about student learning (Stiggins, 1999, 2001a, 2005; Stiggins & Conklin, 1992). Some teacher preparation programs may provide opportunities to learn discipline-specific assessment practices (e.g., Gotwals & Birmingham, 2015; Windschitl et al., 2011); however, more generalizable understanding of effective classroom assessment practices is largely missing from teacher preparation programs (Walker, 2021). Given this lack of preparation, assessment and grading practices are strongly influenced by communities of practice, beginning with preservice field experiences (Nolen et al., 2011; Vass, 2013) and continuing throughout teachers' careers (Brookhart, 2011; Guskey, 2009, 2011; Nolen et al., 2011). In what follows, I briefly summarize how grading, classroom assessment tools, and large-scale testing affect the validity of claims educators make about students' learning.

Classroom Grades and Grading Practices

Grading is a practice that is fraught with validity problems due to typical grading conventions, grading policies mandated by school administrators, and/or policies agreed on by teachers within a school or department. Course or subject area grades represent an attempt to summarize, in a single letter or number, the achievements and behaviors of students over the course of a grading period. A grading policy such as 90–100% is an A, 80–89% is a B, and so forth is one of the mostly commonly used grading conventions in American schools (Brookhart et al., 2016). While grading conventions like this are widely accepted, they provide little information about *what* students have learned. As an analogy, it is as if an individual is saying, "I have filled 80% of this jar," but it does not tell others what is in the jar. Is the jar 80% full of sunflower seeds? Marbles? Water?

In addition to the vagueness of letter grades, research on teacher grading practices suggests there is great variability in what teachers include in summary grades (Brookhart et al., 2016; Cizek et al., 1995; Duncan & Noonan, 2007; Guskey, 2009; McMillan, 2001; McMillan et al., 2002; Stiggins et al., 1989). Most people outside of schools assume that grades reflect academic achievement; however, the majority of teachers include effort, participation, attendance, attitude, and/or other noncognitive factors in summary grades (Frary et al., 1993; Guskey, 2002; Liu, 2008; Llosa, 2008; McMillan, 2001; McMillan & Lawson, 2001; McMillan et al., 2002;

Russell & Austin, 2010; Sun & Cheng, 2013)—all of which can be affected by biases in teachers' observations and beliefs. For some teachers, more than half of summary grades are based on class participation and nonachievement factors (Russell & Austin, 2010).

Many schools require teachers to use grading software to summarize grades. This may lead teachers to turn grading decisions over to the software. However, grading software is not a panacea. Unless carefully programmed, the results from grading programs can significantly misrepresent student learning.[6] In most cases, only teachers (and possibly students) know what is included in grades.[7] Teachers rarely give students a grading policy that tells them what is included in a summary grade. This makes the communication value of grades essentially nonexistent.

> The simple truth is that a single number describing a student's performance in school is just as ineffectual and difficult to interpret as a single number describing someone's physical health. That number or grade combines diverse data, gathered through different means and measuring a variety of different attributes. As such, it's not informative, meaningful, helpful, or equitable. (Guskey, 2020, p. 2)

Despite their poor informational value, grades have powerful effects on students' motivation and self-esteem. For example, poor course grades and grade-point averages in middle and high school are highly correlated with disengagement (Poorthuis et al., 2015) and school dropout rates (Alexander et al., 2001; Allensworth et al., 2014; Barrington & Hendricks, 1989; Bowers, 2011; Bowers & Sprott, 2012).

Given that summary grades are unreliable and uninformative indicators of overall achievement, if teachers are going to ensure fair and valid assessment of students from diverse backgrounds, they must step away from summary grades as primary communication tools and be prepared to communicate more complete pictures of student performance to students, parents/guardians, and other stakeholders. Guskey (2020) recommends a "'dashboard' of information that meaningfully summaries the different aspects of student performance" (p. 40)—a practice that is more common in elementary school than secondary school. Providing an accurate narrative about student learning is far different from marking student work and assigning grades.[8]

Quality of Current Classroom Assessment Tools

Teachers assess students' learning in a variety of ways. Much research suggests that teachers primarily use published tests, quizzes, and homework assignments provided with instructional materials for their assessment tools (Frey & Schmitt, 2010; Frisbie et al., 1993; Madaus & Clarke, 2001;

Madaus et al., 1992). Yet, reliance on textbook assessments is problematic. Publishers pay little attention to the assessment tools included with instructional materials (Beck, 2009; Stiggins, 2001a). Beck (2009) described how assessment development for textbooks (including e-textbooks[9]) is subcontracted to item development companies[10] with little time allotted for the development work. Frisbee et al. (1993) found that published end-of-unit tests for elementary and middle school students were poorly aligned with instruction and with the learning objectives established for the units. Taylor (2009) found that end-of-unit tests from popular elementary mathematics and reading programs were typically of poor technical quality and were not well aligned with either instruction or learning goals.[11]

Although most publishers follow company guidelines for "bias-free publishing" (e.g., McGraw-Hill, 1983), these guidelines are primarily used to guide content development and the selection of primary documents and literature for textbooks. The assessment tools themselves do not receive scrutiny for potential bias. Hence, reliance on published assessment materials is no guarantee that teachers' assessments of their students will be fair and unbiased, nor that the assessment tools will be useful in determining whether students have achieved learning goals.

Research suggests that, when teachers perceive that published assessments will not serve their purposes, they develop their own assessments (Marso & Pigge, 1988). However, researchers have found a negative correlation between teachers' self-reported confidence in their own assessments and the evaluation of teacher-developed assessments by assessment specialists (Boothroyd et al., 1992; Oescher & Kirby, 1990). Problems with teachers' assessment tools are due, in part, to the fact that teachers receive little training on how to develop quality assessment tools (Stiggins, 1991, 2001a, 2002). In addition, teachers may have little time or content expertise for assessment development. Most secondary teachers must teach large numbers of students and multiple course sections. They may have to adapt instruction to the needs of students in different course sections, and they may be required to prepare for more than one course, leaving little time for thoughtfully developed assessment tools. Elementary teachers typically teach multiple subject areas and may lack the subject matter knowledge needed to develop classroom assessment tools for each subject.

Influence of Large-Scale (District, State, and National) Testing on Teacher Assessment Practices

Today, each state and territory in the United States has its own state-level assessment program anchored in the state's academic standards.[12] When states and territories set academic standards, groups of educators and other stakeholders establish aspirations and expectations for what students should know and be able to do based on their experiences in school. Most states' academic standards represent a desire for students to be able to do high-quality work that, from the perspective of those who write the standards, has value beyond school (e.g., analysis of complex text, research reports, scientific investigations, mathematical problem solving). To help educators understand the characteristics of high-quality work, those who write standards describe those characteristics in the form of specific descriptors or standards. Most states then hire testing companies to develop their state-level tests.

Assessment specialists working on state-level tests consider validity and reliability in every step of the assessment development and implementation process. They carefully craft large-scale tests, starting with a meticulous design for each test that is intended to ensure appropriate representation of the breadth of a state's standards. Specialists pay careful attention to every detail that affects whether the results of tests (test scores) are trustworthy (quality of test items, test layout, scoring rules, scoring processes, data collection, data analysis, generating total test scores, validity studies, and other supporting research). Assessment specialists attempt to make standardized tests fit for all students, regardless of their backgrounds.

Despite the thoughtfulness given to establishing academic standards and the care given to developing state-level tests, the very demands of large-scale tests make valid interpretation of results difficult if not impossible to accomplish. Most state-level assessments involve disconnected items that test discrete knowledge and skills. This form of testing can make test scores more reliable; however, a test of disconnected knowledge and skills limits the degree to which assessment scores generalize to the actual work standards are intended to represent. For example, testing students' knowledge of scientific practices does not tell us whether students can use those practices to authentically investigate scientific questions. Testing reading skills and strategies in discrete items does not tell us whether students can thoughtfully engage in a book club or critically evaluate the credibility of an author's claims on the Internet. In short, current methods of testing—whether in the classroom or on large-scale tests—are unlikely to provide valid information about students' learning of important knowledge and skills. Conventional methods of large-scale and classroom assessment fit well within a factory model of education where minimal testing time and rapid return of scores are more important than student learning.

Despite their limitations, as a nation, we have come to trust current methods of assessment and the technologies that deliver them. States use standardized tests to meet requirements for federal funding. Schools and districts use standardized interim tests to assess whether students are making adequate progress through the year. Textbook and e-textbook assessments typically have the look and feel of standardized, large-scale tests. Yet, the factors that have made these tests seem trustworthy—standardization of content, assessment method, and administration—limit their usefulness and detract from the validity of resulting scores for diverse populations of students.

For decades, large-scale tests have had oppressive impacts on classroom instructional and assessment practices—particularly for low-income and minority students. Research suggests that America's primary methods of assessment, whether online or on paper, work best for students who come from communities that share the values and experiences of the developers of instructional programs and standardized tests—most of whom represent the dominant White and middle- to upper middle-class culture. The assessment methodologies used in state and district standardized tests are known to discriminate against students from low-income families, students of color, new immigrants, English learners, and students with disabilities (Coon et al., 2002; Flowers et al., 2011; Madaus & Clarke, 2001; Madaus et al., 1992; McCarty, 2009; Newton et al., 2013; Taherbhai et al., 2012; Taylor & Lee, 2011, 2012).

Educators may complain that large-scale tests "don't test what we teach"; yet, in their own classrooms, teachers regularly emulate the assessment methods used in large-scale testing (Frey & Schmitt, 2010; Stiggins & Conklin, 1992). Some teachers feel pressure to teach and test their students in the same way as large-scale tests, hoping that it will prepare students for those tests (Croft et al., 2005; Haladyna et al., 1991; Nolen et al., 1989; Smith, 1991). Over time, regardless of the incongruity between methods of assessment and the intent of academic standards, educators adapt teaching to prepare students for large-scale tests (Davis & Martin, 2018; Lipman, 2004; Madaus, 1988; Madaus & Clark, 2001; Madaus et al., 1992; McCarty, 2009; Pedula et al., 2003).

> The current environment of high-stakes testing engendered by [No Child Left Behind] has caused many states and local school districts to shift their instructional approaches in ways where satisfactory outcomes on state assessments—not authentic learning and development—become the primary goal. These pressures have also positioned administrators and teachers to appropriate much of the underlying ideology that characterizes African American children as . . . illiterate, using white and Asian student performance as the standard. (Davis & Martin, 2018, p. 53)

As teachers, under pressure to raise test scores, adapt instruction and assessment to prepare students for the demands of large-scale tests, students have fewer and fewer opportunities to engage in meaningful and culturally relevant work that reflects the intent of academic standards. In the long run, classroom strategies designed to increase large-scale test scores can prevent students from learning the knowledge and skills needed for success in school and life beyond school.

IMPROVING THE VALIDITY OF CLASSROOM ASSESSMENT
FOR DIVERSE LEARNERS

For nearly 30 years, educators and assessment specialists have attempted to improve assessment practices in classrooms (Black & Wiliam, 1998a, 1998b, 1999, 2009; Brookhart, 2008; Chapuis & Stiggins, 2009; Heritage & Wylie, 2018; Popham, 2008; Resnick et al., 1995; Stiggins & Chapuis, 2005; Taylor & Nolen, 1996; Wiggins, 1992; Wiggins & McTighe, 2005). Extensive reviews of research have revealed the assessment practices that best support student learning (Black & Wiliam, 1998a, 2009; Hattie & Temperley, 2007; Sadler, 1989; Sadler & Good, 2006). To provide fair and valid assessment of students with diverse cultural and social backgrounds, teachers must step back from conventional "teach-test-grade" assessment practices and engage in purposeful assessment designed to support student learning. Assessment practices that best support student learning include the following:

1. Clarity about learning goals
2. Ensuring that *students* know and understand the learning goals
3. Giving assignments that ask students to demonstrate the learning goals
4. Attending to whether factors unrelated to the learning goals impact students' performances
5. Evaluating student work (whether by the teacher, students themselves, or others) only on students' achievement of learning goals rather than on factors unrelated to learning goals.
6. Providing feedback and opportunities for self-assessment and revision so that students can close the gap between where they are and where they need to be

There are many excellent resources available to help teachers implement effective assessment practices and develop high-quality assessment tools (e.g., Popham, 2020; Stiggins, 2001b, Taylor & Nolen, 2008; Wiggins & McTighe, 2005, 2011). These texts deal with "best practices" for assessment and grading, and many of the practices described in these texts would improve the quality of classroom assessment practices and support teaching and learning in positive ways. Existing assessment textbooks focus on the procedural aspects of assessment: how to give effective feedback, how to develop performance tasks and scoring rubrics, how to observe students during instruction, how to develop different types of test items, how to use fair grading practices, teaching students how to assess their own work, and so on. While the guidance in these books can support efforts to create fair and valid assessments of all students, they do not directly address potential barriers for students with diverse cultural and social identities and how to remove those barriers.

Clearly, given the state of published classroom assessments, the lack of teacher training in assessment, the impact of large-scale testing models on classroom assessment practices, poor alignment of classroom assessments with learning goals, and the problematic nature of course/subject area grading, making assessment tools and processes fair and valid for students from diverse cultural and social backgrounds requires a solid commitment to fair assessment of every student and the willingness to learn how to do so. This commitment is easier to make when assessment is considered an integral aspect of instruction rather than an "after-the-fact" exercise to collect scores for a gradebook (Black & Wiliam, 1998a, 2012; Chapuis & Stiggins, 2002; Heritage & Wylie, 2018; Popham, 2008; Stiggins & Chapuis, 2005, 2006, 2008, 2009).

CULTURALLY RESPONSIVE PEDAGOGY AND THE VALIDITY OF CLASSROOM ASSESSMENT

Culturally relevant pedagogy (Ladson-Billings, 1995a) and *culturally responsive pedagogy* (Gay, 2010) are educational models derived from observations of educators who are successful in teaching students of color. Culturally *relevant* pedagogy is intended to support high academic achievement for all students, "cultural competence," and the ability to "both understand and critique the existing social order" (Ladson-Billings, 1995a, p. 474). The aim of culturally relevant pedagogy is to produce students who can achieve academic standards by using "aspects of students' cultures in an asset-based approach as opposed to deficit-based to make the course material relevant to them, and increase their skill acquisition, engagement, and learning outcomes" (Montenegro & Jankowski, 2017, p. 5). Culturally *responsive* pedagogy uses "the cultural characteristics, experiences, and perspectives of ethnically diverse students as conduits for teaching them more effectively" (Gay, 2002, p. 106).

The processes used to develop state academic standards can lead to standards that privilege knowledge and skills valued by the dominant White middle- to upper middle-class culture (Cumming, 2000) and marginalize the knowledge and skills valued by others. The goal of *culturally sustaining pedagogy* (Paris, 2012; Paris & Alim, 2014) is to help students embrace their own cultural backgrounds and the knowledge and skills valued by their own cultures. Students learn skills, knowledge, and ways of thinking unique to their own cultures. Current thinking about culturally sustaining pedagogy (Ladson-Billings, 2014; Paris & Alim, 2014) suggests that educators must move beyond adaptation of instruction so that students can achieve a state's academic standards. Teachers have to think carefully about how they will teach and how they will evaluate their success in helping students learn about and embrace their own cultures.

In many classrooms, and in teacher education programs, the focus of culturally relevant or culturally responsive pedagogy is on instructional methods. Although there are many resources that can help teachers engage in culturally responsive pedagogy (Banks, 2014, 2016; Banks & Banks, 2020; Gay, 2010; Khalifa et al., 2016; Ladson-Billings, 2009; Taylor & Sobel, 2011), little guidance is available to help teachers develop culturally responsive assessment tools and apply culturally responsive assessment processes (Montenegro & Jankowski, 2017).

While assessment specialists have developed many strategies to minimize bias for or against different groups, only a handful of authors have addressed culturally responsive assessment (Lee, 1998; Messick, 1995; Montenegro & Jankowski, 2017; Qualls, 1998). The assumption in large-scale testing is that, by making assessment tools as standardized and "unbiased" as possible, they will provide fair and equitable assessment of all students. Assessment specialists have not considered nor scientifically investigated the idea that "assessment, if not done with equity in mind, privileges and validates certain types of learning and evidence of learning over others, can hinder the validation of multiple means of demonstration, and can reinforce within students the false notion that they do not belong in [school]" (Montenegro & Jankowski, 2017, p. 5).

> [Assessment] has remained largely unchanged in regards to inclusivity, and little urgency has been given to ensuring that students are provided with just and equitable means to demonstrate their learning. There is a difference between assessing all students in the same way in relation to a specific outcome of interest and making sure assessments are appropriate and inclusive of all students. Being attentive to how students may understand questions, tasks, and assignments differently, as well as feedback regarding their learning, is not only beneficial to students but to internal improvement efforts as well. (Montenegro & Jankowski, 2017, p. 5)

Culturally responsive pedagogy and culturally sustaining pedagogy also provide guidance on learning goals that go beyond state academic standards. If educators want students to attain "cultural competence" and the ability to "critique the existing social order," educators must think about what students will know and be able to do in order to focus their teaching and evaluate their own success in helping students achieve these aims. When teachers are clear about the learning goals and understand who the students are (their background experiences, funds of knowledge, interests, needs, and goals), teachers can work to make sure that assessment practices are appropriate for students so that claims about student learning are valid.

COMMUNITIES OF PRACTICE AND THE VALIDITY
OF CLASSROOM ASSESSMENT PRACTICES

As is evident from the research on the factors that influence classroom assessment practices described earlier in this chapter, assessment practices are situated in particular contexts. Teachers do not work in a bubble; they work in communities of practice (Lave & Wenger, 1991). Any discussion of how to make assessment tools and processes fair and valid for students must take into account the context in which teachers work. In many cases, educators who embrace culturally responsive pedagogy or culturally sustaining pedagogy work in communities of practice that collaborate to achieve these aims.

For a community of educators to work together to support student learning, they must negotiate their practices and their ideas about fair and valid assessment. When educators set goals for cultural competency and critical thinking about issues of justice, they have to negotiate with administrators and colleagues to ensure their efforts are not undermined by overarching systems (e.g., Acosta, 2013; Borck, 2019). The validity of claims about students' learning depends on how people in different communities of practice go about setting learning goals, evaluating student learning, and establishing policies and practices for grading.

As already discussed, the validity of assessment results depends on the meanings given to assessments results and how assessment results are intended to be used (grading, planning instruction, recommending students for instructional interventions, etc.). Meanings and purposes of assessment results are constructed by a range of audiences inside and outside of the classroom. Teachers and students may attach meanings to assessment results in the classroom, but other individuals and groups may interpret them differently and use them for unintended purposes. For example, parents/ guardians use test scores and grades as indicators of their children's school success, college admissions officers use test scores and grades to decide whether to admit students; teachers' peers and school administrators use test scores and grades to decide whether teachers are doing their jobs and whether children should receive special services, be promoted to the next grade level, or be placed in a particular instructional program or course.

That differences in meaning arise from different ideas about the purposes of assessments is not surprising. Nevertheless, teachers must determine how to navigate the boundaries of these diverse contexts in their assessment work. When teachers adjust assessment practices to be appropriate for the cultural and social identities of their students, they must be able to communicate with students, parents/guardians, colleagues, and other stakeholders about how their assessments allow students to demonstrate academic standards; they must be able to demonstrate that student performances on culturally relevant assessment tools have the same meanings and can be used for the same purposes as performances on more conventional assessment tools.

WHERE DO WE GO FROM HERE?

In this book, I focus on fair and valid assessment of diverse learners. I hope to contribute to the literature on assessment by helping educators engage in assessment practices that support diverse learners. The validity of claims about students' learning depends very much on what educators want students to learn, how evidence of learning is gathered, and whether assessment strategies support students' learning. Classroom assessment in schools with culturally and socially diverse students requires careful thinking about the needs of students from a wide range of backgrounds. Will classroom assessment tools and processes support instruction, engage students, and give students opportunities to benefit from schooling, or will these practices continue to suppress students and misrepresent their learning?

In Chapter 2, I summarize research on bias issues in assessment and how they impact the validity of claims about student learning. I examine factors that can affect the fairness of classroom assessment practices within and beyond our increasingly diverse classrooms. I present research on how grading practices can be impacted by implicit biases and result in invalid reports about students' learning and how teachers' implicit biases affect students' progress. I also describe how features of assessment tools and processes (item formats, language complexity, context, and evaluations of students' work) can impact the validity of scores and grades. I describe strategies for minimizing bias and recommend tools educators can use to look for potential bias in the assessment tools they use.

I begin Chapter 3 with a review the literature on culturally relevant, culturally responsive, and culturally sustaining pedagogies. I then consider how assessment tools can become not only opportunities for students to demonstrate traditional learning goals (e.g., state standards) but also how assessment can provide opportunities for students to learn through valued work that connects schools with the communities they serve. Because assessment strategies define the types of work assigned to students, teachers owe it to their students to consider the purposes of schooling. Will schooling demand that students suppress their own ideas, values, and cultural backgrounds in order to succeed, or will schooling support the achievement of marginalized students while helping them develop pride in themselves and their cultural heritages?

In Chapter 4, we present research on factors that impact students' engagement in learning and assessment processes and provide suggestions for how to improve students' engagement with assessment. All too often, assessment is something that is "done to" students, with students as passive receivers of assessment results. However, students are agents in their own learning. They choose whether to engage in learning experiences and whether to show others what they have learned. Students are more able to achieve learning goals when they understand what they are to learn, when they feel some ownership of the learning goals, and when they know how to achieve (Black & Wiliam, 1998b; Brookhart, 2008; Hattie & Temperley, 2007; Stiggins & Chapuis, 2005, 2008). When students understand what they are supposed to learn, they can be more purposeful in their own learning and set goals for themselves that may go beyond the expectations set by educators (Stiggins & Chapuis, 2005). When students are engaged in the learning process, they are more likely to demonstrate their learning during classroom assessment events.

In Chapter 5 of this book, we describe teachers' communities of practice and the situational factors that affect how and what teachers assess and how teachers report about student learning. Recognizing that assessment practices occur in communities of practice and require teachers to negotiate their practices with others (e.g., school policies that impact teachers' grading practices), we describe how teachers navigate within their communities of practice as they choose assessment tools, interpret students' work, and engage with the communities they serve.

We know from research (Dillan & Wiliam, 1998, 2009; Hattie & Temperley, 2007) and our own work as teachers and teacher educators that effective assessment practices can support student learning and create vibrant classrooms with engaged students. Alternately, poor assessment tools and processes, practices that are focused more on generating numbers for a gradebook than on students' learning, can do a tremendous amount of harm: harm to students' learning and well-being, harm to the instructional process, and harm to relationships between teachers, students, and families. Throughout this book, I describe strategies teachers can use to increase relevance and minimize bias in assessment practices to be sure students' work demonstrates the learning goals and is relevant and accessible to all students.

CHAPTER 2

Bias and Sensitivity Issues in Classroom Assessment

In Chapter 1, I introduced the concept of validity. Here, I expand on the primary issue that threatens the validity of claims about student learning—assessment bias. Bias in education has been documented in many different studies from multiple perspectives. For example, students have different opportunities to learn due to tracking (e.g., Ansalone, 2000, 2009; Beard, 2019; Horn, 2008; Palardy et al., 2015) or detracking (Burris et al., 2008; Horn, 2008). The quality of feedback provided by teachers differs based on assumptions about students' abilities (Blackwell, et al., 2007; Taylor, 1979; Tenenbaum & Ruck, 2007). Differences in the quality of textbooks, instructional materials, and facilities in schools that serve predominantly White middle-class students versus schools that predominantly serve low-income students and students of color provide dramatic proof of biases in our educational system (e.g., Entwisle & Alexander, 1988, 1992, 1994; Entwisle et al., 1997; Kozol, 2005; Ladson-Billings, 2006).

Another type of systemic bias has to do with learning goals. In the United States, all states and territories have developed academic standards (learning goals) and state-level assessments associated with the learning goals. These standards and assessments drive instruction and assessment at the district, school, and classroom levels. In the broadest sense, therefore, assessment bias can begin with biases involving what knowledge and skills are privileged in state academic standards (Solano-Flores, 2011; Cumming, 2000; Pollitt, Marriott, & Ahmed, 2000; Solano-Flores & Nelson-Barber 2001; Stobart, 2005).

These overarching systemic biases are beyond the scope of this book; however, biases in educational systems, as well as the potential for bias in the development of educational standards, directly affect large-scale testing and teachers' classroom assessment practices. In this chapter, I focus on one contributor to these bias issues—sources of bias in assessment tools, processes, and practices.

In what follows, I explain assessment bias and describe how assessment bias affects grading and scores on tests and other assignments. I review sources of test score bias found in research on large-scale tests and discuss how these sources of bias can affect classroom assessment practices. I describe how teachers can work to minimize bias in their classroom assessment practices, and I describe strategies that communities of practice (at the school, district, or state level) can use to examine published and teacher-developed assessment tools and processes to look for potential sources of bias.

WHAT IS BIAS IN ASSESSMENT?

In general, teachers expect differences in students' performances on tests, projects, homework, and other assignments due to differences in instruction, study skills, time on task, mastery of content, and a range of other factors that can affect student learning and student performance. For example, suppose educators in a school have adopted science standards that include science investigation skills. If students in one biology class engage in hands-on science investigations as they learn scientific inquiry and thinking skills while students in the class across the hall learn about scientific inquiry and thinking through lectures and teacher modeling, the two groups of students would likely perform differently on a school's end-of-course biology test that requires scientific reasoning, data analysis, and so forth. This type of systematic difference is called *impact*. In other words, systematic differences in performance between two classes of students are caused by differential opportunities to learn concepts and skills rather than aspects of items, tasks, scoring rules, assessment content and contexts, and/or evaluations of students' work. When students have different opportunities to learn concepts and skills for any of a variety of reasons (e.g., tracking, ability grouping, curricular focus), differences in students' performances can serve as messengers of differential educational experiences rather than as evidence of assessment bias.

Assessment bias occurs when students of equal ability from different demographic groups have unequal likelihood of doing well on a particular item, task, test, or other assignment due to features within the assessment tool or the assessment processes. Assessment bias can occur when characteristics of an assessment tool systematically give students from one demographic group a better chance of doing well on the item or task than students from other groups (Nitko, 2004; Popham, 2005). Cultural background, gender, type of community, region, language proficiency, and other demographic variables can affect how students interpret and respond to items, tasks, tests, and other assignments regardless of opportunities to learn. Assessment bias can also occur when educators allow attitudes or beliefs about groups of students to affect their evaluation of students' work and their expectations for students' performance.

Since the late 20th century, a major focus in education has been on implementing academic standards focused on higher level knowledge and skills. Students are expected to comprehend, analyze, and interpret complex text. They are supposed to solve nonstandard mathematical and real-world problems. They are expected to develop complex understanding of disciplinary core ideas, scientific practices, and cross-cutting concepts in science. They are supposed to be able to analyze causes and effects of historical events using primary sources. In short, 21st-century learning goals are much more complex than the basic skills that were the focus of minimum competency testing during the 1970s and 1980s (Huddleston & Rockwell, 2015; Rothman, 1995).

When learning goals are complex, assessment will be complex. In this context, any number of features of assessment tools could lead to bias in the ultimate outcome of assessments—scores and grades. For example, suppose a reading test includes a passage about water rights. The content of the passage might be more familiar to students from rural areas than students from urban areas—making it easier for the rural area students to comprehend the key ideas, details, and perspectives in the passage. A mathematics item or task might involve a context that is familiar to students from cities (e.g., managing time using a city bus schedule) but not known to students in suburbs—interfering with suburban students' comprehension of the mathematical requirements of the task.

Students may systematically differ in their comfort with certain item types, leading to differences in performance due to *response bias*. For example, several studies suggest that boys are more comfortable with multiple-choice items and girls are more comfortable with items and tasks that require written responses (Ben-Shakhar & Sinai, 1991; Birenbaum & Feldman, 1998; Lane, Wang, & Magone, 1996).

Assessment bias can be caused by the perspectives of those who evaluate students' work. Research suggests that educators make assumptions about students' abilities based on their gender, ethnicity, language proficiency, and so forth (Bennet et al., 1993; Copur-Gencturk et al., 2019; Ferguson, 2003).

Teachers might be harsher in evaluating the work of students who write about cultural issues and ideas unfamiliar to the teacher, interpret text or data differently than the teacher, or write a persuasive essay taking a position with which the teacher disagrees (Shores & Wesley, 2007). Theory on implicit bias suggests that vague evaluation criteria leave more room for teachers' implicit biases to influence their judgments. If teachers are evaluating student work and they are unsure what standard to compare the work with, implicit stereotypes can "fill in the blanks." However, studies also suggest that when teachers have explicit criteria for evaluating students' work, discrepancies based on race and gender decrease substantially (Tenenbaum & Ruck, 2007; Uhlmann & Cohen, 2005).

In summary, the primary validity concerns about bias in assessment are whether factors within assessment tools suppress or enhance students' ability to demonstrate what they know and are able to do, and whether assessment processes such as grading and evaluations of students' work are affected by explicit or implicit biases toward students based on their race, class, gender, culture, or social identities.

IMPACT OF TEACHER ATTITUDES AND BELIEFS ON FORMAL AND INFORMAL ASSESSMENT OF STUDENTS

Bias in Grading Practices

Grading is an important part of the teaching profession and unbiased grading practices are essential to ensure fair and valid assessment of students from diverse social and cultural backgrounds. However, grades are a primary source of bias in the assessment of students—particularly when students do not have home support, do not "just know" teacher expectations, or come from cultures that have different ideas than the teachers about adult–child interactions, sharing their own ideas, contradicting others, and so forth.

Grading plays an important part in what teachers communicate to students and parents/guardians about student learning and in how students see themselves. When implicit assumptions about students weigh into grading practices, biased grading is more likely. As discussed in Chapter 1, summarizing students' performance over a grading period in a single grade provides little to no information students and parents/guardians can use to evaluate students' learning or progress. A course or subject area grade of C or U (Unsatisfactory) has very different meaning if the grade is based on nonachievement factors (attitude, effort, behavior, participation) rather than on performance on tests and projects. When teachers are explicit and public about their grading policies and use grading as a vehicle for communication, bias is less likely to creep into the overall grading process.

Bias can occur because of grading policies that privilege some students over others. Research suggests that grading policies tend to favor students from middle- to upper middle-class homes. For example, when a teacher, school, or department has a grading policy that penalizes students for late homework (e.g., "one day late, no credit" or "lose 10% for each day the assignment is late"), educators may be creating a bias against students who provide child care for siblings, work after school to help support the family, or lack parental help when a language other than English is spoken in the home. Nearly one-fifth of students report they are not able to do homework because they don't have Internet access at home (Project Tomorrow, 2017).

Research on teachers' grading practices demonstrate that teachers incorporate many nonacademic factors into grades (see Brookhart et al., 2016, for a review of studies on teacher grading practices). Factors often incorporated into grades include perceptions about behavior, effort, participation, and attitude. Teachers may not espouse stereotypes about students from diverse cultural or social backgrounds; yet, implicit stereotypes can be activated in a teacher's mind during the grading process (Devine, 1989), leading to biased judgments that affect students' grades (Greenwald & Krieger, 2006). When expectations are subjective or ambiguous, implicit or explicit stereotypes have greater potential to influence grading (Quinn, 2020)—particularly when cultural norms for behavior and participation differ between teachers and students.

Research on teacher judgments about student behavior suggests that teachers punish African American and Latinx students more often than White students for subjective infractions such as "defiance" and "disrespect" (Staats, 2014). African American students are more often disciplined for "disrespectful behavior" and "disrupting" class (McFadden et al., 1992; Shaw & Braden, 1990; Zimmerman et al., 1994), whereas White students are disciplined for more objective behaviors such as smoking and vandalism (Skiba et al., 2020).

A national study by Riddle and Sinclair (2019) looked at adults' implicit biases and overt racist attitudes. After controlling for the number of African American students in a community, the data showed that African American students were given detention or suspension more often than White students in communities with high levels of explicit or implicit racism (Chin et al., 2020; Riddle & Sinclair, 2019). In studies looking at teachers' beliefs about students based on race, teachers rated African American students as "poorer classroom citizens" (Downey & Pribesh, 2004). Bennett and his colleagues (Bennett et al., 1993) showed that, after controlling for variables such as test scores and gender, teachers' perceptions of students' behavior constituted a significant component of grades. Yet, teachers' perceptions of students' behavior did not correlate with students' standardized test scores. These studies suggest that African American and Latinx students are likely to get lower grades when perceptions of behavior are included in the grade (Feldman, 2019).

Two other subjective variables often included in grades are attitude and effort. A nationally representative sample of teachers was surveyed on whether students "care about doing well," "get along with teachers," and "work hard at school." Teachers gave African American students lower ratings than White students on all three items (Puma et al., 1993). Gross (1993) found that teachers said African American students were least studious, least prepared, and least likely to have the right frame of mind to attend to instruction.

However, in a study by Casteel (1997), 8th- and 9th-graders were asked who they most wanted to please with their class work. "Eighty-one percent of African American females and 62% of African American males indicated they wanted to please teachers. Only 28% of White females and 32% of White males wanted to please teachers."

Gross (1993) found that, in addition to judgments about students' attitudes, teachers and administrators reported that African American parents were less supportive of the school's mission than White parents. Yet, when parents were interviewed in focus groups, African American parents were more supportive of their children striving for the higher level math classes, even if that meant lower grades. White parents were more prone to say that their children should stay in the top sections only if they were likely to do well (Gross, 1993). Beliefs about family support can impact teachers' judgments about students' attitudes toward school and, therefore, the nonacademic aspects of grades.

If teachers do not have explicit criteria for evaluating behavior, attitude, and effort, or when they apply expectations unevenly across students, bias in grading is highly likely. Research suggests that the best practice for minimizing bias in grading is to minimize the influence of homework and personal judgment about effort, behavior, and attitude on grades (Feldman, 2019). Feldman found that when teachers omit homework grades and judgments about behavior, attitude, and effort from grades, differences in grades between White students and non-White students shrink dramatically. In addition, the correlation between grades and standardized test scores increases (Feldman, 2018).

Some teachers argue that students will not do homework if it is not "graded" and that students need to experience the consequences of poor attitudes, efforts, and behavior. Concerns about attitude, effort, and behavior are best handled by creating a learning climate focused on support for *all* students' learning. If grades are used to punish students for missing homework or perceptions of "bad" behavior, poor effort, or bad attitudes, teachers create an adversarial climate in the classroom. In a learning climate, students can feel safe communicating about personal challenges and can contribute to defining class norms about behavior.

Cultures vary in the social behaviors that are considered appropriate. Teachers must be sure that the classroom community norms and behavioral expectations are respectful of different cultures. Teachers need to involve students in establishing behavioral norms, help students develop these skills and dispositions, assess them consistently and fairly, and ensure that expectations do not violate cultural norms. In Appendix A, I provide recommendations for ways to address nonacademic factors that make their way into most teachers' grading practices.

Self-Fulfilling Prophecy

Bias in teacher judgments of students' ability and behaviors can have powerful effects on students' future performances. Most educators have heard of the concept of *self-fulfilling prophecy*. A self-fulfilling prophecy is a case in which a teacher's expectation regarding a student's performance affects the student's learning behaviors (Rosenthal & Jacobson, 1968a, 1968b). In past studies of self-fulfilling prophecy, researchers gave teachers false information about students' prior achievement—identifying some students as high-performing students and other students as low-performing students.[1] After controlling for actual ability, researchers found that when students were classified as "low performers," their later performance was much lower than the performance of students classified as "high performers," regardless of true initial achievement level (see Smith, 1980 for a meta-analysis of research on self-fulfilling prophecy).

A limitation of prior studies of self-fulfilling prophecy is the lack of controls for racial and cultural backgrounds of students. One study did investigate the influence of race on students' later performances. Jussim et al. (1996) studied the achievement trajectories of over 1,600 6th-graders. The researchers looked at teachers' early judgments about students' academic performance and academic potential. The researchers found that, although teachers' beginning-of-year evaluations were fairly accurate and did not show bias based on race, by the end of the year, there were significant differences in the overall grades for students judged to be less able by their teachers. Low-performing White students tended to gain in performance, whereas African American students lost considerable ground. The impact on African American students was nearly three times that of the impact on White students. Differential outcomes were also significant for girls and for low-income students. The effect accumulated across factors. For example, African American girls from low-income families experienced much greater effects due to compounded biases.

Differential Feedback for Students

Another potential cause of differences in students' grades over time is bias in teachers' support for students' learning. Taylor (1979) conducted an experiment in which a 6-year-old student was watching from behind a screen as preservice teachers taught a given lesson. Teachers were randomly told the 6-year-old was African American or White. Taylor found that, when the student was identified as African American, he received significantly less feedback after mistakes, less positive feedback after correct responses, and significantly less coaching. This study suggests that teachers could be helping White students more than African American students. Over time, these differences may be large enough to have significant effects on students' performance.

Beliefs About Ability

Intelligence tests have had a significant impact on people's beliefs about the abilities of low-income, African American, Indigenous American, and

Latinx students (see Farkas, 2003, for a review). For example, Rheinberg (1983) observed teachers for a year and found that teachers who believed intelligence was an inherent characteristic did not believe they could affect their students' performance. Low achievers in their classrooms began and ended the school year as low achievers. In contrast, when teachers had high expectations for students, students who started the year as low achievers moved up and became moderate or high achievers by the end of the year. Teacher beliefs about students' abilities also impact students' beliefs about their own abilities and their performances in school (Aaronson et al., 2002; Good et al., 2003).

Stereotype Threat

Stereotype threat is another phenomenon that can decrease students' performances over time (Steele, 2010; Steele & Aaronson, 1995). Steele and colleagues conducted studies looking at how messages from assessors impact students' performance. When students were told that a test reflected their abilities, despite equivalent SAT scores, African American students performed more poorly than their White peers, and females performed more poorly than males. However, when students were told they were doing a class exercise, that some tasks might be difficult, but they should do their best, there was no difference in performance between White students and African American students or between males and females with comparable SAT scores. White students appeared to be unaffected by references to ability. Steele and his colleagues considered these differences in performance to be caused by students' awareness of stereotypes about people in their racial group. When the idea of ability was raised, stereotype threat caused *stereotype anxiety*, which interfered with African American students' abilities to attend to tasks.

Stereotype threat can operate for students from any marginalized group. When the stereotype is about ability, individuals can develop fear about performing in ways that might reify the stereotype. They fear the stereotype might become the basis of others' negative judgments. Several studies have corroborated the findings of Steele and Aaronson (1995) for African American and female students as well as Latinx students (Hartley & Sutton, 2013; Nguyen & Ryan, 2008; Rodriguez, 2014; Sherman et al., 2013; Spencer et al., 1999, 2016). Experimental studies investigating the anxiety levels of students in the "stereotype threat" condition supported claims about how stereotype threat can impact students' anxiety levels and performances (Osborne, 2001, 2006, 2007). The primary strategies recommended for decreasing stereotype threat are to

1. decrease emphasis on ability as the determining factor in achievement (Steele & Aaronson, 1995),
2. affirm students' value (Taylor & Walton, 2011),

3. provide mentoring from older students on how to overcome academic challenges (Good et al., 2003), and
4. help students understand stereotype threat and how it can affect their performance (Johns et al., 2005).

Whether the cause of lower grades is a self-fulfilling prophecy based on low expectations, differences in ongoing support for students' learning based on race or gender, or lower performance due to stereotype threat triggered by teachers' implicit or explicit messages about ability, teachers' biases for or against students can have profound effects on students' performances and grades. Although many of the studies reported here are dated, the more recent studies by Chin et al. (2020) and Quinn (2020) suggest that implicit bias is still an issue in teacher assessment and grading practices.

Clearly, teacher beliefs and attitudes play a critical role in their judgments of students and in how students judge themselves. Teachers must be willing to examine their own assumptions and biases (Gay, 2010), and consider how their beliefs affect their grading practices, students' beliefs about themselves, and students' performances.

BIAS IN STUDENTS' SCORES ON TESTS AND OTHER ASSIGNMENTS

In addition to teacher inferences about students' abilities, attitudes, effort, and behavior, there are two other sources of bias in classroom assessment practices. Teachers may be biased in how they evaluate students' work. Alternately, there may be features of assessment tools that interfere with some students' ability to demonstrate what they know and can do.

Addressing Bias in Evaluations of Students' Work

Positive and negative stereotypes about students, based on their social or cultural identities, have been shown to influence the ways in which evaluators judge students' test performances (Babad, 1980; Baron et al., 1985; DeMeis & Turner, 1978; Gershenson et al., 2016; Gross, 1993; Malouff & Thorsteinsson, 2016; Quinn, 2020; Shores & Weseley, 2007). Biases that affect teachers' evaluations of students' work can be much more subtle than overt stereotyping. Teachers and administrators may be influenced by *implicit* beliefs about groups that affect their evaluations of students' work (Quinn, 2017, 2020; Starck et al., 2020; Warikoo et al., 2016), biases of which people are not aware but nonetheless influence judgements about students' work or students' capacities (Chin et al., 2020).

Vague scoring rules have been shown to lead to biases in teachers' evaluations of students' writing. For example, if teachers evaluate a written essay on a scale of 1 to 10, with no criteria to indicate the features that must be present to earn the highest score, teachers may shift their evaluations to idiosyncratic aspects of the writing or personal preferences. However, if the dimensions of writing (writing traits) are defined, and specific criteria are given for levels of performance, teachers are more likely to focus evaluation of students' work on criteria rather than personal biases (Quinn, 2020).

Many other studies have shown that, when expectations are clear and specific, judgments about students appear to be less susceptible to bias (Tenenbaum & Ruck, 2007; Uhlmann & Cohen, 2005). Therefore, the most effective way to minimize bias in evaluations of students' performances is to apply scoring rules that provide specific expectations for students' work. In Chapter 6, I provide examples of how to write scoring rules tied to learning goals.

Addressing Bias in Classroom Assessment Tools

In what follows, I describe strategies publishers and test developers use to minimize bias and some lessons learned from research on bias in large-scale tests. Few bias-reduction strategies are used in the development of published classroom assessments; however, research can provide insight into ways that local educators might apply some of the same strategies used by publishers to minimize the bias in their own assessment tools.

Knowing that biases are hard to see, publishers of instructional programs and large-scale tests have developed systematic processes to control for bias (see, e.g., McGraw-Hill's *Guidelines for Bias Free Publishing*, 1983; Educational Testing Service's (ETS) *Fairness Review Guidelines*, 2003). Publishers have two goals: (1) to ensure that contexts, historical and contemporary situations, and literary characters and situations represent the diversity of social and cultural groups in schools and (2) to avoid negatively impacting any students through stereotyped, demeaning, or condescending representations of individuals or groups. Content specialists use several bias reduction strategies during the content development processes for both instructional materials and assessments:

- Avoiding content, language, and images that promote or demean any group.
- Watching for over- or under-representation of any group.
- Screening passages, topics, themes, and contexts for potentially offensive or upsetting materials.
- Checking for stereotypes and misrepresentations of any individual or group.
- Ensuring that diverse perspectives and authors are represented in literature, primary documents, imagery, and text.

The care that publishers take to ensure that educational materials are appropriate for and represent diverse learners clearly demonstrates that these issues are important to them. Large-scale assessment developers use all of these strategies during development work and then take further steps to have experts examine assessment materials and to use student performance data to look for statistical bias.

STRATEGIES FOR MINIMIZING CULTURAL, RACIAL, GENDER, AND LANGUAGE BIAS IN LARGE-SCALE TESTS

Test items, reading passages, science scenarios, social studies passages, scoring rubrics, and other assessment materials can give some students advantages others do not have. Assessment specialists who develop large-scale tests attempt to minimize bias in every step of assessment development through a wide range of standardized processes. The following is a list of specific strategies content specialists use during large-scale assessment work to even the playing field for students from diverse cultural and social groups:

- Select topics for items, passages, and scenarios that will be familiar to the widest range of students.
- Avoid jargon and technical language unrelated to the targeted learning goals. (For example, a test item could refer to the actions of a "scientist" rather than the actions of a "nuclear engineer.")
- Avoid sensitive topics and controversial issues unless the sensitive topics or controversial issues are central to a discipline (e.g., natural selection, climate change, immigration). When students are confronted with images, stories, or contexts that are highly charged, their performance is likely to decrease (Educational Testing Service, 2003).
- Minimize language complexity in test items and tasks in order to support English language learners. Several aspects of language complexity have been shown to negatively impact the test performances of English learners as described later in this chapter.
- Avoid contextual information that is not necessary for correctly responding to test items. Avoiding unnecessary contextual information does not mean that test items do not need context. For example, students are more likely to engage with the data in a graph if the reason for engagement is relevant to their own lives (Taylor & Lee, 2004).[2]
- Apply principles of "universal design" to remove barriers for students with special needs. (For example, if an online test item requires a "drag and drop" interaction, students with fine motor or visual disabilities may not be able to respond to the item.)

In addition to development strategies for minimizing bias and increasing access, large-scale test developers also convene groups, called bias and sensitivity review (BSR) panels, to look for potential bias. BSR panels review all assessment materials—stimulus materials (e.g., reading passages, images, timelines, science scenarios), items, task directions, and writing prompts—for any potentially biasing factors that might affect students' ability to interact with the material and respond to test items.

Large-scale test developers also collect field test data to investigate statistical bias in items, tasks, and stimulus materials. Statistical indices flag items that systematically function differently for students from different racial, ethnic, or gender groups. If there is no statistical bias in a test item or performance task, students from different groups (e.g., males and females) who have the same total test scores are expected to have the same likelihood of performing well on a given item or task. If their performances are quite different, items or tasks are flagged for bias. The results of statistical investigations of bias are routinely presented in the technical reports for large-scale tests. Test items and tasks that demonstrate potential bias, either through BSR panels or statistics, are carefully reviewed, revised, or eliminated.

As is evident from the processes large-scale test developers use to minimize bias, assessment specialists do not intend to infuse bias into the materials. They apply all of the development criteria used in published instructional materials and rigorously investigate potential bias through BSR panels and through statistical analyses. However, when assessment developers are culturally different from students, no matter how carefully they and the publishers examine materials, unintended biases are likely to creep into assessment materials.

In the following sections, I describe some of the discoveries made during routine procedures to investigate bias in large-scale tests. The patterns and phenomena revealed in these routine practices are enlightening and can highlight why research on bias in published classroom and district assessment tools could improve the validity of students' performances on classroom assessments.

Lessons Learned From Bias and Sensitivity Review Panels

Taylor (2008) conducted a study observing BSR panels that were reviewing large-scale and classroom-based assessment materials in multiple subject areas for a state in the Pacific Northwest. Observations took place over the course of a year. Here, I briefly describe the study and review results to highlight how subtle features of passages and items can cause bias in assessment tools. In providing key results from this study, I hope to encourage educators to apply similar scrutiny to classroom and district assessments.

Panelists for the BSR panels were selected by the state to represent the state's diversity in race/ethnicity, cultural background, economic status, political orientation, and students with special needs. The BSR panel included individuals who were experts on sensitivity issues for their own groups, some representing nongovernmental organizations in the community (e.g., Urban League, NAACP, El Centro de la Raza) and others representing special school populations (e.g., homeless students, English learners, special education students). A pool of 30 reviewers contributed over the course of a year; however, each panel was composed of about 15 reviewers representing the range of demographic groups. Facilitators for the panels were professionals with expertise in bias and sensitivity issues and in group facilitation. Facilitators trained panelists on how to recognize sensitive content (content that may upset students) and potential sources of bias (see Chapter 7, Table 7.1) through demonstrations and practice (see Appendix C for a bias and sensitivity review protocol and resources).

Because the assessment contractor and the state had been quite vigilant in screening the work for obvious biases and sensitivity issues before the BSR panel began their work, the panelists found few of the typical problems for which they had been trained. The job for BSR panelists can become more difficult because of the close attention given to potential sources of bias during the development process. However, in this case, that difficulty was a blessing. The panelists found several issues that were not represented in published bias and sensitivity review guidelines.

"Othering." Reading assessment specialists attempt to reflect the diversity of students by using passages written by or about individuals from diverse backgrounds. However, not all passages reflect diversity in an appropriate way. For example, in this state, the assessment contractor selected biographical sketches about famous Americans who represent diverse groups (e.g., race, culture, socioeconomic status, and disabilities). The passages described how all of these famous people had to overcome public reactions to fundamental aspects of themselves such as disability (e.g., Helen Keller), ethnicity (e.g., Jim Thorpe), and skin color (e.g., Jackie Robinson). One reviewer commented,

> All of these bios are about people who were treated badly for being Black or handicapped or things like that. The bios play up the fact that they triumphed over hate—over being different. In the end, these bios are about how we have to overcome our differences rather than showing our accomplishments. It's just another way to put us in the 'other' category.

The examples of racism and maltreatment of individuals described in these passages had the potential to upset students and negatively affect their performances. This is an example of unintentional bias. Reading passages and other stimulus materials must be carefully scrutinized for potentially demeaning content, even when the intent of the texts is to represent and possibly celebrate diversity.

Inconsistency With Culture. Among the reading passages reviewed by the BSR panel were legends and folk tales from all over the world. Indigenous American tribes in the Pacific Northwest had translated legends from their oral traditions to print for the first time. The panelists identified three problems with the way these legends were handled by the assessment contractor. First, all folk tales and legends, regardless of culture, were called "folk tales." Indigenous American reviewers found this to be offensive because folk tales are fiction and legends are believed to be true.

Second, the Indigenous American legends had been altered slightly to fit a more typical Western story structure. Each legend had a conclusion with a statement reflecting the "moral of the story." The Indigenous American panelists noted that this was a violation of the original intent of legends— that the lessons to be learned can be different at different times and for different people; the reader/speaker or listener is to draw his or her own conclusions and lessons from a legend, which might be different for different individuals or at different times in an individual's life. Clearly, a multiple-choice item focused on drawing conclusions from these passages would be inappropriate.

A third example of cultural inconsistency was caused by changes in language usage. For example, authors of a passage on First Peoples of the Pacific Northwest changed the term "first feast" to "barbeque," which changed the significance of the first meal after a successful hunt. These examples of cultural inconsistency show how important it is to learn about and honor the norms of the cultures from which primary documents are drawn.

Multiple Interpretations. It is very common for reading, math, and science tests to have items asking students to identify reasonable conclusions, interpretations, or inferences based on information presented in text, graphics, or tables. However, interpretations are influenced by background knowledge and experiences (Brooks & Browne, 2012; Copenhaver, 1999; Rosenblatt, 1976; Spiegel, 1998). A reading passage proposed for the State's tests illuminates this issue. The story was of an African village in which a feral cat was eating the villagers' chickens. The villagers wanted to kill the cat. A young man suggested that they feed the cat instead. By the end of the tale, the cat was guarding the chickens from other predators.

One multiple-choice question asked students to draw a conclusion from the story. According to the scoring key, the correct answer was that the villagers had learned the benefits of being kind to animals. Reviewers interpreted the passage differently. One reviewer argued that feeding the cat was not at all kind—that farm cats keep the rat and mouse population under control; feeding cats worked counter to their functions. Another reviewer thought that the item writer was missing the point of the story: treating an enemy with respect. It is apparent from this example that readers bring their own prior knowledge and experiences to bear on how they interpret the ideas and information in a text (Rosenblatt, 1976).

As with the Indigenous legends described earlier, given that lessons learned can change over time and through diverse experiences, multiple-choice items asking students to identify a conclusion could never be valid; they do not allow for a diversity of valid text-based interpretations. Instead, they ask students to identify the conclusion that represents the views of the item writer—typically a White, middle-class educator.

Culturally Inappropriate Tasks. Assessment developers often create item templates that guide their work. Using templates, they can efficiently generate large numbers of items and tasks. Sometimes, templates can backfire. Taylor (2008) observed three examples of reviewers' concerns about using standardized templates. First, nearly every set of items associated with a literary passage included an item asking students to summarize the main events of the passage. A panelist noted that summarizing Indigenous American legends would not be appropriate. Coming from an oral tradition, legends are to be repeated in full, allowing listeners to construct their own interpretations.

The second example involved a mathematics item asking students to plan a statistical survey. The structure of items was standardized, only the topic changed. For one particular example, the focus was on how to obtain an unbiased sample for a survey; the topic of the survey was students' fears. While the purpose of the item was not controversial, the topic generated an extended discussion. Panelists representing several cultural groups noted that a survey about fears was not appropriate since the topic represented an issue that could cause students to lose face in their communities.

As a final example, the test developers routinely paired boys and girls in many test items in order to avoid gender associations with a particular science or mathematics activity. In response to a scenario in which a boy and girl were partnered to do a science investigation, a reviewer noted that, for the most conservative members of his culture, boys and girls should not work together. He suggested that test developers alternate between pairs of boys and pairs of girls as actors rather than including both boys and girls in the same activity.

As these examples show, lack of understanding of the values and norms of diverse groups can result in assessments that are problematic for students. Despite significant efforts by assessment developers to minimize bias in the assessments, subtle factors can still impact the cultural appropriateness of the materials.

Some readers might suggest that it is impossible to represent the values and norms of all cultural, racial, and gender groups. Given the volume of large-scale and classroom-based assessments, how can assessment developers ensure that all materials are appropriate for all students? This is a valid concern. Asa Hilliard, a renowned educational psychologist, noted,

> The acceptance of the reality of diversity is to undermine the possibility for standardized, mass produced, universally applicable measurement instruments. Agree or disagree, it is a fundamental scientific flaw to ignore this particular challenge. (Hilliard, 2003, p. 9)

Fortunately, classroom assessments are not limited in the same way that "mass produced" assessments are. While it may not be possible to eliminate bias due to cultural differences, more attention could be placed on learning about the norms of local cultural groups. Teachers can invite input from students and their families; teachers and school leaders can invite input from local communities. In a classroom focused on student learning, students may feel safe bringing their experiences and knowledge to bear on items, tasks, and other assignments. The principles of culturally responsive pedagogy (described in some detail in Chapter 3) emphasize the need for teachers to get to know the cultural values, beliefs, strategies for communication, and so forth for the students in their own classrooms.

In Chapter 7, I describe how educators can work together to conduct bias and sensitivity reviews of published classroom assessments prior to curriculum adoptions and of items and tasks within interim and benchmark assessment tools. Table 7.1 shows the primary issues reviewers look for in bias and sensitivity reviews. Appendix C provides protocols and resources for running bias and sensitivity reviews.

Assessment Format and Bias: Investigating Potential Bias Through Statistical Analyses

Some large-scale assessment research suggests that *features* of large-scale assessment tools (e.g., standardization, test item formats, language complexity, and contextual biases)—features often replicated in published classroom assessments and teacher-developed assessments—may have systematically suppressed test performances of female, minority, and English-learning students for nearly a century (Abedi & Lord, 2001; Boone & Adesso, 1974; Butler-Omololu et al., 1983; Garner & Engelhard, 1999; Long & Anthony, 1974; McNiel, 1975; Mendez-Barnett & Ercikan, 2006; Taylor & Lee, 2011, 2012; Wright & Isenstein, 1977). Large-scale test developers conduct statistical investigations of bias. Statistical investigations are rarely, if ever, done for textbook-embedded assessments. However, an understanding of how statistics are used to reveal potential bias can inform more informal assessment reviews of classroom and district assessments.

To look for statistical bias, test developers conduct research called *differential item functioning* (DIF) analyses. As the name suggests, the purpose of DIF studies is to see whether items or tasks function differently for students from different groups. In a DIF study, an item or task is flagged for DIF if it statistically "favors" one group over another. In other words, if students from two groups have equal total scores (suggesting similar levels of achievement) yet, students from one group outperform students from another group on a particular item or task, the item or task "favors" the higher performing group. DIF studies identify a reference group (usually the economically/socially dominant group) and focal groups (groups for which there are concerns about test score bias). In DIF studies, only two groups are compared in each analysis (e.g., White students and Indigenous American students). DIF can favor either the focal (nondominant) groups or reference (dominant) groups. The greatest concerns arise when items, tasks, or stimulus materials favor reference groups over focal groups. Looking at items and tasks that favor nondominant groups can provide clues about how to more fairly and validly assess students.

Taylor and Lee (2011) investigated DIF in reading tests comparing White students (reference group) with students from Indigenous American, Latinx, African American, and Asian American backgrounds (focal groups). They used state assessment data from 5 years and three grade levels (grades 4, 7, and 10) in their study.

Taylor and Lee found a striking pattern in the data. The majority of multiple-choice items flagged for DIF favored White students; while the majority of open-response items flagged for DIF favored students from Indigenous American, Latinx, African American, and Asian American backgrounds. This pattern was strongest for items asking students to develop interpretations of text (e.g., draw inferences, interpret characters, draw conclusions, compare and contrast ideas, determine cause or effect, and so forth). The pattern was more extreme for older students than for younger students, and the statistics were more extreme for students from Latinx and Asian American backgrounds compared to other focal groups.

These statistical results would not be surprising to proponents of reader response theory (Brooks & Browne, 2016; Copenhaver, 1999; Rosenblatt, 1976; Sloan, 2002). Spiegel (1998) stated:

> The making of meaning from reading is a dynamic, reflective, introspective process. Readers don't discover "the" meaning in a text. In the past, meaning was assumed to reside in the text, but now the reader has replaced the text as the most central element in reading (Purves, 1975). Meaning is *made* [emphasis added] by the reader, not found (Probst, 1981). . . . Meaning is constructed, interpreted, and revised by readers themselves, not by literary critics, professors, or even authors. (p. 42)

When reading items ask students to develop interpretations, it is likely that readers' prior experiences, particularly experiences related to the information or events described in passages, will impact their responses to items. For multiple-choice items, readers must recognize the "correct" conclusion, inference, or interpretation; however, for open-response items, readers are allowed to develop their own inferences and interpretations. In reader response theory, even though meaning is personal, it is grounded in text. Multiple grounded interpretations of text may be valid. Spiegel (1998) wrote, "Because meaning is constructed by unique individuals, multiple meanings are to be expected and even celebrated. Within any group of peers, many different interpretations of the same text are likely to, and indeed should, occur" (p. 43).

If multiple-choice text interpretation items tend to favor White students over students from other groups, the inferences, interpretations, or conclusions represented in the correct answer choices are "more correct" for White students than for students from other groups. When students' valid interpretations of text are not represented in multiple-choice answer choices—or, worse, if their own interpretations are provided as "wrong" answers—the item is biased against those students and threatens the validity of their test scores.

The fact that individuals differ in their interpretations of text, based on prior experiences, does not automatically lead to measurable DIF. DIF occurs when examinees in defined groups differ in *systematic* ways when responding to test items. The DIF question is not whether all students within a focal or reference group think alike but rather whether students in the focal group think *differently* than students in the reference group. In the Taylor and Lee (2011) study, the results do not suggest that students from Indigenous American, Latinx, African American, and Asian American backgrounds were unified in their thinking about text, only that their interpretations of text were not consistent with those of the multiple-choice item writers. This could occur if item writers came from cultural and economic backgrounds similar to that of the White students.

Learners' experiences within their (sometimes multiple) cultures provide them with rich knowledge that may not be tapped by assessments. These effects are not limited to reading assessments. Saxe's (1988) work on the mathematical understanding of young street vendors in Brazil is an early example of this: When given traditional math problems involving arithmetic operations the vendors used in their work daily, they performed poorly. When the same problems were framed in terms of that daily work, the vendors were quick, accurate, and flexible. In other words, the item framing either elicited or blocked use of well-learned mathematical knowledge. Lave (1988) reports similar results for American adults using everyday mathematics in actual grocery stores as compared to their (apparent) inability to use that same math in story problems set in grocery stores. In the Lave study, being physically in the store enabled complex cognitions that were not tapped in the school-like setting.

When Taylor and Lee (2011) examined ethnic/racial DIF in mathematics items, although some items exhibited DIF, they found no discernable patterns in the DIF. When Taylor and Lee (2012) examined gender DIF for reading and mathematics items, they found patterns of gender DIF similar to the ethnic/racial DIF patterns in reading.[3] Multiple-choice reading items asking students to identify valid text-based conclusions or interpretations favored boys, and open-response items asking for text-based conclusions and interpretations favored girls. In mathematics, the open-response items favoring girls tended to assess statistical analyses, logical reasoning, and nonroutine problem-solving; multiple-choice items favoring boys tended to assess more abstract mathematical applications.

Classroom-based and large-scale tests have employed multiple-choice items as the main item type for over 100 years. It is likely that this has led to systematic suppression of students' performances in unknown ways. Taylor and Lee (2011, 2012) recommend that reading and mathematics tests balance the use of multiple-choice and open-response items and that text interpretation items primarily be in open-response format.

Open-response items present their own potential for bias. For example, Smitherman (1993) found that when student written responses on National Assessment of Educational Progress included African American vernacular English, students were likely to receive lower scores. As I discussed earlier in this chapter, valid assessment of students' learning requires valid *evaluation* of students' responses. Prior research suggests that when evaluators lack specific scoring criteria, positive and negative stereotypes about students can influence teachers' evaluations (for reviews of previous research, see Malouff & Thorsteinsson, 2016; Quinn, 2020).

In large-scale testing, detailed processes are used to ensure that all valid responses are credited, from development of scoring criteria to selection of sample responses that support scoring rules. Open-response items and performance tasks on large-scale tests typically require students to anchor their answers in presented text or data, which helps evaluators better understand students' thinking. Evaluators are trained to look for valid responses that are not represented in training materials.

Classroom teachers can also look for valid responses that differ from their own analyses, interpretations, inferences, and conclusions or those expected in scoring guides. When teachers do not understand how students have drawn a particular conclusion, made a certain interpretation, or solved a problem in a particular way, they have the benefit of direct contact with students. They can ask students to explain their thinking. Students' inferences, interpretations, conclusions, and solutions are likely to draw upon students' prior knowledge relevant to the context as well as the information and ideas presented in text, data, or investigation results.[4]

Many other studies of gender DIF have corroborated the results found by Taylor and Lee (2012). Several researchers found that multiple-choice mathematics items flagged for DIF tended to favor boys, whereas open-response mathematics items flagged for DIF tended to favor girls (Bolt, 2000; Garner & Engelhard, 1999; Noble, 1992). Henderson (2001) examined DIF in multiple subject areas and found that multiple-choice items flagged for DIF favored boys, and open-response items flagged for DIF favored girls. Zenisky, Hambleton, and Robin (2004) found that multiple-choice science items favored boys, and open-response science items favored girls.

Alternate Explanations for Differences in Students' Responses. A possible alternate explanation for gender DIF shown in previous studies has to do with response demands. Multiple-choice items require students to locate and mark a correct response (or, in the case of text interpretation, a "best" response), whereas open-response items often require some sort of written response, graphic representation, or demonstration of problem-solving strategies. In a study of students' responses to open-response mathematics items, Lane et al. (1996) found that middle-school girls were more likely than boys to explain their thinking and show their solution strategies. Other studies have found that boys have a greater preference for multiple-choice items than do girls (Birenbaum & Feldman, 1998) and are also more likely to guess when they do not know the answer (Ben-Shakhar & Sinai, 1991).

The consistency of the results of these studies across subject areas has implications for how teachers assess students from different racial, cultural, or gender groups. Teachers can examine published assessments to see if multiple-choice items predominate and whether students are being asked to identify someone else's interpretations of text or problem-solving strategies. Teachers can look at the scoring guides that come with published assessment materials to compare how best responses in teachers' guides align with the interpretations, conclusions, and problem-solving strategies of their own students. If students develop viable responses that are not represented in scoring guides, teachers can adjust scoring guides as needed.

Minimizing Language Complexity Bias in Assessment

Many students in today's schools come from families that speak languages other than English in the home. Research suggests that it takes from 5 to 7 years or even more for most English language learning (ELL) students to gain sufficient mastery of academic English to join English-speaking peers in taking full advantage of instruction in English (Hakuta et al., 2000). While ELL students are learning English, their limited English proficiency affects both learning and assessment performance. Learning content-based knowledge in a new language cannot occur at the same rate as for native speakers.

ELL students may also have difficulty understanding teacher's instructions and test questions. Students may understand concepts taught in language arts, mathematics, science, and social studies classes, but may not yet have sufficient mastery of the English language to interpret the intent of test items and tasks or to express their understanding in English.

In the context of today's educational emphasis on real-world applications of knowledge and skills, any number of linguistic features of assessment tools could present challenges for English learners. Abedi and his colleagues (Abedi, 2006, 2011; Abedi et al., 2005; Abedi et al, 2001; Abedi & Hejri, 2004; Abedi & Lord, 2001; Abedi & Sato, 2008) conducted studies to determine what accommodations provide the best assessment support for English learners. Primary among the strategies they investigated were (a) giving students more time to complete assessments, (b) reading items, tasks, and directions aloud,[5] (c) giving students glossaries that translate vocabulary unrelated to the subject area, and (d) linguistic simplification. They found that giving students more time when their language proficiency was very poor provided little help, particularly when the language demands in assessments were high.

In a report to the U.S. Department of Education LEP[6] Partnership, Abedi and Sato (2008) concluded:

> [Research] on the assessment and accommodation of ELL students shows a substantial performance gap between these students and their native English-speaking peers, which could be attributed at least partly to the impact of linguistic biases in the assessments. . . . Among the language-related accommodations, linguistic modification is the most promising as it does not affect the validity of assessment and at the same time helps to narrow the performance gap between ELL and non-ELL students. (p. 4)

Language complexity is a significant issue in assessment. Assessment items, tasks, and directions can include vocabulary and syntactic structures that are unique to testing and very challenging. Assessment items and tasks may include technical terms and vocabulary unrelated to targeted learning goals.

Table 2.1 provides a list of different linguistic challenges, examples of test items that demonstrate those challenges (shown in italics), and suggestions for how to linguistically simplify the questions to be more accessible to English language learners.

Although the examples in Table 2.1 may seem unlikely, sentence structures and vocabulary usage similar to these examples are common in both large-scale and classroom-based assessments. Abedi and his colleagues found that attention to these linguistic factors, through language simplification, can improve LEP students' performances while having little to no effect on the performances of native English speakers.

Table 2.1. Language Complexity Issues in Assessment

Issue	Example Item	Language Simplification
Technical vocabulary unrelated to the targeted mathematics concept	An *engineer* is *designing* a suspension bridge to *span* the distance between the banks of a river. The bridge must be at least 1320 feet long. How long must the bridge be, in miles?	Eliminate unrelated technical language: The city needs a new bridge over the river. The bridge must be 1320 feet long. What will be the length of the new bridge in miles?
Multimeaning words within the subject area	*Graph* these data using a bar chart.	"Graph" as a verb is an infrequent use of the term. Remove it from the sentence: Create a bar chart to represent the data.
Multimeaning words unrelated to the subject area	The *banks* of the river are 1320 feet apart. How many miles are they apart?	Eliminate unrelated multimeaning words: The river is 1320 feet wide. How wide is the river in miles?
	Teresa put $100 in an *account*. After a year, her money had earned 10% in interest. How much money does she have now?	Replace unrelated multimeaning words: Teresa had $100 in the bank. Her money earned 10% interest in 1 year. How much money does she have now?
Idiomatic phrases unfamiliar to English learners	In the story, Mia is angry with her sister. Why is her *patience running out*?	Replace unfamiliar idiomatic phrases: In the story, Mia is angry with her sister. Why is she angry?
Sentence length	Jose wants to build a rectangular garden for his vegetables and he wants an area of 36 square feet. What dimensions will give him 36 square feet for his garden?	Break up sentences and decrease reading load: Jose wants to build a rectangular garden. He wants an area of 36 square feet. What dimensions will give him 36 square feet for his garden?

Issue	Example Item	Language Simplification
Dependent clause	If Jamal is going to build a garden with an area of 36 square feet, what dimensions can he use for his garden?	Separate clauses into sentences: Jamal is going to build a garden with an area of 36 square feet. What dimensions can he use for his garden?
Multiple prepositional phrases	Maria needs an area *of 36 square feet to build a garden in her backyard to grow vegetables.* What dimensions will give her 36 square feet of garden?	Break up sentences or eliminate unnecessary information: Maria wants to build a vegetable garden in her back yard. She needs an area of 36 square feet. What dimensions will give her 36 square feet of garden?

Even simple language issues can affect students' performance. For example, Solano-Flores and Trumbull (2003) analyzed the different ways students interpreted mathematics items. The following is a "lunch money" item from the National Assessment of Educational Progress:

> Sam can purchase his lunch at school. Each day he wants to have juice that costs 50¢, a sandwich that costs 90¢, and fruit that costs 35¢. His mother has only $1.00 bills. What is the least number of $1.00 bills that his mother should give him so that he will have enough money to buy lunch for 5 days? (National Assessment of Educational Progress, 1996)

This item is intended to measure proficiency with addition, multiplication, and rounding. However, interviews with students from three student subgroups (high-SES suburban White, low-SES inner-city African American, and low-SES rural Indigenous American) about their interpretation of the question revealed great variation. Eighty-four percent of White students read the question as intended, whereas only 56% and 52%, respectively, of Indigenous American and African American students read the sentence as intended. Solano-Flores and Trumbull found that 10% and 18%, respectively, of the Indigenous American and African American students interpreted the word *only* as restricting the number of dollars (i.e., "His mother has only one dollar").

In another study, Moschkovich (2008) observed a 3rd-grade group problem-solving conversation during a math class. She recorded conversations among ELL students and found that different students often had different interpretations of problems. In questioning students' thinking the teacher discovered the different interpretations. Rather than dismissing differences in reasoning as a lack of understanding of mathematics concepts, she used students' interpretations to bridge their transition to formal vocabulary and concepts.

POTENTIAL FOR BIAS IN COMPUTER-ADMINISTERED TESTS

Computer-administered testing tools are often provided with e-textbooks and other computer-based instructional materials. In addition, most district interim and benchmark assessments are administered to students via computers. At this time, bias and differential item functioning are largely unexplored in computer-based tests. Of the limited number of studies investigating potential bias in computer-based testing, the research suggests that students with disabilities, females, and African Americans perform more poorly than their counterparts on computer-based tests (Coon et al., 2002; Flowers et al., 2011; Newton et al., 2013; Taherbhai et al., 2012).

Research also suggests that students with more computer skills perform at higher levels on computer-based tests than students with fewer computer skills (Csapó et al., 2010; Poggio et al., 2005; Thompson & Weiss, 2009). During the COVID pandemic that began in 2020, it became evident that access to computers was highly related to race and income level. Lake and Macori (2020) summarized research from a wide range of sources:

> While pinning down specific national numbers is difficult, what is painfully clear is that a disproportionate share of those who lack access to a reliable internet connection and devices are Black, Hispanic, live in rural areas, or come from low-income households.

Students with regular access to computers outside of school are more likely to develop better computer skills and, therefore, perform better on computer-administered tests regardless of true achievement levels.

Many new item interaction types have been created for computer-administered tests (e.g., drag and drop, sorting, highlighting, graphing); however, little to no research has been conducted to investigate bias due to interaction types similar to that found for multiple-choice and open-response items. In addition, a close look at computer-administered classroom assessment tools shows that most of the item types are the same as those found in paper-pencil tests and quizzes. Therefore, educators are likely to find the same issues with computer-administered classroom and district tests as are found with paper-based classroom assessments. Educators at all levels of the education system—from classrooms to testing professionals—should be looking for potential biases from computer-administered tests related to gender, ethnicity, socioeconomic status, special education status, and cultural background.

POTENTIAL FOR BIAS IN PUBLISHED CLASSROOM ASSESSMENTS

The type of research conducted and reported for large-scale tests (bias and sensitivity reviews and statistical analyses) rarely occurs for published classroom assessment materials. Although educational publishers work hard to minimize bias in instructional materials, they typically do not review assessment materials with the level of scrutiny they use when choosing passages, selecting original documents, writing text, and developing lessons (Beck, 2009). Yet, the likelihood of bias arising within classroom assessments is just as high as it is for large-scale tests.

Despite the fact that teachers use published classroom assessments as their predominant tools for judging students' achievement (Frisbie et al., 1993; Madaus et al., 1992; Stiggins, 2001a), educational publishers rarely collect data to investigate potential bias in textbook and other published classroom assessments (Beck, 2009; Stiggins, 2001a). Tests, quizzes, and homework assignments provided with published instructional materials are typically developed within tight timelines and do not undergo the same scrutiny as do items and tasks from large-scale tests (Beck, 2009). Few classroom assessment materials go through the rigorous procedures used to control bias in large-scale assessments. Nor are the items and tasks in published instructional materials reviewed by bias and sensitivity panels composed of racial/ethnic/cultural experts who are trained to recognize possible biases, insensitivity, and stereotyping.

The same is true of teacher-developed assessment tools. Unless as part of a school or district-wide effort to improve the quality and fairness of classroom assessments, teacher-developed assessments are not reviewed for or tested for potential bias.

MINIMIZING BIAS IN CLASSROOM ASSESSMENTS

An important tenet of validity theory is whether factors unrelated to the assessed knowledge and skills impact student performance on items, tasks, and assignments and/or how students' performances are evaluated. When those factors systematically impact some demographic groups more than others, the assessment tool, process, or event is biased. Bias is one of the greatest threats to the validity of scores and grades for students. However, educators can take control over potential sources of bias and work to improve assessment and grading practices by minimizing biasing factors.

The first step in dealing with bias is to recognize that most bias is unintentional. The studies reviewed in this chapter suggest that, even with the best intentions, bias can be an insidious factor in large-scale tests, grading practices, and classroom assessment tools and processes. Bias analyses are rarely, if ever, done for published classroom or district assessments. Hence, the degree to which students' classroom assessment performance is suppressed or enhanced by factors unrelated to the learning goals is unknown. Grading practices are typically guided by conventions rather than best practices. Grading practices that incorporate subjective evaluations of students' effort, behavior, attitude, and so forth are prone to bias. In what follows, I describe steps educators can take to minimize bias in classroom assessment tools and processes.

At the Classroom Level

The most important strategy for ensuring unbiased classroom assessment is teacher self-assessment and observation. Teachers can examine their own thinking to assess whether they have subtle biases for or against any students. Self-awareness about beliefs and attitudes is critical for unbiased classroom assessment practices. Teachers can take a hard look at their grading practices to see if practices are fair to all students—whether all students can meet grading expectations.

Classroom teachers can look for potential sources of bias due to item context, language, and formats. They can look at their own assessment tools to identify ways to decrease bias.[7] They can look for patterns in their students' work where performance on an item or group of items appears to differ for students based on gender, race, ethnicity, cultural background, or other demographic variables. They can also ask students to help them find instances of bias.

Sensitivity and Relevancy of Context and Content. Teachers can ask their students to talk about any materials perceived as offensive or culturally inappropriate.[8] They can interview students about their interests and ask students to share information about family histories, cultural norms, and values (if sharing cultural norms and values is appropriate for students) to create real-world contexts for assessment tasks. Teachers can engage with community members to find materials to help create culturally relevant classroom assessments and to understand cultural norms.

By applying strategies for culturally relevant pedagogy (as described in Chapter 3), educators can alter published classroom assessments to be more relevant to their students. It is common practice for states to release sample items from state tests to help educators understand what standards mean and how they are assessed at the state level. Educators can review released items and determine how to structure questions that target state academic standards. Teachers can develop similar items, changing stimulus materials to be more culturally appropriate and to represent the diverse backgrounds of their students. For example, asking students to identify main ideas, describe features of character development, interpret figurative language and so forth can be done in relation to a wide range of reading materials. Table 6.2 in Chapter 6 provides examples of generic item stems that could be used for a variety of reading passages, allowing teachers to choose culturally relevant passages and passages written by authors from diverse cultural groups. Fair use laws allow teachers to use copyrighted materials if they are being used for educational purposes and not for profit-making purposes.[9]

Mathematical problems, science scenarios, and social studies concepts can be situated in culturally and socially relevant contexts. In a study investigating reading as a potentially biasing factor in mathematics assessments, Taylor and Lee (2004) found that students classified as struggling readers performed much better than expected when mathematics problems were put in contexts familiar to students and relevant to their developmental levels.

Item and Task Formats. Given the range of studies that have found DIF in multiple-choice versus open-response item types, classroom teachers should look at item-level performance on their classroom tests to see if similar patterns emerge. If open-response items are not available, teachers can alter items to allow students to develop their own answers. For example, if the focus of the assessment is on interpretations, conclusions, and inferences in any subject area, teachers can convert multiple-choice items to open-response items. However, when doing so, it is essential that students also be asked to refer to relevant data or text to support their interpretations, conclusions, and inferences. Scoring rules must allow for a range of viable responses (see examples in Table 6.3 in Chapter 6).

Published classroom assessments often include brief, short-answer items. It is common for teacher guides to provide vague evaluation criteria such as "answers may vary." Teachers can develop scoring rules for short-answer items that help them stay focused on the targeted standard and minimize the impact of internal biases. If teachers' guides suggest that items have only one right answer, the guides may be misleading. If teachers find that students are systematic in their "wrong" responses, students may be having difficulty interpreting the intent of an item. Students may be interpreting information in a scenario, graphic representation, or passage in a way that differs from the item writers. In other words, "right answers" may not be right for all students. Teachers can ask students to show their work or explain their answers so that teachers can assess whether items and tasks are clear and whether there might be more than one right answer.

To address response bias, teachers can teach students about the genre of testing. If teachers believe they need to prepare students for the

multiple-choice items that will inevitably populate tests, they can use
multiple-choice items as teaching tools, asking students to discuss among
themselves why they think answers are correct or incorrect based on the
relevant text or data and then present their ideas to the whole class.

Teachers can help students understand how background knowledge
affects responses to multiple-choice items that require interpretation,
analysis, and conclusions. They can give students items requiring interpretations or conclusions and ask them to choose their answers and describe how their background knowledge influences their answers. Next,
teachers can give students the "correct answers" and ask them to hypoth-
esize what background knowledge would be needed to choose the correct
answers.

Teachers can also prepare students for open-response items by having
them generate their own responses, comparing their responses to the scoring
rule and to "correct" responses. Observations from state-level tests suggest
that a common reason for low scores on open-response items is because
responses are incomplete. Students do not or cannot read all the requirements of an item; therefore, they omit some aspects of a complete response.
Teachers can model how to read items and ensure complete responses.

Language Complexity. Given issues with language complexity, especially
in items and tasks targeting real-world situations and higher levels of understanding, teachers can ask students to identify language that is confusing;
they can work with students to ensure they understand what items and tasks
are asking of them. Although not studied in systematic ways, language complexity could also impact the performances of students with cognitive disabilities. Students with reading difficulties may struggle to understand the
requirements of items and tasks. If needed, teachers can simplify the language in the published assessments provided with instructional materials.
Teachers should use care in developing their own items, tasks, and assignments to make sure that language complexity is not a factor that prevents
students from demonstrating their knowledge and skills.[10]

In short, one of the most powerful ways to make assessments more
fair and valid for students is to involve students in the assessment process.
The idea that students should not know what will be included on a test is a
problematic holdover from standardized testing. This thinking is antiquated
and unrelated to the purpose of education. Students should know what they
are expected to learn and how they will be assessed. When the purpose of
schooling is student learning, students' involvement in the assessment process is simply another way to show students that their achievement is valued
and expected.

As teachers work to minimize sources of bias in their classroom assessments, key to their success will be creating a safe space for students to share

their experiences. Teachers can learn a great deal by observing students and listening to their ideas. In addition, change takes time. Teachers will need to work to improve their assessments over time—choosing the most important assessments as the early focuses of improvement.

At the School or District Level

Educators in the classroom and at the school and district levels can and should take the time to examine assessment materials for potential bias during and after curriculum and district assessment adoptions. Too often, educators implicitly give authority to educational publishers as experts in curriculum and instruction. However, that trust is not warranted when assessment materials associated with curricula are not handled with the same care as other curriculum materials.

To make classroom and district assessments appropriate for students from diverse backgrounds, teachers and their communities of practice can use the findings from past research to guide local evaluations of published classroom and district assessments to ensure that tests, performance tasks, and other assignments are free of bias for or against any demographic group. Specific steps communities of educators can take include the following:

- Conducting local bias and sensitivity reviews of all assessment materials using the guidelines provided in Table 7.1 and the protocols provided in Appendix C
- Reviewing published classroom assessment materials to ensure that items requiring analyses, interpretations, conclusions, and problem-solving allow students to develop their own responses (anchored, of course, in text, data, etc.)
- Evaluating scoring criteria (rubrics) to ensure that they
  » provide specific guidance on how to evaluate student work rather than vague guidelines such as "answers may vary";
  » allow for multiple valid interpretations of text, data, scientific results, and multiple viable solutions.
- Examining classroom and district assessment materials for linguistic complexity using guidelines provided in Table 2.1 and the protocols in Appendix D
- Considering factors that may affect accessibility for students with disabilities using information provided in Appendix E

When schools have schoolwide grading policies, educators must consider whether aspects of these policies privilege some students over others and work to eliminate those biases.

In Teacher Preparation Programs

Teacher educators can use a variety of activities to help preservice and in-service teachers understand potential or hidden sources of assessment bias. Activities might include the following:

- Engaging in mock bias and sensitivity review processes looking at published assessment materials using the protocol and tools given in Appendix C
- Reviewing items, tasks, and directions for assignments for linguistic issues using the protocol and tools given in Appendix D and then revising assessment tools to minimize language complexity
- Altering assessment tools to incorporate culturally relevant stimulus materials (e.g., reading passages, science investigations, and contexts for mathematical problems, primary texts for history and social studies courses)
- Considering factors that may affect accessibility for students with disabilities using information provided in Appendix E
- Developing fair grading policies that minimize the influence of biasing factors such as perceived participation, effort, attitude, and behavior

THE ROLE OF COMMUNITY IN REDUCING BIAS IN ASSESSMENT

Reducing bias in assessment is an arena in which a community of practice is necessary to address biasing factors. If educators are to minimize bias and optimize the validity of students' performances on district, school, and classroom assessments, it falls to teachers, departmental teams, district curriculum committees, and school leaders to deal with potential assessment bias. Educators must be prepared to communicate with and collaborate with students, parents/guardians, colleagues, and school administrators in their efforts to minimize bias in assessment tools and processes. Students from historically marginalized or disenfranchised groups and their parents/guardians need to understand sources of bias and how bias can affect grades and performance in school so they can respond when they see unfair assessment and grading practices.

Change is uncomfortable. White, middle- to upper middle-class students have benefited from the biases in assessment and grading practices for many generations. These students and their parents/guardians may react negatively to policies or practices that focus more on student learning than on competition. Students who are accustomed to outperforming other students, because of biases in their favor, may believe that unbiased practices are "unfair" to them. If all students do well on tests and other assignments and earn good grades because barriers have been removed, parents/guardians, peer teachers, and school administrators may think that teachers are "giving away" grades or see the results as "grade inflation." When teachers create classrooms focused on student learning rather than on competition, they will need to be able to assure students, parents/guardians, colleagues, and school administrators that all students are achieving high expectations (Gay, 2010).

CONCLUSION

The purpose of assessment in the classroom is to find out whether students have learned what their teachers want them to learn so they can further support students as they learn and grow. The heart of validity is truth—do the results (students' responses, test scores, grades) truly reflect what students have learned? Any factors in items and task directions that systematically detract from students' abilities to show their knowledge and skills (whether in the choice of stimulus materials, the item type, the scoring rules, language demands) and any factors in grading policies that incorporate implicit biases or favor students in some groups over others, can result in invalid scores and grades. Fair and valid assessment results require a commitment to making sure that assessment tools and processes are fair to all students.

The dominance of standardized testing has supported the marginalization and oppression of students from diverse cultural and social backgrounds for a century. For the past 50 years, classroom instruction and assessment have been driven by standardized testing. The research presented here shows that valid assessment of students is not possible in the context of standardization—no matter how hard educational publishers and test developers work to minimize bias. It is time to push back against the myth that standardization in testing supports fair and valid assessment of students and begin the hard work of making sure that classroom assessment tools, processes, and practices support learning and benefit all students.

CHAPTER 3

Culturally Relevant and Socially Responsive Assessment

In Chapter 1 of this book, I introduced validity theory to frame the assessment of students with diverse social and cultural backgrounds. However, as was evident from the research presented in Chapter 2, "Bias and Sensitivity Issues in Classroom Assessment," one-size-fits-all assessment tools and processes incorporate factors that detract from valid assessment of many students (Hilliard, 2003). Culturally sensitive and culturally appropriate assessment practices are needed to serve the diversity of students in our schools. When supported by teachers' communities of practice, classroom teachers can develop or modify classroom assessment tools and implement classroom assessment processes to make assessments more relevant and appropriate for students from diverse cultural and social backgrounds. However, making traditional assessments more culturally sensitive and less biased is not sufficient to meet the needs of students from culturally and socially diverse backgrounds.

Critical to the validity of claims about students' learning is clarity about what students are expected to learn. In today's standards-based educational world, state academic standards represent a set of learning goals that are crafted and agreed-on by a representative group of educators in each U.S. state or territory. These state-level academic standards influence curriculum adoptions, the professional development of teachers, and the content of state and district-level assessments. One of the key ideas of the standards-based movement has been that, although *what* students learn may be defined at the state level, *how* students achieve those standards can be locally determined. One might think this is an ideal situation for culturally responsive teaching and assessment. A model that puts emphasis on *what* students learn rather than *how* they learn should give teachers quite a bit of autonomy in how they teach—so long as their instruction helps students achieve a state's academic standards.

Many years have passed since the advent of the standards-based educational reform in the 1990s. Over that time, in an effort to ensure all students achieve state standards, school districts have adopted instructional materials that define not only what is taught each day but also how teachers teach. These materials are called "scripted" curricula or "teacher-proof" curricula. School administrators have come to believe that if all teachers teach exactly the same curriculum using the same instructional methods at the same pace, all students will achieve the same learning goals.

The National Assessment of Educational Progress (NAEP), a national "report card" that provides state-to-state comparisons of students' performance, has been used to track student achievement since the 1970s. Data from NAEP suggest that efforts to standardize curriculum have failed to serve students of color, English learners, and low-income students (Sleeter, 2012). Many researchers claim that scripted instructional programs work best for students from White middle- to upper middle-class backgrounds (Esposito & Swain, 2009; Howard & Rodriguez-Minkoff, 2017; Royal & Gibson, 2017; Sleeter, 2012). NAEP data would seem to support this claim. While the performance of White students on NAEP has steadily increased since the beginnings of standards-based educational reform, the performance of Black/African American and Latinx students has plateaued (Lee, 2002; Sleeter, 2012).

At about the same time the standards-based education movement emerged, Ladson-Billings (1995a) proposed *culturally relevant pedagogy* to better serve African American students. Culturally relevant pedagogy uses students' backgrounds, experiences, cultural resources, and "funds of knowledge"[1] (Moll et al., 1992) to frame instruction so that students from diverse cultural backgrounds can be academically successful. Ladson-Billings's (1995a) research suggested that culturally relevant content helped African American students achieve high academic standards. The idea is that, if students can identify with the literature and contexts used for teaching, they can more easily engage with content. In its simplest form, instructional and assessment materials are adapted to include literature, contexts, scientific phenomena, local examples of social studies concepts issues, primary documents, and historical texts relevant to the students within a classroom. In its most sophisticated form, all instruction is completely grounded in the lived experiences and learning needs of students (Gay, 2000); learning goals include both the state academic standards and goals focused on students' development of cultural knowledge as well as civic and cultural pride.

In this chapter, I present theories about culturally relevant pedagogy (Ladson-Billings 1995a), culturally responsive pedagogy (Gay, 2000), and culturally sustaining pedagogy (Paris, 2012). I explain how the use of culturally relevant pedagogy helps students achieve academic standards, and I describe how culturally responsive practices can be used to improve the quality of assessments for students from diverse social and cultural backgrounds.

CULTURALLY RELEVANT PEDAGOGY

For generations, the goal of schooling in the United States was to assimilate students into a "monocultural and monolingual society" (Paris, 2012, p. 39). Diverse cultural and social groups were viewed in terms of their "deficits" in demonstrating the values, language, and literatures of mainstream culture. Their own languages, literatures, and culture were considered to be of lower quality and have less value than that of the dominant Eurocentric languages, literatures, and cultures.

> Simply put, the goal of deficit approaches was to eradicate the linguistic, literate, and cultural practices many students of color brought from their homes and communities and to replace them with what were viewed as superior practices. (Paris, 2012, p. 93)

Shepard et al. (2018) note that "countless studies have documented the lack of learning that occurs when students are treated as deficient or when members of non-dominant communities . . . are asked to park their identities at the door to join a mainstream school" (p. 24).

Beginning in the 1970s and 1980s, social and educational practices moved toward honoring the cultural values and experiences of poor communities, particularly communities of color, as resources for helping students attain the language, literature, and culture of the mainstream curriculum. Ladson-Billings (1995a) coined the phrase *culturally relevant pedagogy* to describe classroom strategies that could support students' achievement through the use of content and contexts relevant to the lives and experiences of students.

> Culturally relevant pedagogy rests on three criteria or propositions: (a) students must experience academic success; (b) students must develop and/or maintain cultural competence; and (c) students must develop a critical consciousness through which they challenge the status quo of the current social order. (Ladson-Billings, 1995b, p. 160)

Ladson-Billings (1995b) studied teachers who were successful in helping African American students achieve high academic standards. She found that all of the teachers she studied "demanded, reinforced, and produced academic excellence in their students" (Ladson-Billings, 1995b, p. 160). All of these teachers used students' home and community cultures as vehicles for learning, including parents and community members as resources for the classroom.

Gutiérrez (2008), also writing about culturally relevant pedagogy, proposed a "third space" in classrooms. Rather than use students' families, communities, and experiences only as resources for instruction, teachers should develop a pedagogy "grounded in the historical and current particulars of students' everyday lives, while at the same time oriented toward an imagined possible future" (p. 154). She argued that this type of teaching is not just about building bridges for students between the knowledge, cultural values, traditions, and beliefs of community and the academic goals of schooling but that a new reality must be formed, integrating the language, literatures, and cultures of school and home.

Academic Success

Beckett (2011) noted that culturally relevant teachers focus on what is essential in education—"not what students *should* learn . . . or *must* unlearn but what teachers and students learn together" (p. 74, emphasis added). Effective culturally relevant teachers do not have a single teaching philosophy or method of teaching; they use whatever strategies are most effective in supporting the students in their own classrooms (Beckett, 2011). The teachers in the Ladson-Billings studies viewed knowledge as something that is "continuously recreated, recycled, and shared" (Ladson-Billings, 2009, p. 340). She found that culturally relevant teachers participated in a reciprocal relationship with their students. Teachers used their professional knowledge and skills to support students academically, socially, and culturally, and students used their cultural and community knowledge to help teachers integrate into their communities (Beckett, 2011).

In many ways, culturally relevant teaching is "just good teaching" (Ladson-Billings, 1995b, p. 159). It is consistent with constructivist teaching practices focused on helping students develop new knowledge through their own direct experiences with the content they are to learn.

Constructivism is a theory about learning—that learning occurs when people actively construct or develop knowledge through interaction with people and things. Knowledge is gained by the direct experiences of the learner (Elliott et al., 2000). Learning is a social activity—something humans do together, through interaction with each other (Dewey, 1938). Vygotsky (1978) noted that community plays a central role in the process of "making meaning." For Vygotsky, the environment in which children grow up will shape how they think and what they think about. From a constructivist perspective, all teaching and learning involves sharing and negotiating socially constructed knowledge.

Cultural Competence

Theories about culturally relevant teaching are consistent with research on effective teaching and learning practices. What differs for culturally relevant teaching is how teachers go about integrating with the families and communities of children and bringing students' experiences, knowledge, and culture into their lessons in school. Most White teachers come from similar families and communities as their White students. However, given that the public school teaching force is predominantly White and middle class and the students are becoming increasingly diverse, teachers must learn about their students' cultures, families, and communities from direct efforts to connect with the communities in which students live.

Ladson-Billings (1995b) found that all of the successful teachers in her studies became involved in the communities of their students. The teachers saw teaching as giving back to the communities and encouraged their students to do the same. Foster (1993, 1995, 1997), in her studies of highly successful African American teachers, found that effective teachers saw themselves as part of the communities they served. They used cultural patterns that would be familiar to students (especially "equality" and "collective responsibility," Foster, 1993, p. 577) in classroom activities. In addition to high academic achievement, a central aim of culturally relevant pedagogy is to help students develop a deeper understanding of and respect for their own histories and cultures.

> By "cultural competence," Ladson-Billings was speaking of supporting students in maintaining their community and heritage ways with language and other cultural practices in the process of gaining access to dominant ones. (Paris, 2012, p. 94)

This is accomplished by incorporating texts and content that is relevant to the social and cultural histories of students. Texts and historical content must go beyond stories and histories of the struggles and oppression of people from socially and culturally diverse backgrounds (Gay, 2010). Content must include high-quality literature by authors with backgrounds similar to students; math and science courses must include information about the contributions of different groups to science and mathematics; histories must expand beyond a Eurocentric focus.[2] Understanding of the histories and cultural contributions of students' social and cultural groups must go beyond "culture days" where special events are created to celebrate different cultures (Sleeter, 2012) and beyond attention to a few, high-profile African Americans (Gay, 2010).

Critical Consciousness

A third aim of culturally relevant pedagogy is development of critical consciousness so that students can (1) think critically about the factors that cause racism and oppression, (2) work for change, and (3) develop a sense of civic responsibility. This third aim of culturally relevant pedagogy may seem outside the scope of public education; however, both critical thinking skills and civic responsibility are part of most state's academic standards. In the context of culturally relevant pedagogy, teachers focus critical thinking and civic responsibility on the issues facing students in their classrooms.

> For culturally relevant teachers . . ., the main task is community building: students are seen and are taught to see themselves as valued members of important ethnic communities, and academic learning is embedded in activities and projects which appeal to students' desire to help their communities. (Beckett, 2011, pp. 68–69)

Several researchers (e.g., Dutro et al., 2008; Paris, 2012) stress the importance of getting to know students and the languages, literatures, and cultures of their communities directly rather than "essentializing" students based on race, ethnicity, religion, gender, and so forth (e.g., assuming all Black students have historical roots in slavery). According to Beckett (2011), culturally relevant teachers work with students on projects that benefit the local community immediately. The projects are partnerships between teachers, students, and community members. Students can rely on teachers for knowledge and organization and teachers can rely on students and community members to make sure projects support the community.

Many studies examining the effectiveness of culturally relevant pedagogy show positive impacts on student learning and on students' attitudes toward learning (Au & Kawakami, 1994; Foster, 1993, 1995; Gay, 2000; Farinde-Wu et al., 2017; Hollins, 1996; Ladson-Billings, 1995b, 2009; Love, 2016; Risko & Walker-Dalhouse, 2007; Wiggan & Watson, 2016; Young, 2010). To date, most research involves small-scale studies of effective teachers or successful students in urban, minority, or low-income communities. Sleeter (2012) has noted that larger scale studies would be helpful to convince policymakers and school administrators of the efficacy of culturally relevant pedagogy. Ladson-Billings (2006) recommended demonstration projects wherein educational researchers apply their research directly in schools that serve students from Black/African American, Latinx, and Indigenous American communities.

CULTURALLY RESPONSIVE PEDAGOGY

Culturally responsive pedagogy (CRP), as defined by Gay (2002), involves "using the cultural characteristics, experiences, and perspectives of ethnically diverse students as conduits for teaching them more effectively" (p. 106).

> [The t]heory of CRP is that students learn best when they are engaged in their environments and with the information to be learned. This engagement happens when students feel validated as members of the learning community and when the information presented is accessible to them. Students feel validated

and capable of learning presented information when their learning environments and the methods used to present information are culturally responsive to them. (Rychly & Graves, 2012, p. 45)

As with culturally relevant pedagogy, culturally responsive pedagogy responds to the social and cultural identities of the students actually present in a classroom. Fixed definitions of cultures (essentializing cultures based on race or ethnicity) are avoided due to the heterogeneity of beliefs, practices, educational levels, and experiences within groups (Nortvedt et al., 2020) as well as the ways the practices of groups change over time and due to media, social media, and interactions among communities (Nortvedt et al., 2020; Paris & Alim, 2014). To create culturally responsive classrooms, teachers explore their students' cultural and social identities and make connections with students' communities; they get to know individual students, their families, and the values, beliefs, practices, and funds of knowledge each student brings to the classroom.

Culturally responsive teachers do not use the same teaching methods or materials year to year based on assumptions about students' backgrounds and experiences. They draw from a broader pool of multicultural resources, some of which may be provided by the students themselves, based on the individual needs, cultures, and experiences of the students in the classroom (Gay, 2010; Irvine & Armento, 2001; Ladson-Billings, 1994).

Commitment to Achievement

For culturally responsive teachers, academic success is a "non-negotiable mandate for all students" preparing them to be "productive members" of "their respective ethnic communities" (Gay, 2000, p. 36). Teachers must connect new information to students' background knowledge and present knowledge in ways that respond to students' "natural" ways of talking, thinking, and intellectual engagement (Gay, 2002, p. 111). Culturally responsive teaching practices attend to the specific cultural characteristics that make students different from one another and from the teacher. According to Gay (2000), culturally responsive pedagogy involves adapting classroom routines and learning experiences to the values, traditions, language, communication styles, and relationship norms of the students.

Gay claims that when academic knowledge and skills are situated within lived experiences and students' frames of reference, knowledge and skills are more personally meaningful, have higher interest appeal, and are learned more easily and thoroughly. From her perspective culturally responsive teaching (CRT) *validates*, *affirms*, and *empowers* diverse students (Gay, 2000). To attain this level of integration, teachers must deeply understand the values, interests, traditions, communication styles, and relationship patterns (e.g., child–adult interactions, gender role expectations) within the cultures of students (Gay, 2010).

Addressing Controversial Issues

Culturally responsive pedagogy goes beyond including familiar cultural and familial contexts and content to support learning of accepted academic standards. Gay (2002) urges teachers address controversial issues such as racism and poverty and to avoid focusing only on a "few high-profile individuals" within certain racial or ethnic groups (p. 108). She cautions against "decontextualizing women, their issues and actions from their race and ethnicity" (p. 108). She states that culturally responsive teaching deals directly with social controversies; contextualizes them within race, class, ethnicity, and gender; and includes multiple perspectives on these issues. Culturally responsive pedagogy is also *emancipatory*, releasing "students of color from the constraining manacles of mainstream canons of knowledge" (Gay, 2000, p. 37). Finally, it is both *multidimensional*, encompassing all aspects of classroom climate, curriculum, teaching, learning, and assessment, and *comprehensive*, encouraging students' "intellectual, social, emotional, and political learning" (p. 32).

Culture of Caring

A third key aspect of culturally responsive pedagogy is a culture of caring (Gay, 2000; Nieto, 2004). Teachers must affirm students' cultural backgrounds (Nieto, 2004), have a strong belief in the capacity of all students to learn, and be willing to go to whatever length is necessary for students to achieve high academic standards (Farinde-Wu et al., 2017; Foster, 1993, 1995; Rychly & Graves, 2012; Ladson-Billings, 1995a). Culturally responsive teachers hold students accountable for their own and for each other's learning; they have empathy for their students, maintaining the ability to understand the classroom from students' points of view (Rychly & Graves, 2012). Gay (2002) claims that, while Western White male culture focuses on competition and personal achievement, many social and cultural groups value collaboration and community more than independence—focusing on the good of the community rather than the higher achievement of any one member.

Symbolic Curriculum

Gay (2002) also speaks of the symbolic curriculum and the societal curriculum. For example, she discusses ways to avoid creating nonverbal cues that marginalize students (e.g., images, icons, mottos, awards, celebrations, religious observances, music, art, and other artifacts), symbols that are regularly incorporated into the images and routines of schools. She states that teachers must address the teaching that comes from mass media such as impressions of different cultural, racial, gender, and economic groups on television shows and the Internet (e.g., portraying Latino boys and men as gang members; women doctors, lawyers, detectives as sexy; etc.).

Teacher Self-Awareness

Finally, Gay (2002) discusses the importance of teachers being self-aware about their own biases and assumptions. Teachers will be unable to fully do the work of culturally responsive pedagogy if they do not first reflect on their own attitudes and beliefs about other cultures (Grant & Asimeng–Boahene, 2006; Nieto, 2004). Jemal (2017) states that this reflection must involve thinking critically about one's own beliefs and feelings, looking for hidden assumptions and beliefs, and identifying how historical events have impacted contemporary thinking that perpetuates systems of inequality.

Nuri-Robins et al. (2006) have found that many teachers claim to be "color blind" or "culture blind" (p. 89); however, they noted ways in which attempts to ignore social or cultural differences can cause unintended harm to groups "perpetuating the sense that they are invisible" (p. 88) or that there are "no talk rules" about social or cultural identities and issues.

Rychly and Graves (2012) conducted a literature review to identify the characteristics of teachers who have successfully implemented culturally responsive pedagogy. They found four characteristics that were common among successful teachers:

> (1) that teachers are empathetic and caring, (2) that they are reflective about their beliefs about people from other cultures, (3) that they are reflective about their own cultural frames of reference, and (4) that they are knowledgeable about other cultures. (p. 45)

Faarinde-Wu et al. (2017) examined the teaching strategies of award-winning culturally responsive urban teachers. In their research, they found four themes in the practices of these teachers:

> (1) implement RACCE (i.e., they respect, act immediately, communicate, celebrate, and encourage students); (2) co-create a familial-style classroom culture of success; (3) establish student-first learning; and (4) utilize critical multicultural content delivery. (p. 287)

A recent Stanford University study explored the role of culture in student learning (Love, 2016). This study revealed that embedding student culture into the curriculum and pedagogy is beneficial for all students. Participants in the Stanford study showed increased attendance and academic achievement. Researchers found that when Latino students had the opportunity to take courses in ethnic studies, their achievement and attendance increased (Depenbrock, 2017; Romero, 2010).

As daunting as Gay's (2002) criteria for culturally responsive pedagogy appear to be, it is evident from research that, when teachers are self-reflective about their own biases, work to connect lessons and coursework to the lives and experiences of their students, embed aspects of students' cultures into the daily routines of teaching, and focus on the best interests of their students—both in the short term and the long term—they are successful in supporting the academic and personal development of students from diverse cultural and social backgrounds.

CULTURALLY SUSTAINING PEDAGOGY

Culturally sustaining pedagogy involves helping students attain the academic standards of mainstream culture *and* develop deep knowledge of and appreciation for their own literature, languages, and cultures. Learning goals go beyond those of state academic standards and include learning goals related to students' development of a strong commitment to sustaining their own cultures (Bernal, 2010). Paris's (2012) conceptualization of culturally sustaining pedagogy refocuses the "stance and practice of asset pedagogies" (Paris & Alim, 2014, p. 87) toward more explicitly multilingual, multicultural outcomes. Cultural sustaining pedagogy "seeks to perpetuate and foster—to sustain—linguistic, literate, and cultural pluralism as part of the democratic project of schooling" (Paris, 2012, p. 93).

Alim (2007) distinguishes between curricula based on students learning the culture, language, and literature of their own cultures and one that is based on curriculum that uses students' literature, language, and culture as resources for learning the "acceptable curricular cannon" (p. 27). Paris (2012) notes that a curriculum may be relevant or responsive to students' language, literature, history, and culture without ensuring that language, literature, and culture continue as part of students' "repertoires of practice" (Gutiérrez & Rogoff, 2003, p. 22).

> For too long, scholarship on "access" and "equity" has centered implicitly or explicitly around the question of how to get working-class students of color to speak and write more like middle-class White ones. Notwithstanding the continuing need to equip all young people with skills in Dominant American English (DAE) and other dominant norms of interaction still demanded in schools, we believe equity and access can best be achieved by centering pedagogies on the heritage and contemporary practices of students and communities of color. (Paris & Alim, 2014, p. 87)

In addition, as students grow older, they begin to create new versions of culture (e.g., hip-hop culture) that influence both local language and culture and the languages and cultures beyond the local community (Alim & Reyes,

2011; Paris, 2009), especially in the age of social media. Paris and Alim (2014) claim that these emerging aspects of culture also merit exploration and inclusion in students' repertoire of knowledge:

> Youth cultural and linguistic practices are of value in their own right and should be creatively foregrounded rather than merely viewed as resources to take students from where they are to some presumably "better" place, or ignored altogether. (p. 87)

A primary goal of culturally sustaining pedagogy is to empower students from historically and socially marginalized groups and to help them engage (in partnership with their teachers) in a "collective struggle against the status quo" (Borck, 2019). Culturally sustaining pedagogy is intended to help students develop positive racial/cultural identities (Graves, 2014; Jemal, 2017; Sanders, 1997; Yosso, 2005), develop critical consciousness about the sociocultural contexts in which they live, and embrace academic achievement as a form of social resistance (Carter, 2008; Floyd, 1996; Graves, 2014; Sanders, 1997). Carlson et al. (2006) noted that individuals with the highest levels of critical consciousness are aware of reality and of their responsibility for either sustaining that reality or changing it.

In a study of an urban alternative high school that has been successful with African American youth, Borck (2019) found that teachers had four key perspectives on how to support urban, low-income youth consistent with the notions of culturally sustaining pedagogy. First, the teachers believed they had to be honest about structural inequality and its relationship to race and class. Second, teachers believed they needed to shift the explanation for students' previous failures away from the idea of individual limitations and toward structural inequality. Third, students had to recognize that, even though there are structural inequalities in society, they are valuable, worthy, and legitimate. Finally, students needed to learn how to "code switch" (p. 383) between their home language and culture and the language and culture of dominant society in order to access the resources they needed to be successful in life.

Sanders (1997) interviewed a sample of 8th-graders from across 10 middle schools in a large city in the southeastern United States. The students represented high achievers, middle-level achievers, and low achievers. As part of the interview, Sanders asked the students questions about their future plans and how they thought racism and racial discrimination might influence their plans. The majority of students in the low-performance group denied that racism would be an issue for them. Most students in the high-performing group were strongly aware of racism. High performers saw their achievement as proof that African Americans are equal to or superior to Whites. They also believed that they would have to work twice as hard as Whites to attain the same goals; however, they were committed to do so because it would improve opportunities for all African Americans.

Another instance that demonstrates the success of culturally sustaining pedagogy was reported on National Public Radio. Tucson, Arizona, began offering a Mexican American studies program in the 1990s. Educators in the district stated that the program had been very effective in addressing the achievement gap between White and Latinx students. Although all of the courses in the program were electives, those who took the courses scored higher on state tests and had a higher high school graduation rate (Romero, 2010).

SUMMARY OF CULTURALLY RELEVANT, RESPONSIVE, AND SUSTAINING PEDAGOGY

The previous review outlines the characteristics of classrooms that incorporate culturally responsive pedagogy. Clearly, from the research to date, efforts to create culturally responsive classrooms have supported students' learning as measured by state tests, grade point averages, graduation rates, and teacher and student self-reports.

The research and writing to date has focused on culturally responsive pedagogy for Black/African American, Latinx, and Indigenous American students; however, the principles of culturally responsive pedagogy apply to new immigrants, English learners, LGBTQ students, and students with disabilities. English learners bring their own literatures and cultures to school, yet schools primarily focus on assimilating these students into the dominant language, literature, and culture. As EL students work to learn academic content while developing a new language, their success is likely to be influenced by how much educators respect and honor their backgrounds and lived experiences and incorporate their histories and literatures into educational experiences.

LGBTQ students routinely face discrimination, denigration, and hate crimes by mainstream culture. Their lived experiences and social/political issues may be treated as taboo in schools. Yet, LGBTQ individuals have contributed to social and political history, literature, and economic progress (e.g., author James Baldwin, astronaut Sally Ride, scientist Sir Francis Bacon, artist and scientist Leonardo DaVinci, actress/comedienne Ellen DeGeneres), served with distinction in the military (e.g., U. S. Secretary of Transportation, Pete Buttigieg, General Tammy Smith), and contributed to our nation's ongoing movement toward justice for all (e.g., Congresswoman Barbara Jordan, tennis champion Billy Jean King).

Individuals with disabilities have also contributed to social and political history, literature, science, mathematics, and culture (e.g., President Franklin D Roosevelt, actress Whoopie Goldberg, actor Robin Williams, physicist Albert Einstein, artist Pablo Picasso, activist Greta Thunberg, musician Ludwig van Beethoven, scientist Temple Grandin). Clearly there is no shortage of opportunities to incorporate the histories, literature, language, and cultural backgrounds of students from all marginalized groups in culturally responsive classrooms. Therefore, creating a safe educational space and getting to know students and their families/communities is critical to effective use of culturally responsive pedagogy. In the next section, I propose strategies for culturally responsive assessment.

CULTURALLY AND SOCIALLY RESPONSIVE ASSESSMENT

Culturally and socially responsive assessment practices must be effective in helping teachers gather valid evidence about whether students have achieved learning goals—whether the goals are set by state academic standards, teachers, students themselves, or are related to cultural knowledge and pride. Culturally and socially responsive assessment practices must give students opportunities to show their learning in ways that honor their cultural and social identities, backgrounds, and experiences.

A simple strategy for creating a culturally and socially responsive reading test might be to select texts from several authors with culturally and socially relevant backgrounds and develop test items that can be used across texts to measure reading comprehension, text analysis, and text interpretation (see Chapter 6 for an example of this strategy). However, selecting culturally and socially appropriate texts in a reading assessment without looking at potential biases in the types of questions students face can defeat the goals of culturally responsive pedagogy (see research on multiple-choice and open-response test items reported in Chapter 2). Hence, culturally and socially responsive assessment tools will likely differ from standardized tests or textbook assessments while targeting the same academic standards.

The Impact of Teacher Beliefs on Assessment Practices

Teachers may believe that all students can attain challenging learning goals, or they may believe that achievement is limited by students' ability. Research shows that culturally responsive teachers have high expectations for students and insist that students achieve them. Teachers work in partnership with students. They communicate "respect, honor, integrity, resource sharing, and a deep belief in what is possible" (Gay, 2000, p. 52). This perspective is in direct contrast to the types of deficit thinking that have negatively impacted the performance of students from diverse cultural and social backgrounds.

For much of the 20th century and beyond, classroom assessment followed the model of large-scale tests. This model is based on concepts of intelligence growing out of the work of eugenicists and social Darwinists in the late 19th century (e.g., Sir Francis Galton, a psychologist and statistician; Karl Pearson a mathematician; and Charles Spearman, a psychologist). Standardized achievement tests, designed on the same principles as intelligence tests, were intended to discriminate between "more and less able" students. The assumption behind achievement testing was that students who learned the content did well on the tests; students who did not learn the content did not do well on the tests. Students with high IQs would learn; students with low IQs would not learn. Test scores were assumed to be based on how "smart" students were. Educators believed that responsibility for success or failure fell directly on students' abilities based on a *theory of individual differences* (see Revelle et al., 2011 for information about the origins of the theory of individual differences). Many teachers still teach, test, and move on to the next lesson, whether or not students have achieved learning goals. This model of teaching is consistent with a belief that students' achievement is solely the responsibility of students.

Since the late 20th century, more and more educators reject the intelligence theory model of education and consider it the responsibility of teachers to create contexts wherein all students can learn. Research shows that, when effective formative assessment practices are used, more students achieve high academic standards. Effective formative assessment practices include (1) ensuring that students know the goals of instruction and the criteria for high-quality work; (2) ensuring that assessment tools and practices are focused on students' attainment of learning goals; (3) using teacher, peer, and self-evaluation strategies to help students know where they are in relation to the learning goals; and (4) helping students take the next steps toward success. Teachers are coaches rather than gatekeepers (Sadler, 1989; Sadler & Good, 2006). As coaches, their job is to identify, for each student, strengths and areas in need of improvement and then help each student move toward attainment of learning goals. Students and teachers work together to improve student learning (Black & Wiliam, 2012). Research also suggests that, when students engage in peer and self-assessment, they have a better understanding of the goals of instruction, the criteria for high-quality work, and their current status in relation to the learning goals (Hayward 2012; Heritage & Wylie, 2018; Nortvedt et al., 2020). Assessment that is used to support students' learning has been called *assessment for learning* (Gipps, 1994; Wiliam, 2011).

> The introduction of [assessment for learning] not only changed the purpose of assessment but also brought to the forefront student involvement in assessment

practices, clarity regarding assessment criteria and expectations, and high-quality assessment procedures. (Nortvedt et al., 2020, p. 13)

Assessment for Learning

Effective assessment for learning involves feedback that is purposeful and directly related to the targeted learning goals. Teachers provide opportunities for students to apply the feedback soon after receiving it (Black & Wiliam, 1998a, 1998b, 2009; Hattie, 2009; Hattie & Timperley, 2007; Leahy & Wiliam, 2012). Assessment for learning contributes to equity and learning for students from diverse cultural and social backgrounds because it allows teachers to identify the needs of different students and provide feedback that responds to their varying needs (Heritage & Wylie, 2018; Norvedt et al., 2020). Assessment for learning strategies apply whether an assessment tool is a performance task or a test composed of traditional test items. For traditional tests, teachers can identify patterns of misunderstanding and change how concepts are presented based on insights from students' work (Foster & Poppers, 2011) and/or give students opportunities to self-assess to better understand their own thinking. Students can retake tests as they improve their understanding. From the research on the effectiveness of formative assessment practices, it is likely that culturally responsive teachers who are committed to the success of their students are growth oriented and use assessment (whether formal or informal) to support students' learning.

Concerns About Assessment in Culturally and Socially Responsive Classrooms

Two primary concerns raised by critics about the role of assessment in culturally responsive teaching are *fairness* and *representation*. Representation refers to the question of whose learning goals are privileged by a system. Fairness refers to whether culturally and socially diverse students can be fairly assessed using conventional modes of assessment. Fairness also refers to whether students have had the opportunity to learn what is assessed.

Fairness. Testing companies use bias and sensitivity reviews and statistics to minimize bias and unfairness. However, Stobart (2005) claims that fairness in assessment is a sociocultural issue rather than a technical one. Fair assessment cannot be considered separate from both the curriculum and students' opportunities to learn all that is assessed. If children do not have equal opportunities to learn particular concepts and skills, any assessment targeting those skills will be unjust, regardless of how much attention is paid to bias and sensitivity issues in the development of the assessment (Gee, 2003).

Generally, the question of whether students have the opportunity to learn that which is tested is raised in discussions about large-scale external tests. Most people assume that what is assessed in the classroom is the same as what is taught. However, differences in students' classroom assessment performance may be due to differences in background knowledge and mismatches between what has been taught and what is assessed. As I demonstrated in Chapter 2, background knowledge can lead to classroom assessment results that are biased against students with backgrounds that differ from the dominant middle- to upper middle-class White culture (e.g., complex language and vocabulary that is not familiar to English learners, test items or tasks requiring background knowledge that has not been taught to all students, the topic of a reading passage that is more familiar to some students than others). For example, Moschkovich (2007) found that English learners had diverse interpretations of mathematical problems due to language usage. In addition, research on text-embedded assessment materials shows there is often a mismatch between the focus of instructional materials and the associated assessment tools (Frisbie et al., 1993; Taylor, 2009)—making it difficult for students to assess their own progress or for teachers to fill the gaps.

In short, fair assessment involves making sure that students know what is being assessed, have the background knowledge necessary for the contexts and texts used in assessment tools, and have ample opportunities to learn and prepare for any assessment event. When assessment practices are intended to support students' learning, teachers fill in gaps in background knowledge or adapt assessment content and contexts to fit the background knowledge and experiences of students.

Fair and equitable assessment requires teachers to abandon historically accepted, standardized methods of assessment (e.g., the belief that tests and other assessment tools are "neutral" measures of targeted knowledge and skills, the practice of concealing the content of tests until the testing event, testing only a sample of all the knowledge and skills taught, having all students complete the same items or tasks so that scores can be compared). In assessment for learning, assessment tools are not treated as "dip sticks" used to determine how much students have learned before moving on to the next topic or unit of instruction. Instead, in culturally and socially responsive classrooms, where teachers make a commitment to high achievement for all students, teachers will use assessment tools and practices to find out what students have learned and what they still need to learn and help students close the gap between current performance and achievement of the learning goals (Black & Wiliam, 1998a, 1998b, 2009; Hattie, 2009; Hattie & Timperley, 2007).

Linn (1994) recommends allowing students to choose content, context, and tasks (within specified limits) to "decrease the likelihood of disadvantaging students from diverse cultural and social backgrounds" (p. 572). If given a choice, students are likely to choose the test items or assessment tasks that are grounded in familiar contexts (Hood, 1998). Baker and O'Neil (1994) agree, suggesting that students are more likely to engage with assessments when they can select items and tasks directly related to their lived experiences and prior knowledge.

Another aspect of fairness has to do with the phenomenon of testing itself. Testing is a cultural phenomenon that differs across countries. Students who are new to the United States may not understand the genre and may need to learn how the *genre* of testing works (Hornof, 2008). Understanding the genre of testing is not limited to new immigrants. Witness the fact that, simply by teaching students how to take the SAT or ACT, students, on average, can raise SAT scores by more than 100 points (one standard deviation) (Strauss, 2017a) and raise ACT scores by 3–5 points (a little less than one standard deviation).[3] Culturally and socially responsive teachers can help students understand the genre of testing in much the same way they help students learn the criteria for high-level performance in persuasive writing or how to comprehend and interpret expository texts. Teaching students about the genre of testing is not the same as "teaching to the test" or "teaching the test" (Madaus & Clark, 2001; McCarty, 2009). Similar to teaching students the structure of haiku or the how to interpret data in a scatter plot, teaching the genre of testing involves making sure that students understand (a) how items and tasks are framed, (b) strategies for eliminating wrong answers in multiple-choice items and figuring out which answer is "correct" when there may be more than one possible interpretation of what is correct, (c) how to carefully read open-response items to understand the requirements for student-constructed responses, and (d) the meaning of assessment vocabulary. For example, Appendix F provides a list of terms frequently found in test questions across subject areas (Mitchell et al., 2015) that can be taught, modeled, and practiced as part of regular instruction and reinforced during activities designed to prepare students for standardized tests (Hornof, 2008).

In sum, for culturally and socially responsive assessments to be fair, students must have the opportunity to learn targeted knowledge and skills. Assessment tools and processes must be aligned with learning goals and be respectful of students' background knowledge and experiences. Students must understand the language of assessment, the expectations for assessment performance, and how to engage with assessment tools. Teachers' assessment practices must be focused on supporting student learning.

Representation. Another primary concern about assessment in culturally and socially responsive classrooms has to do with content representation— what content is to be taught and learned? The question of representation must be addressed by individual teachers and within communities of practice (see Chapter 5 for a discussion of how communities of practice influence learning goals and classroom assessment practices). When the aim of schooling is to achieve state academic standards, the role of assessment in culturally and socially responsive classrooms is to assess whether students are attaining those standards; however, the assessment tools, literature, language, and contexts can be adapted to be appropriate for and familiar to the specific students in a class (e.g., selecting culturally and socially relevant texts to assess students' reading skills and strategies, placing mathematics tasks in contexts that are familiar and relevant to students, anchoring science concepts in local contexts).

Some writers criticize the focus on state academic standards as the primary aim of education.

> Even in societies that recognize multiculturalism as part of society there is rarely recognition of the specific and unique knowledge of the different groups in schools. Thus, multiculturalism becomes lip-service as there is no "de facto" recognition of it as legitimate knowledge; educational leaders continue to strive for homogeneous knowledge to be owned by all. (Shohamy, 2000, p. 3)

Messick (1995), in a paper discussing validity and assessment, addressed the role that social values have played in defining academic standards as well as defining what is considered acceptable evidence to support the validity of claims about students' learning. Messick's writing about validity and assessment raises several questions: "How much have cultural values defined the educational constructs some in U.S. society hold so dearly (e.g., academic achievement, intelligence, etc.)? Whose culture and whose values have defined these constructs? Could it be that these constructs would be defined differently if they were defined by people with different cultural backgrounds?" (Hood, 1998, p. 191). Since the validity of claims about students' learning is based on clarity about what students are to learn and what it looks like when students have learned, to what extent do educators need to explore new definitions of what it means to be a literate adult within diverse cultural and social contexts?

Proponents of culturally responsive and culturally sustaining pedagogy see other important aims of schooling such as developing racial and cultural pride; understanding the impact of racist, sexist, homo-sexist policies and practices on students from diverse cultural and social backgrounds; and developing deep knowledge about students' own cultures' histories and contributions to mainstream representations of history (Alim & Paris, 2014; Gay, 2010; Ladson-Billings, 1995a).

To effectively apply culturally responsive pedagogy, educators must be clear about the aims (goals) of education (Ladson-Billings, 1995a)—especially goals that go beyond state standards. Clarity about learning goals is a validity issue. In order to make valid claims about students' learning, educators must be very clear about what students are to learn. If the aims of education are for students to achieve academic standards defined by a state, assessment will be focused on how well students are achieving state standards; instructional processes will provide support for students to learn the targeted knowledge and skills. Instructional and assessment materials can be adjusted to be relevant to students' cultural and social identities. If educators want students to achieve culturally sustaining goals—focused on students' knowledge of their own language, literacies, cultures, and histories—instruction must support students' attainment of these goals, and assessment must be focused on students' attainment of these goals. In short, as I emphasized in Chapter 1, validity is truth about students' learning. When instruction is focused on cultural knowledge and assessment is focused on the knowledge and skills taught in textbook materials, teachers will not have valid information about students' learning.

DEVELOPING CULTURALLY AND SOCIALLY RESPONSIVE ASSESSMENT TOOLS

Most thinking about culturally and socially responsive assessment practices has been concerned with students' attainment of typical academic standards. Educators have written about how to adapt traditional tests to meet the needs of students from diverse backgrounds (e.g., Linn, 1993). Others have proposed the use of performance-based assessments as the most effective strategy for integrating culturally and socially responsive assessment in classrooms (Qualls, 1998; Lee, 1998; Messick, 1995). Still others have expressed concerns about the cultural relevance of performance-based assessments (Lee, 1998; Pollitt et al., 2000; Stobart, 2005) and whether performance-based assessments are fair to English learners and minority students (Stobart, 2005). Finally, some authors express the belief that assessment, in and of itself, is a mechanism designed to control people and force them to assimilate into the dominant culture (Baker & O'Neil, 1994).

Each of these perspectives approaches culturally responsive assessment in a superficial manner. Simply using culturally relevant literature, histories, and contexts as resources for assessment avoids the more important question: What are students supposed to know and be able to do, and what does it look like when they have achieved? Only by starting with learning goals can any discussion of culturally and socially responsive assessment take place. If traditional assessment tools test content and skills that are not important using testing methods that are biased, improving the literature and contexts will not make the assessment tools more valid.

Similarly, making the claim that performance-based assessments are the best way to make assessment culturally and socially relevant ignores a the more important question—what performances? Early efforts to develop performance-based assessments simply used contrived classroom activities and turned them into performance tasks. To develop culturally responsive performance assessments, educators must ask: What valued performances do we want students to know how to do as result of their experiences in the classroom? Are those performances of value to students regardless of cultural or social background? Are there valued performances unique to specific cultural and social groups?

Questioning whether performance-based assessment is fair to English learners and minorities sets the stage for potential bias. In early efforts to develop performance assessments, English learners, African American students, and Latinx students performed more poorly on standardized performance tasks than did White, English-speaking students. However, poor performance may be a message about opportunities to learn. To deny students the opportunity to learn how to do such valued performances because of historic inequalities in performance based on race, cultural background, language proficiency, or prior achievement is to deny students future opportunities in school and life beyond school. Denying students the opportunity to learn how to do important work is also denying them the opportunity to help their children succeed in school (Ladson-Billings, 2006). Fortunately, in the classroom, students can learn how to do valued performances that are central to subject area disciplines (e.g., persuasive writing, scientific investigation, tracing the causes of historical events) and, with effective use of feedback, can become proficient.

Finally, claims that the assessment process itself is a tool for oppression is a notion based on testing for sorting and selecting. Recent research on the efficacy of formative assessment reveals the power of using assessment to support learning.

Just as educators must be clear about learning goals in order to teach, they must be clear about what achievement of those goals looks like in order to validly assess (Brookhart, 2009). By clearly defining, prior to instruction, what students are expected to know and be able to do based on the learning goals, teachers will have a clearer focus for instruction and assessment; teachers can be sure to provide the conditions and activities that will support students' achievement of targeted knowledge and skills (Qualls, 1998).

Culturally and socially responsive assessment tools should be designed based on tasks that are most suitable for demonstrations of the targeted knowledge and skills (Kane et al., 1999; Messick, 1995). To ensure that assessments are culturally and socially relevant, both teachers and students should contribute to the assessment development process. Teachers define what it looks like when students demonstrate the targeted knowledge and skills and what valued performances students should be able to do. Students can generate ideas about culturally and socially relevant tasks and contexts wherein knowledge and skills can be applied.[4] Taylor and Nolen (2008) suggest that students should generate ideas for performances based on the activities of adults in their families and communities—describing a range of performances relevant to everyday life and work that involve application of targeted academic standards. Teachers can use culturally and socially relevant resources (e.g., stories, historical texts, community issues) in both instruction and assessment.

When learning goals involve higher order thinking skills, assessment tasks must elicit students' thinking so that teachers do not have to make inferences about students' thinking, reasoning, and problem-solving strategies. Culturally and socially responsive teachers must consider an array of strategies for students to show their thinking and reasoning (e.g., drawings, interviews, observation during group work). Finally, as with any assessment, student work must be carefully analyzed in relation to learning goals so that teachers (and students) can draw reasonable inferences about what students know and can do (NRC, 2001).

Culturally and Socially Responsive Performance-Based Assessment

State academic standards represent (either explicitly or implicitly) valued performances that have been disaggregated into smaller components (standards) to help educators focus instruction. For example, the ability to write or speak persuasively has applicability in many settings outside of school (e.g., proposals, letters to the editor, letters to legislators, presentations to a city council), and most states' standards include persuasive writing as a learning goal. To ensure that multiple aspects of persuasive writing are taught, the educators who craft standards have decomposed persuasive writing into different elements (e.g., providing a claim or position, presenting arguments and counter arguments, providing evidence to support arguments, using persuasive language strategies, etc.). Similarly, authentic reading and mathematics activities have been decomposed into discrete skills that, in the aggregate, represent valued performances but, when disaggregated, create a dizzying array of academic standards.

Historically, classroom, district, and large-scale tests have focused on assessing students' mastery of the disaggregated knowledge and skills. An implicit assumption has been that, by testing the disaggregated knowledge and skills, we can make inferences about students' abilities to do the valued performances (Shepard, 1991). Unfortunately, this has led to a history of testing wherein assessments do not adequately represent the valued performances (Qualls, 1998).

Since the 1990s, educators have argued for the use of performance-based assessments, rather than test items, to assess valued performances (Resnick et al., 1995; Spalding, 2000). For example, Messick (1995) claimed that performance-based assessments are "less stigmatizing, more adaptable to individual student needs, less narrow and more faithful to the richness and complexity of real-world problem solving, more instructionally relevant, more useful for public and parental reporting, and more reflective of the actual quality of student understanding" (p. 21). Writers have also suggested that performance-based assessments could be valuable tools for integrating students' language, literature, and cultures into assessment events (Baker & O'Neil, 1994; Hood, 1998; Koelsch et al., 1995; Lee, 1998; Messick, 1995). Not only can performance-based assessments provide opportunities for students to understand the purpose of the learning goals, culturally and socially relevant performance tasks can improve students' interest and engagement (see Chapter 4 for a more thorough discussion of student engagement).

Lee (1998) suggests the essential characteristics of culturally responsive performance-based assessments include the following:

- Be linked and integrated directly with curriculum and instruction
- Involve tasks that draw on culturally based funds of knowledge from both the communities and families of the students as well as the knowledge the students bring from their youth culture
- Address some community-based authentic need and, as a result, may well have political linkages
- Demand that students draw on knowledge sources from several disciplines
- Involve students in working together as well as working with others from outside their schools

Koelsch et al. (1995) state that the criteria for developing culturally responsive performance-based assessments should include connection with students' lives, allowing students to show learning in a culturally responsive way, with a clear connection between what is learned in school and the world outside of school.

If teachers are clear about what performances they want students to learn how to do and are explicit about the criteria (expectations) for students' work, creating and using culturally and socially responsive assessments involves making sure contexts and content are relevant to the students within the classroom. Table 3.1 provides examples of learning goals, performances that could demonstrate the learning goals, and suggestions for how the performances could be made relevant to students.

Each of the examples given in Table 3.1 is focused on learning goals that are represented in nearly every state's academic standards. Since the learning goals are skills and knowledge that can be applied in many situations, the primary strategy for providing culturally and socially responsive assessment is to focus the content of the tasks on ideas, authors, issues, and events that are relevant to the students' lived experiences and cultural/social

Table 3.1. Learning Goals and Valued Performances

Subject Area	Learning Goal	Performance	Making the Performance Relevant to Students
Mathematics	Students learn how to represent data on coordinate grid. Students learn how to identify a line of best fit. Students learn how to write linear equations to represent a line of best fit.	Ask students to plot data, draw the line of best fit, and write an equation to represent the line of best fit.	Provide students with data from a real-world scenario relevant to their lives (e.g., the relationship between measures of toxins in the water supply in different communities and incidence of disease in the community). Have students write a proposal or letter to a legislator about the trends shown in the data.
Language arts	Students learn how to think critically about how authors communicate their messages.	Students read an expository text, analyze the author's strategies for communicating the message, present their analyses in a mode of their choice (e.g., a poster similar to a science fair, a written essay, a dramatization, an oral presentation), making sure that each performance option allows students to show their analysis.	Students choose from authors that represent the cultural/social backgrounds of students or choose from topics that represent local social, political, or economic issues.
Language arts	Students learn how to write persuasive arguments.	Students write letters to the editor of the local newspaper or a state legislator presenting their positions on an issue (Garcia, 2020).	Anchor the writing in local community issues, giving students the opportunity to research local issues and interview community members before writing.

Subject Area	Learning Goal	Performance	Making the Performance Relevant to Students
Language arts	Students learn how to write narratives.	Write a story, memoir, or biography using narrative strategies (e.g., description, sequence, voice, dialogue).	Give students an opportunity to write about a cultural event, a family member, or their experiences at a local event.
Social studies	Students learn the causes of events at a certain time in state history.	Write or present a historiography or report to describe events during a certain time in history and explain their causes via essay, oral narrative, visual representation, or dramatization.	Ask students to learn about a person from their cultural/social group during the historical era. Add the person's experiences and/or contributions to the historiography or report.

backgrounds. To generate these types of assessments, teachers would need to understand the meaning and intent of the academic standards *and* identify real-world contexts, relevant to their students, in which those standards can be demonstrated.

For any assessment, particularly performance-based assessments, teachers need to be clear about the criteria for good work and communicate those criteria to students. Performance criteria can be drawn from specific academic standards relevant to the performance. For example, if students are to research a particular historical era from the point of view of someone from their cultural background, teachers would have to be clear about what is to be demonstrated in the report (e.g., person's name, age, ethnicity, location, description of the individual's contribution to or personal experiences during the era). If students are writing a story, teachers would have to be clear about whether the story is a simple narrative describing a series of events or if the story needs a plot line, description of setting and characters, beginning and conclusion, and so forth. If students are graphing data, details about what is presented in a graph of data must be clearly stated (e.g., title, titles for axes, units, accurately plotted data, line of best fit, linear equation). Alternately, students and teachers can work together to compare good and poor examples of performances and identify criteria for high-quality performances together. If the performances are unique to a given culture, students and teachers can work together to identify criteria for the performance that are appropriate for students' cultural backgrounds. (Chapter 2 provides an example of how the narrative structure of some Indigenous American legends differ from a Western narrative structure.)

Each of the tasks described provides a real-world opportunity to use knowledge and skills defined in state academic standards. The targeted standards are important enough to merit the time and focus needed for students to develop deep understanding of the concepts and skills. Neither the learning goals nor the tasks are trivial. The reading materials, research topics, mathematical contexts, and so forth can be adapted to the specific cultures, experiences, and concerns of the students in the class.

Teachers can use performance assessment as both an opportunity to explore culture and as a teaching opportunity. Students can generate ideas for culturally and socially relevant performances, contexts, and literatures. Teachers can organize lessons prior to work on a task to help students unpack and define characteristics or criteria for good work. Appendix B provides guidelines for developing a performance-based assessment.

Project-Based Learning (Assessment as Learning)

Rather than have performance tasks be culminating events after a unit of instruction, performance tasks can also be the centerpiece of instruction. As students engage in projects and tasks, they learn the targeted knowledge and skills. As students use feedback from teachers and peers to improve their work to better meet criteria, assessment becomes an opportunity for students to learn *while* doing projects and tasks. This type of assessment has been called assessment *as* learning (Dan, 2014).

When projects and performances are the centerpiece of instruction, projects and performances can be used to make connections between the classroom and the students' cultures and communities and even geared toward service to the community. As with any assessment tasks, teachers can ensure that the targeted knowledge and skills are central requirements of the project or performance. Teachers can help students internalize the criteria for high-quality performance so that they know what to demonstrate in their work and how to develop more proficiency over time. When students do authentic work characteristic of adults in various disciplines, students can develop understanding of the criteria by which similar adult work is evaluated. "Internalizing what criteria mean in a particular discipline is not just about learning the rules for grading—it literally means learning the discipline itself" (Shepard et al, 2005, p. 298).

Examples of culturally and socially responsive projects are given in Table 3.2.

Again, when using assessment *as* learning, a project or performance becomes both a learning experience and an assessment of that learning: an opportunity to develop targeted knowledge and skills and to demonstrate the knowledge and skills via the project or performance. Culturally and

Table 3.2. Culturally Responsive Projects That Give Back to the Community

Subject Area	Learning Goals	Performances	Connection to Community
Language arts	Students learn how to write effective expository essays: voice, organization, descriptive language, a range of vocabulary, and so forth.	Write a biographical sketch. Write an informative letter to a legislator. Write an article for the local paper.	Interview a favorite neighbor or family member. Learn about a community issue. Interview a local artist or activist.
Mathematics	Students learn how to organize data into graphs, compute descriptive statistics, and interpret results.	Collect data and represent it in both a graph and in statistics (mean, median, mode); summarize and draw conclusions from the data.	Collect data from community members about their perspectives on a local issue; present a report to the mayor or city council.
Social studies	Students learn economic concepts related to distribution of wealth.	Investigate and present results of research on economic policies and how they affect communities.	Research how local regulations and ordinances have impacted economic conditions for members of the community (e.g., home and business ownership, or employment). Present findings at the local library or community center.
Science	Students learn concepts of human/environmental interaction.	Investigate the impact of human activities on the environment; provide results of the investigation in presentation, essay, news article.	Research how local economic activity (e.g., building, mining, fracking, industrial pollution) has affected the health of a community's environment and its citizens. Present results at the local library or community center.

socially responsive projects that integrate community with valued work can also speak to the "political dimension of education" (Lee, 1998, p. 277). Community-based projects can be designed to provide an opportunity to learn valued knowledge and skills, address the authentic needs of "disenfranchised and marginalized communities," as well as help students to develop a sense of community responsibility (Lee, 1998, p. 277). Gruenewald (2003) and Smith (2007) call this type of experience "place based" pedagogy: a pedagogy that departs from

> [the] presentation of standardised knowledge associated with established disciplines, reliance on teachers as primary information sources, assessment procedures based on ease of marking and justification, and the control of students (Smith, 2007, p. 189)

Caveats About Culturally and Socially Responsive Performance Assessment

Although, educators have recommended the use of performance-based assessments in culturally responsive classrooms (e.g., Messick, 1995; Norvedt et al., 2020; Qualls, 1998), writers have also noted that, if instruction and assessment are to be culturally responsive, it is imperative that the performances are culturally responsive (Hood, 1998; Moschkovich & Nelson-Barber, 2009; Norvedt et al., 2020). If a particular type of performance is inconsistent with students' cultural values, educators must find other ways for students to demonstrate their learning.

Early critiques of performance-based assessments for students from diverse cultural and social backgrounds have focused extensively on the appropriateness of the contexts for performance assessments (e.g., Lee, 1998), the degree to which classroom teachers are capable of constructing performance assessments that truly tap into high-level academic standards (Qualls, 1998), and whether teachers can reliably and fairly evaluate students' performances (Bond, 1995). Bond (1995) states that teachers, like anyone else, can "hold purely prejudicial beliefs that can affect their objective assessments of others" (p. 24).

Much has changed since the late 1990s when performance assessments were first explored in education. Since that time, many efforts to construct performance assessments have emerged—from including short-answer items in traditionally multiple-choice tests to incorporating direct writing assessments; including structured performance-based assessments similar to those in the more recent large-scale tests (e.g., Smarter Balanced assessments); and California's efforts to incorporate authentic science investigations in its state tests. Teachers have participated in large-scale scoring operations wherein they have learned how to apply systematic scoring criteria to students work. School districts have provided workshops for teachers to help them learn how to look closely at students' work, provide effective feedback, and apply other assessment for learning strategies in the classroom assessment process.

Still, development of culturally and socially responsive assessment tools may be a challenge for teachers. As Lee (1998) has pointed out, just including performance-based assessments doesn't ensure that the assessments are either culturally relevant or sensitive to the lived experiences of students. She notes that, if a fundamental concern of culturally responsive teaching is to enhance the ability of youth to engage with rich texts and construct generalizations from texts that they can then apply in some way to their own lives, educators must ask themselves what role the selection of texts and genres plays in students' performance?

Lee describes early examples of performance-based assessments that were focused on what was considered rigorous and demanding to academics rather than real students. She gives, as an example, a performance assessment asking students to write an essay responding to Winston Churchill's statement that the U.S. Civil War was both the "last romantic war and the first horrendous modern war." Lee points out that asking students to write an analytic essay responding to Churchill's statement was inappropriate for students of color—particularly African American students. She notes that the topic of the essay is clearly geared to the perspectives of academics and not to the world views of non-White cultures. As Lee's example shows, although analytic writing is a valued form of writing, the topic of the performance task is erudite and shows clear bias in favor of highly educated, primarily White students.

> The challenge of building performance tasks that link academic skills with everyday contexts is answering the question of whose everyday context. (Lee, 1998, p. 273)

Culturally responsive assessment must also consider students' cultural ways of communicating and accomplishing tasks and their cultural perspectives on achievement. If culturally and socially responsive assessment is to be student and culture centered, educators must respect cultural norms about group or individual work, success and competition, gender, and adult–child interactions (Hood, 1998). Here are some examples:

- Some cultures believe that knowledge belongs to the collective rather than the individual (Moschkovich & Nelson-Barber, 2009). Therefore, teachers must consider ways to have students do performances that require group efforts—at least for some aspects of the work. For example, students could work in small groups to analyze a text for different themes and different strategies authors used to communicate those themes. Students could then take the ideas from the group and complete a task that shows their personal response to the text—building on the ideas of the group.

- Teachers must consider whether it is appropriate for students to work in mixed-gender groups and organize groups accordingly.
- Teachers must consider perspectives on individual versus group achievement. Research suggests group projects requiring contributions from all members of a group benefit all learners, regardless of their initial level of achievement (Cohen, 1998).
- Many cultural groups eschew competition. By focusing on the success of all students, teachers can allay concerns about competition. Using draft-feedback-revision cycles as students complete assignments communicates a belief in the success of all learners and creates a noncompetitive classroom climate.

In short, culturally and socially responsive assessment must be "sensitive to cultural variations in ways of participating, thinking, and learning" (Norvedt et al., 2020, p. 11).

Lee (1998) points out that developing and implementing performance-based assessments brings educators into highly politicized territory. Assessment specialists raise concerns about the quality of tasks and the accuracy of teacher evaluations (Qualls, 1998; Linn, 1993, 1994). Policymakers and school leaders raise concerns that focusing on performance-based assessments takes up class time that should be dedicated to students learning a broad array of knowledge (Ryan, 2006).

> The research base suggests that context is important, but the politics of the curriculum—and, by association, assessment content—rears its figurative head in any efforts to design and implement both culturally responsive pedagogy as well as culturally responsive performance-based assessments. (Lee, 1998, p. 274)

Lee (1998) describes two bodies of support for the proposition that culturally responsive assessments will be useful and empowering for students from culturally and social diverse backgrounds. First, several researchers have found that the contexts in which individuals apply knowledge and skills impact their success (e.g., Lave et al., 1984). For example, Lave et al. (1984) found that although individuals might not be able to show their mathematical skills on traditional classroom tests, they are able to effectively use the same mathematical skills when applied in their community contexts. Such research suggests that "cognitive competencies are situated rather than absolute—that everyday representations and operations are neither incorrect nor impoverished, merely different" (Lee, 1988, p. 273).

The second body of research has to do with authenticity. Real-world problem solving is often ill-structured and requires learners to draw on multiple strategies, resources, and funds of knowledge to solve particular problems. In contrast, school-based tasks are often contrived; successful performance may not generalize beyond the classroom (Lee, 1998). In addition, everyday tasks require complex thinking and may require students to draw on knowledge and skills from across disciplines—again making performance more likely to be generalizable beyond the classroom. For example, the mathematics and social studies performance tasks described in Tables 3.1 and 3.2 require integration of language arts skills (writing, speaking, presenting) into the performances in order to give students an authentic audience for their work. In addition to these arguments, when performance tasks are integrated with instruction (assessment as learning), instructional time and assessment time are not separated into discrete aspects of instruction (Dan, 2014). Shepard et al. (2018) use the phrase *horizontal coherence* to describe situations wherein curriculum, instruction, and assessment provide mutual support and are codesigned.

A final caveat has to do with the nature of authentic work. Solomon (1993) notes that authentic work beyond school often requires input from more than one person, each with different levels of expertise. Thinking and problem solving are shared across group members. The skills required to complete culturally and socially responsive performance tasks that require groups to solve problems or explore ideas together are more likely to generalize beyond the classroom. The challenge for culturally and socially responsive teachers is to balance successful performance by a group with assessment of individual students' knowledge and skills. If feedback and revisions are to be appropriate for individual students, group tasks must be carefully crafted to allow for both group success and individual demonstrations of knowledge and skills.

CULTURALLY AND SOCIALLY RESPONSIVE ASSESSMENT: LAST THOUGHTS

This chapter has reviewed the research and writing about culturally relevant, culturally responsive, and culturally sustaining pedagogy. Research on the characteristics of teachers who have successfully implemented culturally responsive pedagogy show that their practices lead to high academic achievement for students from low-income and culturally diverse backgrounds. Their work is grounded in an unequivocal belief in what is possible for children (Acosta, 2012; Gay, 2002; Romero, 2010).

> Culturally responsive caring is *action oriented* in that it demonstrates high expectations and uses imaginative strategies to ensure academic success for ethnically diverse students. Teachers genuinely believe in the intellectual potential of these students and accept, unequivocally, their responsibility to facilitate its realization without ignoring, demeaning, or neglecting their ethnic and cultural identities. They build toward academic success from a basis of cultural validation and strength. (Gay, 2002, p. 110)

It is evident from the literature on culturally responsive assessment that efforts to align assessment practices with culturally responsive pedagogy have been limited. Most of the writing and thinking about how to make assessment more culturally relevant was written in the 1990s. Little has been done to address this issue since that time. After the reauthorization of the Elementary and Secondary Education Act (ESEA) in 1994 and again in 2001 (No Child Left Behind; NCLB), thinking about classroom-based assessment was overshadowed by the demands of large-scale testing (Davis & Martin, 2018). The intense focus on large-scale testing has dominated state activities and local educators' work (McCarty, 2009). The onerous features of NCLB drove educators away from focusing on student learning to thoughts about how to raise test scores—leaving serious thought about classroom-based assessment far behind (Davis & Martin, 2018).

Fortunately, recent research on the factors that most support student learning has shown that assessment for learning is one of the most effective strategies for improving student achievement. As more educators learn about assessment for learning strategies, educators have given renewed attention to classroom-based assessment. The most recent reauthorization of ESEA in 2015—the Every Student Succeeds Act (ESSA)—shows a recognition that large-scale test-driven education has failed to achieve the ESEA goals. Educators at all levels of the educational system are trying to figure out how to use classroom assessment throughout the school year to monitor students' learning so that the claims made about student learning can be trusted. In this context, it is time to rethink culturally and socially responsive instruction and assessment.

This chapter is an attempt to integrate the best thinking about culturally responsive pedagogy, formative assessment practices, and culturally responsive assessment. The bottom line is that the principal aim of all these literatures is to identify the practices and methods that are most likely to support the learning of culturally, socially, and linguistically diverse students and to ensure the validity of claims about students' learning.

We may still suffer from a century of educational practices driven by theories of intelligence perpetrated by eugenicists of the 19th century. These practices threaten the validity assessment results for all students, but especially for students with diverse cultural and social identities. However, we can change this trajectory by rejecting rigid, racist, classist, and sexist thinking about students' abilities, gaining clarity about what students truly need to learn, and ensuring that all instructional and assessment decisions support student learning of important, nontrivial knowledge and skills.

There is no such thing as a neutral educational process. Education either functions as an instrument that is used to facilitate the integration of the younger generation into the logic of the present system and bring about conformity to it, or it becomes "the practice of freedom," the means by which men and women deal critically and creatively with reality and discover how to participate in the transformation of their world. (Freire, 1970/2000, p. 34)

In this chapter, I am recommending the use of performance assessments as the most effective way to create culturally and socially responsive assessments that provide valid information about students' learning of valued knowledge and skills. When well developed, not only can performance assessments integrate knowledge and skills in authentic ways, they can become practices of freedom where students engage in work that helps to transform their worlds.

High-quality performance tasks that have value in and of themselves can help teachers focus their teaching of the dizzying array of standards they are expected to teach. Most academic standards are, in truth, derived from valued performances that have been decomposed to help focus instruction. Attention to academic standards, while developing high-quality performance assessments, can help teachers (1) determine the knowledge and skills (criteria) for high-quality work, (2) write directions for tasks that clearly communicate expectations (so students will show what they have learned), and (3) help teachers focus feedback as students learn how to do valued work. Grounding valued performances in the context of community, family, and culture gives the work (and the standards) meaning and purpose and strengthens the validity of claims we make about students' learning. Chapter 6 provides a strategy for developing performance-based assessments and associated scoring rules along with tools to guide the process.

The primary purpose of schooling should be the success of every child. Simply following the agendas of published instructional materials and using text-embedded tests and quizzes will not support students' learning nor prepare students for the world beyond school. Spending instructional time preparing students for large-scale tests rather than helping them learn how to accomplish valued performances not only undermines student learning but wastes precious time with students, leading to invalid test scores that have no meaning. Hopefully the ideas in this chapter can inspire new thinking about culturally and socially relevant assessment tools and practices that support students and that support teachers who wish to create responsive classrooms.

In Chapter 4, Susan and I review the research on instructional and assessment practices that are most likely to encourage student engagement. Only if students engage in the educational process can teachers be sure that assessment results validly reflect students' learning. Many of those engagement-oriented practices are consistent with ideas presented here.

In conclusion, valid assessment will tell educators whether students are learning what they are expected to learn—however the learning goals are defined—and will allow students to make progress toward achieving the goals.

CHAPTER 4

Student Engagement and Assessment

No matter how well we develop tools that can tap into the knowledge and skills we want students to learn, students have to *engage* with these tools to demonstrate their learning. When students believe they have a solid chance of succeeding, their work is worthwhile and their success is valued by others, they are more likely to learn and demonstrate their learning. Earlier chapters in this book describe how assessment tools (the tasks and assignments given to students) and processes (e.g., strategies for evaluating students' work) can meet the needs of the diversity of students in American schools *and* remove barriers and biases that prevent students from demonstrating their learning during assessment events. In this chapter we review the factors most likely to encourage engagement of diverse students and describe how attention to these factors supports engagement with assessments as well as instruction. We begin with an overview of research on student engagement. We then present a set of recommendations for those who are developing or modifying assessment tools and processes to optimize student engagement.

STUDENT ENGAGEMENT: A REVIEW OF RESEARCH

The term *engagement* has been used in a variety of ways by educators and researchers. Two broad categories are particularly relevant to assessment. *School engagement* refers to a sense of belonging in school; feeling part of a school community, valued and welcomed. In the history of schooling in the United States, many groups of students have been marginalized, shunned, or seen as "other" for their social identities, including race, ethnicity, sexual orientation, and disability status. School engagement describes students' feelings, behaviors, and thoughts about their school experiences and is an important predictor of outcomes such as academic success and high school completion.

A second, related use of the term engagement refers to *task engagement*—how students approach school tasks: their actions, effort, persistence, and emotions during learning activities (Skinner et al., 1990). Because attention, effort, and persistence are all associated with positive outcomes related to learning and assessment tasks, task engagement is considered "a highly desirable goal with positive outcomes for all parties [students and teachers]" (Bryson & Hand, 2007, p. 354). This positive relationship assumes quality learning and assessment tasks and activities. Engagement in trivial or meaningless tasks is unlikely to result in much learning or useful assessment. Task engagement is related to school engagement in that it results from an interaction between individuals, their histories, and people and things in their classroom and school communities.

Both school engagement and task engagement are socially constructed. People (teachers, students, parents, and others) create environments in which students feel valued and welcomed (or rejected and marginalized) and the environments in which learning tasks and assessment tasks have their meanings. Are assessments understood to provide useful feedback to learners and their families, or are assessments judgments on students' worth? Are test scores indicators of current levels of student mastery or skill, or indications that students or their families do not care or are not capable of learning? In our experience as teacher educators, for example, many teachers of young children are wary of classroom assessment tools, fearing that it will discourage students and cause them to disengage or give up. This fear is grounded in a definition of assessment as separate from learning, something that is done at the end of a learning period to judge students' capabilities. Institutional and governmental uses of standardized assessment scores to judge and classify students, teachers, and schools (rather than to support student learning) contribute to this definition. Further, assessment tools and scores have frequently been used to marginalize groups of students and have served to reinforce White supremacist ideologies and racist policies (Au, 2016; Davis & Martin, 2018; Lipman, 2004).

Assessment can also be framed as a way to support students' learning, if the processes and tools used really do provide students with usable information that they can use to improve skill or deepen understanding, and if the context provides meaningful opportunities to engage. Student engagement can be improved through positive changes in teachers' relationships with students, effective modifications of instructional strategies, and culturally and developmentally appropriate alterations in the nature of tasks and assessments (Dotterer & Lowe, 2011). In the following sections, we review research that supports this claim. Although these factors have usually been studied separately, it is important to remember that they work in concert. The use of high-quality, culturally, socially, and developmentally appropriate tasks, designed and implemented to support ongoing student learning, and embedded in a context of positive personal relationships where diverse perspectives and contributions are valued, can work together to increase engagement by changing the meaning of assessments for teachers, learners, and their families.

FACTORS THAT IMPROVE ENGAGEMENT OF STUDENTS

Social Context of the Classroom and School

Schools and classrooms are deeply social spaces. Students and teachers spend the majority of their waking hours interacting in school communities that provide the contexts where young people form their academic identities. We begin by locating student engagement within classrooms and schools as a function of how students come to identify with school and school subjects, through interaction with the people, materials, and ideas there. Through actions and words, students develop both disciplinary knowledge (of mathematics, literature, science) and a knowledge of their own position and status within that community (Nasir, 2011; Nasir & Hand, 2008). Students' social identities and histories play a role as well; Nasir (2011) uses the term *racialized identities* to indicate that in the United States and many other countries one's race is always a part of one's identity. Likewise, students with disabilities often find that their disability is seen as a defining aspect of their identity, whether or not it is relevant to any particular task. The "default" or "unmarked" identity (able-bodied, White, often male) becomes a source of largely unexamined privilege. Varelas et al. (2012) argue that for "Black students in mathematics and science classrooms . . . three intersecting identities are particularly important: disciplinary identity (as doers of the disciplines, i.e., mathematics and science), racial identity (emerging understandings of what it means to be Black), and academic identity (as participants in academic tasks and classroom practices)" (p. 319).

Because schooling reflects the inequitable society in which it is embedded, educators, parents, and students must work to create educational spaces that allow all students to see themselves as valued and welcomed members of the school and classroom community (Connell et al., 1994).

> No matter what material resources are available, no matter what strategies districts use to allocate children to schools, and no matter how children are grouped for instruction, children spend their days in social interaction with teachers and other students. As students and teachers immerse themselves in the routines of schooling, both perceptions and expectations reflect and determine the goals that both students and teachers set for achievement, the strategies they use to pursue the goals, the skills, energy, and other resources they use to implement the strategies, and the rewards they expect from making the effort. (Ferguson, 2003, p. 460)

As an indicator of what a community values, assessment tools and processes play an important role in establishing the roles and identities of students and teachers. Students are more likely to engage in instruction and assessment when they believe they can benefit (they can be successful in activities that have real value) and when they believe that teachers care about their success. We have long known that students who feel a sense of belonging and social support are more likely to be engaged and participate in school (Deci & Ryan, 1985, 2000; McCormick et al., 2011; Wentzel, 1997). Many researchers agree that the social, instructional, and organizational climate of schools influences both students' engagement and their academic achievement (e.g., Eccles et al., 1998; NICHD Early Child Care Research Network, 2005; Patrick et al., 2007; Ryan & Patrick, 2001).

Teachers play an essential role in creating positive climates through the intellectual work they design, their interactions with students, and in how they establish norms for students' interactions with each other. Engagement increases when students believe that educators care about their success and when teachers create a climate conducive to learning and success through the clarity of learning goals, helping students set personal goals, opportunities for self-assessment, and opportunities for students to close the gap between current levels of achievement and targeted levels of performance (Black & Wiliam, 2009; Wiliam & Thompson, 2007). Students who are in conflict with their teachers, who do not feel connected or supported, often disengage from classroom activities (Skinner et al., 1990). Ladd and Burgess (2001) found that when teacher–child conflict was greater, students were less engaged in the classroom, were less likely to enjoy school, and were at increased risk for poor academic performance. Further, Baker (2006) found that teacher–child conflict was associated with lower report card grades and standardized test scores, while classrooms rated as having a positive climate were associated with children being more engaged in classroom activities and greater learning (Cornelius & Herrenkohl, 2004).

Work Students Believe Is Relevant to Their Own Lives

For assessment to be a useful tool in supporting learning, students and teachers must see it as providing actionable information that can help students develop valuable knowledge and skills. Students in schools today come from diverse cultural, social, and economic backgrounds. With the standardized education provided in textbooks, anthologies, and other educational materials, many students do not "see" themselves or their communities in the materials and information they use at school. The tasks they are asked to do are often removed from the issues and needs important to students' families and communities. Chapters 3 and 6 describe a number of ways that culturally and socially relevant materials can improve the relevance of classroom assessments, give students opportunities to integrate classroom work with their communities, and allow students to investigate issues of race, class, and gender oppression.

Many standardized and classroom assessments use decontextualized items and tasks to "even the playing field" among students. Claiming that decontextualized tasks "even the playing field" or make assessment tasks neutral is actually dishonest (Adair, 2008; Freire, 1970/2000). There is nothing neutral about assessment. Compartmentalizing and carrying out decontextualized tasks seems to privilege students from White, upper-class backgrounds and disadvantage students from culturally diverse backgrounds (Darling-Hammond et al., 2008). Students bring their background knowledge to assessment events. Students from White and affluent backgrounds are more likely to infer connections between decontextualized tasks and their own lives—possibly because they know they will benefit the system that constructs these tests (Gutstein & Peterson, 2006).

In a study by Cawthon et al. (2011), the researchers used teachers' self-reports and classroom observations to assess students' engagement. Their research showed that the percent of students engaged in lessons increased from 68 to 91 percent when students did "activities that encourage students to draw on their previous knowledge and experiences, engage in critical thinking, and apply what they learn to their own lives" (p. 1).

Assessments that are relevant to students' lives provide important opportunities for students to connect school learning with the world outside of school, which is important for both engagement and learning. Students are more interested and attentive, but also are able to use prior knowledge to make sense of and interact more deeply with materials and problems that relate to their lives and histories (Flores-Dueñas, 2003; Walkington et al., 2012). For example, research on mathematics test performance suggests that, when contexts are relevant to students' lives, struggling readers perform much better than expected on mathematics test items even when substantial reading is involved (Taylor & Lee, 2004).

Personalizing student work also appears to improve engagement and performance (Meier, 2008). For example, Walkington et al. (2012) found that personalization increased student performance on algebraic word problems. They studied algebra classes where teachers used a computer-based tutoring system to individualize instruction through adaptive problem selection, hints, and feedback. Students in the experimental group solved algebraic word problems matched to their self-reported interests (e.g., sports, music, art, games) from student surveys and interviews. Personalization increased student performance, especially with more cognitively challenging problems and for typically struggling students. These findings suggest the importance of relevance in choosing assessment topics, and the possibilities for improving student engagement and performance through personalization and relevance.

Autonomy and Authorship

Meaningful learning can also occur when students participate in shaping the work that they do. Student engagement improves when classroom activities and assessments support students' autonomy (Olivier et al., 2020; Ryan & Deci, 2020). Autonomy has been defined as "freedom from control" or "self-determination" (Assor, 2012, p. 421). Katz and Asor (2007) state that:

> People feel autonomous when they feel and/or understand the value or relevance of the task in which they are engaged, and therefore can identify with it. Feelings of autonomy are particularly strong when the task is perceived as being closely connected to the values, interests, and goals that constitute the core of one's authentic self and identity. (p. 431)

One frequently described way for teachers to strengthen students' sense of autonomy is to offer choice within or among tasks. Choices can increase engagement by productively tailoring learning and assessment tasks to the needs or interests of students, particularly when teachers help students choose tasks that are moderately difficult but achievable, communicate confidence in students' abilities to succeed, and teach students how to assess their own progress (Kostons et al., 2012; Patall et al., 2008). Choice reduces the perception of extrinsic control in learning activities and creates a feeling of "ownership" in students (Schraw et al., 2001). When autonomy (either of an individual or a group) is supported in the classroom, self-regulation and behavioral engagement increase (Adams & Palmer, 2017; Connell & Wellborn, 1991; Hafen et al., 2012), and students perceive a better fit between their own values and academic content and express less boredom when faced with challenging content (Plunger et al., 2019). Choices are not always engaging in school settings, however. For example, some cultural groups (e.g., highly collectivist or hierarchical cultures) may find it *less* motivating to be given choices than to have trusted authorities guide tasks (Katz & Assor, 2007). In addition, researchers have found that, for children, when options become more complex, children tend to respond by using the less-complex strategies characteristic of younger children and even resort to random selection without consideration of the options (Bereby-Meyer et al., 2004; Davidson, 1991).

Supporting student autonomy can take many forms. In project-based learning (PBL), for example, students learn and are assessed through their work on teacher-guided, complex projects (Brookhart et al., 2006) in which there are many opportunities for students to make decisions within a structure (e.g., about strategies, information sources, topic, presentation). Such projects can provide opportunities for student authorship of knowledge through their research and critical thinking, at the same time developing a sense of self that includes developing expertise as a scientist, writer, environmental citizen, or other important role. Opportunities to be recognized as a knowledge contributor or expert may be particularly important for increasing the engagement and sense of belonging of students who have been marginalized in school. PBL also provides opportunities for community engagement, which helps students connect school learning with their own lived experiences (Smith, 2007).

> In classrooms or schools where place-based education is well-established, inquiry into local concerns and problem-solving shape teaching and learning activities more than a standardised curriculum, and teachers and students function more as collaborative team members than as bosses and employees (Smith, 2007, p. 190).

Framing assessment and other educational tasks is also important in supporting student autonomy. Autonomy-supportive teachers frame and design tasks in ways that highlight why completing tasks and learning specific content are useful and relevant to students (Nolen, 2001; Nolen & Nicholls, 1993; Nolen et al., 2020; Tierney et al., 2018); encourage independent thinking, questioning, and constructive criticism; and convey respect for students (Deci & Ryan, 2000). Opportunities for autonomy and authorship with structured support can strengthen students' sense of the efficacy of their own learning strategies, their perceptions of their own abilities to learn, and their sense that achievement is under their own control (Olivier et al., 2020).

Authentic Intellectual Work

Authentic intellectual work asks students to construct new knowledge using disciplined inquiry processes—doing work that has value beyond the classroom (Newman, 1996; Newman et al., 2001). Newman et al. (2001) claim that if students are asked to do authentic intellectual work, they will find the work more valuable and will engage with it. Students may find a topic or subject uninteresting; however, if they are given an opportunity to do tasks they see as valuable, they may develop situational interest in the task. Then, by engaging with the task, they may develop personal interest in the task and the subject area (Høgheim & Reber, 2017).

Authentic intellectual work can occur in both instruction and assessment. When authentic intellectual work is the centerpiece of instruction, instruction and assessment are merged. As students engage in authentic intellectual work, they manipulate information and ideas to arrive at conclusions that produce new meanings for the student, even if those "meanings" are well known in particular disciplines (Hernandez & Darling-Hammond, 2019). For example, scientists may have already established principles related to the genetic transfer; yet, when students conduct their own scientific investigations and develop models to describe sources of genetic variations, they are more likely to develop "deep understanding" of genetic transfer principles. Direct instruction may seem like an efficient way to impart knowledge; however, when students construct knowledge themselves—while engaging in work that is authentic to the subject discipline (e.g., scientific inquiry, literary analysis)—they construct knowledge in the same way as professionals in the given discipline. Shepard et al. (2018), in their description of the goals of the Next Generation Science Standards, state, "proficiency involves much more than being able to recite core ideas of the discipline; it requires application of those ideas to explaining phenomena in the world and solving problems using the kinds of practices that disciplinary experts use" (p. 24). This gives students ownership of knowledge and skills—they are learning for themselves rather than attempting to memorize facts for a teacher or a test. Newman (1996) found the following:

- When students had opportunities to learn, through their investigative skills, using strategies that are central to a discipline (e.g., reading primary documents to research the causes and effects of the American Civil War), students were more likely to retain knowledge.
- When students had opportunities to engage in dialogues and debates with peers and teachers, proposing new problem-solving pathways, grappling with contemporary or historical controversies, and so forth, they were more likely to develop deep understanding.
- When the concepts and skills learned in school had immediate relevance to the larger context in which students lived, students were more likely to understand the relevance of knowledge and skills learned in school.

Learning how to write persuasive arguments, for example, is one of the core writing purposes included in most contemporary state academic standards. A teacher might give students an assignment to write a persuasive essay on a topic assigned by the teacher (e.g., "Write a persuasive essay about whether we should have school uniforms"). Alternately, the teacher might have students investigate local community issues, develop their own perspective on the issue and write a persuasive letter to a newspaper editor or a proposal to a city council. Newman and his colleagues found that when students in elementary and middle school classrooms engaged in this type of authentic work, the quality of academic performance increased regardless of SES, ethnicity, gender, or prior achievement level.

Making school learning more meaningful for students "requires strategies for breaking down the barriers between school activities and mature sociocultural activities, for making visible, accessible, and personally relevant the knowledge, skills, and practices of those mature activities. It makes the learning that can go on in school more meaningful and purposeful" (Shepard et al., 2018, p. 24).

Inquiry-Based Learning Experiences

Studies of inquiry-based classrooms in science (e.g., Chang & Mao, 1999; Schwartz et al., 2004) showed that students developed deeper conceptual understanding and showed increased engagement, interest, and positive attitudes toward science compared with classrooms where lecture was the primary mode of instruction. Students in these studies were able to engage in authentic scientific work: frame research questions, design and conduct investigations, collect data, and draw conclusions (reasoning from evidence).

Murray and Summerlee (2007; Summerlee & Murray, 2010) found that the use of inquiry-based instruction significantly affected the learning behaviors of students, led to greater motivation to succeed, and led to enhanced reasoning and processing skills that transferred to other courses. In the Murray and Summerlee studies, all students, regardless of prior achievement level, benefited from inquiry-based instruction in terms of achievement, engagement, and their ability to access and use resources to support learning.

In contrast, a focus on teaching to standardized tests tended to undermine teachers' and students' focus on student learning, trivialize the targets of learning, and discourage inquiry teaching (McCarty, 2009). In studies of classroom assessments, Madaus et al. (1992; Madaus, 1988) found that assessments in low-income schools focused on low-level skills and mirrored the types of test questions found on standardized tests while assessments in middle- to upper-income schools focused on reasoning and inquiry.

Active Learning and Collaboration

All learning is active. That is, all learning requires the learner to make sense of incoming information, relating it in some way to what is already known (National Research Council, 2000). However, there are instructional techniques that require more than relatively passive mental work. Active instruction involves students in actively manipulating or discussing new information, doing hands-on activities (e.g., science investigations, applying mathematics to solve real-world problems), or authoring new knowledge (e.g., writing histories or historical fiction). A study of engagement trends over 4 years for freshmen and seniors found that high engagement scores were associated with more focus on active and collaborative instruction (McCormick et al., 2011).

The most effective collaborative learning experiences are occasions during which all members of a group are engaged in investigations and problem solving (Cohen, 1984, 1994; Herrenkohl, 2006; Herrenkohl et al., 1999; Herrenkohl & Guerra, 1998). In peer learning experiences, students "learn with and from each other without immediate intervention from the teacher" (Boud et al., 1999, p. 413). Chan and Leijten (2012) found that students involved with peer learning were deeply engrossed in examining other students' approaches to tasks and in evaluating the processes undertaken to complete tasks and solve problems. Other studies have shown that learning experiences in small groups—whether with worksheets and textbooks or with high-quality performance tasks—increase engagement, while passive learning decreases student engagement (Cooper & Speece, 1990; Greenwood, 1991, 1996; Greenwood et al., 1989).

Collaborative learning and assessment tasks are not simple to implement. However, there is an abundance of research and practice related to crafting tasks and creating classroom norms around equitable collaboration (see Horn's 2012 book *Strength in Numbers* for a good resource on these issues). Students with disabilities, students with low social status, English learners, students of color and others may be marginalized within groups without thoughtful planning and instruction (Cohen & Lotan, 1997; Kurth et al., 2002). This may be subtle, including ignoring suggestions or ideas, orienting bodies to exclude particular groupmates, or maintaining control of materials. Kurth et al. (2002) provide a particularly clear case study of a group of elementary science students in which the two White students' domination of the task was not initially apparent to teacher or researcher until the marginalized students (an African American girl and a Latino boy) were interviewed and the video data was reexamined.

Tasks that have single correct answers or require straightforward application of known strategies are not good candidates for collaborative work. Instead, tasks that require the legitimate intellectual contributions of all members of a group (multiple perspectives, different kinds of knowledge, different skills) are what Cohen and Lotan (1997) call "groupworthy tasks" that work against the domination of work by one or two students. Some otherwise groupworthy tasks might still make it difficult for all members of a group to engage (e.g., if a student with limited use of hands cannot manipulate objects or equipment), requiring some adaptation. In any case, it is necessary to establish social norms that encourage meaningful engagement by all participants, stressing the importance of everyone's contributions to a successful task.

Feedback and Opportunities for Improvement

Feedback is one of the most effective interventions to support engagement, autonomy, and student learning (Black & Wiliam, 1998b, 2006; Brookhart, 2008; Butler & Winne, 1995; Hattie, et al., 1996; Hattie & Timperley, 2007; Kluger & DeNisi, 1996). Feedback can be supplied from the environment, as when students design and test a simple machine or write a poem and read it to an audience. It can also be supplied by more knowledgeable others, like teachers or coaches. Quality feedback is a very effective way for teachers to communicate their belief in their students' abilities to learn and succeed, supporting both learning and identity development (Nasir, 2011). If students are encouraged to apply feedback soon after receiving it, they are more likely to benefit from it (Brookhart, 2008; Handley & Williams, 2011). The opportunity to apply feedback not only improves students' performance, it contributes to student learning and communicates that students' success is expected (Gay, 2010).

Minimizing Stereotype Threat

Chapter 2 presented information about the influence of stereotype threat (Steele, 2003) on student performance. Stereotype threat can also affect student engagement when students believe that assessment results are likely to reinforce negative societal stereotypes about them based on group membership. Steele and his colleagues also found specific ways of presenting tasks and tests that minimize stereotype threat and encourage engagement. For example, minimizing competition, telling students that they are likely to do well on a test or performance task, or telling students that work will be challenging but doable increases student engagement and performance.

STRATEGIES FOR INCREASING STUDENT ENGAGEMENT DURING ASSESSMENT EVENTS

We know that engagement during instruction supports learning and engagement during assessment events supports performance. Therefore, educators should consider what they can do to increase students' engagement in both instruction and assessment.

In the first half of this chapter, we presented a brief summary of the strategies research suggests can improve student engagement. In what follows, we use the information from the research to recommend strategies for developing and/or improving assessment tools and processes to foster the engagement of students from diverse backgrounds. Fortunately, classroom teachers can adapt assessment tools and processes to meet the needs, interests, and experiences of their students so that students are more likely to be engaged during assessment events.

Use Assessment to Support Learning

A primary way to create a positive assessment climate is to create a learning environment. When students believe the purpose of assessment is to help them learn, they are more likely to be engaged with the assessment process. Just as an athlete is more likely to listen to a coach if the purpose of feedback is to improve the athlete's game, students are more likely to engage with feedback when the purpose is to improve students' performance.

- Frame assessments as providing students and teachers with useful information that can be used to support further learning. Design assessments to provide this information and give students the opportunity to act on it.
- Communicate high expectations for all students (e.g., "This task may be challenging but there are many paths to success. I know you are up to this challenge").
- Begin assessment events by telling students their success is valued and expected.
- Give students strategies for engaging with assessments (e.g., "There are many different ways to accomplish the tasks in this assessment; choose one that works for you." "If you get stuck review the questions and information provided to see what you have already answered, then try again." "If you get stuck, skip to the next question and then come back when you've finished another question." "Read the questions to see what you will be asked to think about before you read the passage.")
- Ask students to provide feedback on test items or task directions if they don't understand what they are being asked to do.
- Demystify multiple-choice items. For example, rather than giving students a published test, have students discuss (individually or in small groups) why they would select a particular multiple-choice answer and why other answers are not correct.

Use Feedback as a Vehicle for Assessment and Teaching

Feedback and opportunities to improve performance increase students' engagement with their work. Three factors have been shown to influence the effectiveness of feedback: clarity, timeliness, and focus.

First, students must be able to make sense of feedback. If feedback is given in language that is unfamiliar to students or uses terms that differ in meaning across disciplines, understanding is hampered (Brookhart, 2008; Wormeli, 2006). In the same way that effective teachers craft explanations and other forms of instruction in multiple ways (e.g., language, images, models) to reach diverse learners, they find ways to communicate feedback to students who may be new to a discipline, to English, or to discipline-specific vocabulary.[1]

Second, students are most likely to engage with feedback when it bears on what they do next. Structuring assessment activities as a way for students to develop competency (rather than as a measure of achievement) is critical. In athletic coaching, feedback is typically given in the moment, often with both a physical demonstration and an explanation. Players are encouraged to immediately try new strategies. Feedback and revision are common strategies for teaching writing; however, feedback and revision can also be effective in other subjects. For example, providing guidance, then allowing students to self-evaluate their mathematics homework or a mathematics test for patterns of errors, and then giving students an opportunity to redo the homework or test can help students deepen their understanding and eliminate errors on future work. Providing opportunities for students to act on feedback also communicates to students that they can *be* an author, an athlete, a scientist (Nasir, 2011).

Finally, feedback should help students accomplish high-quality work (Brookhart, 2008). Students cannot effectively use feedback if they don't understand the criteria (expectations) for the work. Three ways to help students internalize the criteria for high-quality work include the following:

1. Giving students an opportunity to analyze the characteristics of good work so that they understand the ultimate goals of instruction
2. Teaching students to give and receive peer feedback using disciplinary notions of good work as well as providing teacher feedback
3. Allowing students to revise their work as they apply what they have learned from feedback

Feedback is not the same as "correcting students' work." Students may need to improve many features of their work; however, focusing on every mistake can overwhelm students and lead to a sense of failure. In addition, correcting students' work leads to compliance rather than learning. Students may do what they are told to do—particularly if the feedback is prescriptive—without actually learning how to make their work better in the future or how to generalize conceptual understanding to future situations. Similarly, feedback must provide more than a score. "It does little good to tell a 4th-grader that his essay is a '2' or that he needs three more items correct to reach mastery on a numeracy test" (Shepard et al., 2018, p. 28).

For feedback to effectively engage students, it has to be used in a meaningful manner. Feedback is more likely to benefit students when it helps them know how to improve their work. Focusing on a few areas of improvement and giving students an opportunity to revise their work based on the feedback results in longer term retention of knowledge and skills (Brookhart, 2008). When improvement is recognized in formal grades, students learn that their achievement is valued and expected.

As teacher educators, we have noticed that practicing and preservice teachers are uncomfortable giving students' credit for final performances after a feedback cycle. It is common for teachers to tell us that it is unfair to students who do well in the first effort if students who need more time and feedback are graded based only on their final work. An unfortunate school grading practice is to give students the "average" score between first efforts and revised work. There are at least two significant issues with this model. First, in a learning-centered classroom, the point of education is *that* students learn rather than *when* students learn. Second, averaging scores from initial efforts with scores after continued instruction (e.g., feedback and revision) results in invalid scores or grades—the final grade does not reflect what students' have *learned*. We ask our pre-service teachers two questions: (1) Which student did you actually teach? and (2) How is it fair to make assessment and grading a race where some students begin the race ahead of others (Ladson-Billings, 2006)?

Hattie and Timperley (2007) suggest that the feedback cycle requires three stages of feedback to be effective and useful to students: clarifying learning goals, assessment of progress, and deciding what to do next. When done well, feedback is one of the most powerful ways to engage students, show belief in their abilities to succeed, and improve achievement (Black & Wiliam, 1998b; 2006; Hattie, 2009; Hattie & Timperley, 2007; Sadler, 1989).

Make Assessment Tasks Relevant to the Lives of Students

Research suggests that student engagement increases when students believe classroom activities are relevant to their own lives (Cawthon et al., 2011). To make tasks relevant to students, teachers can do the following:

- Create or modify assessments so they reflect contexts relevant to students' own lives and developmental levels. As Lee's (1998) example in Chapter 3 demonstrates, an assessment task may be authentic intellectual work but not authentic to students' lived experiences.
- Present situations and problems that are relevant to the issues in students' lives and communities. Chapter 6 provides several examples of making assessment tasks relevant to students' communities.
- Whenever possible, avoid the use of abstract or decontextualized items and tasks. There is rarely a good reason to assess concepts in abstract, decontextualized ways—unless a teacher is attempting to narrow down the cause of students' errors or misconceptions in order to provide targeted follow-up instruction.
- Have students connect science or social studies concepts (e.g., water cycle, landforms, energy cycle, social (in)justice, human–environmental interaction, economic inequality) to their own community contexts.

Give Students Authentic Intellectual Tasks

Research clearly supports the use of authentic intellectual work in terms of students' engagement during instruction (Newman, 1996; Newman et al., 1992). In addition, when students engage with tasks that are authentic to various disciplines (e.g., using principles of design to create a logo for a business, using scientific inquiry to develop understanding of a scientific phenomenon, using geometric transformations to create animations), students learn how adults use the knowledge and skills they are learning in school. Students have opportunities to construct new knowledge rather than simply memorizing knowledge others have constructed. Authentic intellectual work makes it easier for teachers to create opportunities for students to connect knowledge and skills learned in school to their own lives, interests, personal goals, and communities. The following provides steps teachers can take to ensure that students are being asked to do authentic intellectual tasks:

- Look at items or tasks before they are given to students and ask, "Does this really happen? Does this task occur outside of school (in the world of work, play, daily life, or research) or is it contrived?" To make sure a task is worth doing, teachers can do the following:
  » Ask whether the task is important enough for students to spend time completing it.
  » Focus on important ideas rather than specific facts or details that will be forgotten after a test.
  » If possible, integrate assessment and instruction so that students develop new knowledge while engaging in tasks that demonstrate conceptual understanding. Ideas about how to integrate assessment and learning are described in Chapters 3 and 6.
- Use performance assessments whenever possible. Here are some examples:
  » Students can do a well-structured research project to demonstrate the same reading standards as multiple-choice and short-answer test items.
  » Students' understanding of scientific phenomena can be demonstrated through their write-ups after scientific investigations.
  » Students' understanding of the causes and/or effects of historical events can be demonstrated through an investigation into how historical events affected their own histories, communities, families, and/or cultures.
- Be sure tasks require students to apply disciplinary thinking skills in authentic ways (to solve problems, to draw conclusions from data, to build causal arguments, to create something).

- Whenever appropriate, have students integrate concepts and skills across subject areas (e.g., applying mathematics skills to analyze social science data relevant to students' lives, writing an essay making an argument about the causes of a particular historical or contemporary event, representing the results of scientific investigations in graphs and statistics).
- Give students opportunities to develop new knowledge.

Adults who engage in authentic intellectual work (scientists, historians, mathematicians, literary critics) do not present "right answers" but rather draw valid conclusions and/or make defensible arguments *based on the evidence available*. In situations where students do authentic work, teachers need to use high-quality analytical scoring rubrics that focus on the features of responses that are authentic to the given disciplines (e.g., effective use of scientific practices, viable interpretations of passages anchored in the text, reasonable and evidence-based arguments for causes of events). Scoring rubrics for authentic intellectual work must be designed so that responses from students from diverse backgrounds and with diverse life experiences are recognized and valued.

Assessment that involves authentic intellectual work is best when teachers integrate instruction and assessment. As students learn how to do a particular type of work, the work becomes an opportunity for both learning and assessment. For example, as students learn how to write historical narratives, they can demonstrate their abilities to write historical narratives and show their understanding of historical events. As students learn how to write persuasive arguments, they also demonstrate their persuasive writing skills. As athletes develop skills and strategies for a particular sport, they also demonstrate their skills and strategies in real time. As students create animations using geometric transformations, they are learning and demonstrating their understanding of geometric transformations.

Promote Student Autonomy and "Authorship"

Autonomy and authorship are best fostered by giving students choices in the tasks they complete, helping them manage their choices, and helping students make connections between learning goals, assessment tasks, and their own interests, values, and goals. The following examples show ways to promote autonomy and authorship.

- Give students opportunities to choose the focus of a task and how to complete a task. See the following examples:
  » Give students options for how they present their work. Many modes of presentation can demonstrate the same concepts and skills (e.g., presentation at the local library, op-ed for the local

paper, proposal to the city on results of an investigation of environmental health).

» Allow students to choose from among texts for an assessment of comprehension, analysis, and interpretation of text. (Chapter 6 provides examples of generic items and tasks that can be used with any literary or informational reading passage.)

» Allow students to choose the specific research questions to investigate related to particular scientific phenomena and give students opportunities to develop their own research designs, interpretations, and conclusions to investigate those questions.

- Have students develop their own examples to show mathematics, science, or social studies concepts.
- Give students opportunities to do tasks that are connected to their values, interests, goals, and identity and that directly benefit the students.

In general, students' perceptions of the assessment task (interest, value, importance), perceptions of their ability to accomplish it (self-efficacy), and perceptions of the reasons they might want to accomplish it (goal orientations) are interrelated. These motivational variables, in turn, influence the effort students will expend on the task and their actual achievement. (Brookhart et al., 2006). Giving students choices requires careful thought:

- Students must be given a limited number of choices that are relevant to their own backgrounds and are comparable in difficulty.
- Teachers must be sensitive to the needs of students who are not comfortable making choices.
- Tasks must not be too complex, leading students to disengage.
- Teachers may need to scaffold moderately complex tasks or model how tasks can be done.
- Teachers need high-quality analytical scoring rubrics that focus on the essential features of effective responses (e.g., effective interpretations of results from a scientific investigation, viable interpretations of passages anchored in the text) rather than evaluating students' work based on specific "correct" answers or based on students' agreement with the teacher's analyses, interpretations, or conclusions.

Provide Opportunities for Active Learning and Collaboration

Assessments can allow for collaborative activities for a segment of the assessment task. It is important to note that collaborative activities require attention to inclusion. Careful attention to classroom norms for collaborative work can help prevent the marginalization of individuals or groups. Assessment tasks with higher stakes make it more likely that the work will be dominated by one or two higher status students. Several researchers have focused on ways to ensure that all students' contributions are needed for successful collaborative work, particularly marginalized students and students with disabilities (Cohen, 1984, 1994; Cohen & Lotan, 1997; Kurth et al., 2002).

During performance tasks, teachers must balance group collaboration with individual accountability for conceptual understanding and skill. For example, students can work together to brainstorm different ideas, and then students can work individually to do culminating work. Students can do individual preparation for aspects of a project or performance and then work with other group members to integrate individual contributions into a coherent whole.

THE CHALLENGES OF MAKING ASSESSMENT ENGAGING FOR ALL STUDENTS

A primary goal of classroom-based assessments in a standards-based culture in the 21st century is to have students demonstrate critical thinking, problem solving, and deep conceptual understanding. Assessment experts have focused research on how to create standardized assessments that are the same for all students. Sameness is enhanced when tasks are brief, easily controlled (e.g., multiple-choice and short-answer test questions), and have a limited number of correct responses. However, having all students complete brief, decontextualized, common tasks will not engage all students. In addition, standardized tasks are likely to privilege the background knowledge and perspectives of the dominant culture (Darling-Hammond et al. 2008).

Educators have demanded more complex and authentic tasks; however, assessment experts have pushed back on this demand because of costs, perceived inefficiency, and questions about reliability. Still, an increasing number of assessment programs include performance tasks with well-developed scoring rubrics to guide evaluation of student work.

Assessment experts have also questioned the equivalence of assessments when they are personalized to fit the interests and backgrounds of students or when students are given choices about which tasks to complete. Similarly, student collaboration during an assessment raises questions about whose work is being evaluated and whether the performance of a group represents the work of all group members. While fairness is, indeed, a major concern in assessment, these issues have to do with models of education based on competition rather than learning. Real-life problem solving involves choice and collaboration.

Most current standardized assessments, whether large scale or classroom based, are not fair. As long as tests present contexts and scenarios

that privilege the cultural values, ideas, and experiences of White and upper income students, testing will continue to foster the marginalization of
students. Fortunately, classroom assessments do not have to fit standardized
testing models. They can be designed to support students' learning rather
than simply judge students' achievement at a particular moment in time.

In this chapter, we recommend research-based strategies teachers can
use to encourage student engagement in classroom-based assessment events.
Well-developed performance tasks give students opportunities to engage in
authentic work, where they apply knowledge and thinking skills to explore
and analyze developmentally appropriate real-world problems relevant to
their own lives. When students with diverse cultural and social identities
believe those tasks are authentic and have value to them, they are more
likely to engage with the tasks because of their intrinsic value to students.
Allowing students to improve their work through self-evaluation and feedback communicates an expectation that all students can achieve high expectations. The recommendations provided in this chapter break away from
"one-size-fits-all" assessment, focusing instead on creating environments
where assessment is intended to be relevant to students with diverse cultural
and social identities and to support all students' learning.

CHAPTER 5

A Situative Perspective on Assessment in Diverse Classrooms

The assessment practices promoted in this book are grounded in extensive research. They require teachers to transition from traditional approaches to assessment (teach, test, grade), to practices that are respectful of and more effective for students with diverse cultural and social identities. The goal of these efforts must be to support student achievement of important learning goals and to ensure that assessment results truly reflect students' learning rather than many of the biases that are built into our current assessment systems.

Teachers do not work in vacuums. They work in communities of practice that influence their everyday work and can influence the validity of claims we make about students' learning. Teacher education programs and professional development opportunities attempt to prepare teachers to make good instructional and assessment choices in their own classrooms. Much research has focused on the degree to which teacher preparation programs and professional development make a difference in teachers' classroom practices. Research shows that the most effective professional development programs provide sustained coaching and mentoring as well as opportunities for collaboration, feedback, and reflection, particularly when professional development occurs in a learning community (see Darling-Hammond et al., 2017 for a review). The most effective teacher preparation programs give preservice teachers opportunities to use the strategies they are learning in field-based experiences and to receive coaching and feedback from mentor teachers, coaches, and program faculty (Dunst et al., 2020). These studies clearly show the importance and influence of the communities in which teachers work.

Throughout this book, we have often used a situative lens to understand teacher practice and provided guidance on how teachers can make assessment practices more fair and responsive to the diversity of students in schools through the work of the communities of practice. Chapter 2 describes how communities of practice can influence the validity of grades and the fairness of grading practices. It also describes how educators can work together to review assessment materials for potential bias. Chapter 3 describes the power of communities of practice in creating schools focused on the success of all students through the implementation of culturally responsive instruction and assessment practices. In Chapter 4, we describe strategies teachers can use to engage students and how educators, working together, can encourage student engagement during instructional and assessment events. The degree to which students' performances during assessment events provide valid information about student learning depends, in part, on teachers working together in communities of practice committed to the success of all students. This chapter is intended to shine the spotlight on the situative perspective itself and argue for its relevance to those who want to work for educational change.

A SITUATIVE PERSPECTIVE

Learning is a social activity—something humans do together, through interaction with each other (Dewey, 1938). Vygotsky (1978) noted that community plays a central role in the process of constructing meaning. The environment influences how we think and what we think about. Individuals do not act in isolation, even when apparently acting alone. Their thoughts, motives, skills, feelings, learning, and identity emerge from and are situated within cultural systems, through activity with cultural tools, and in response to others' activity. Their activity (speech, writing, physical activity, thinking) has meaning through its relationship to the systems of meaning in which it is embedded. For example, the same action (say, a student questioning the teacher's interpretation of a piece of literature or disagreeing with the teacher's assertion that a college education is the path to success in life) may be interpreted differently depending on both the race of the student and that of the teacher, by virtue of the relationship between culture and privilege (see Farkas, 2003, for a review). This relationship feeds and is fed by socially constructed cultural beliefs and actions.

How a person's behavior is interpreted is grounded in the norms and meaning systems of a given space (Lantham, 2016). When a student of color questions the ideas of a White teacher, the teacher may interpret the behavior as "thinking independently" or "being disrespectful" or even personally threatening to the teacher's sense of authority and expertise. The interpretation depends in part on the ongoing individual relationship of the teacher to the student, but also draws on local and cultural ideas and beliefs about how young people should or might behave toward adults. The images from the dominant culture feed implicit biases in perception (Farkas, 2003; Quinn, 2020). Further, through their effect on teachers' and students' interactions, these cultural images influence the interpersonal relationship itself. Similarly, cultural systems can influence students' interpretations of teacher feedback. Students may discount negative feedback from teachers of another racial or ethnic group because they suspect bias (Borck, 2019; Fordham & Ogbu, 1986). Conceptualizing human activity in this way leads us to explore assessment practices in the context of local meanings, identities, learning, or engagement as well as larger societal frameworks.

Distribution Across People, Things, and Time

To take a situative approach means seeing activity, even individual activity, as *distributed* across people, things, and time. Individual teachers, working alone in a room think *through* the tools they use: through the laptops they are using to prepare lesson plans, through the symbol system of their written language, with the conceptual tools of their disciplines. As they plan, they take into account their relationships with their students and anticipate their responses. Their thoughts reflect the meaning systems in which they live and work and their thoughts reflect on those same systems. As teachers plan, their ideas are distributed across notes, sources, memories, and other resources that reflect their analytical processes as well as their results. Their motives for the specific lesson plans are affected by the value systems of peer teachers, their schools, their local variations, their social identities, and the relationship between their social identities and the work they are trying to do. What is "in their heads" is important but only as one piece of a complex picture.

To illustrate, consider the case of Mr. Franklin. A traditional, individual approach to thinking about teacher assessment practices might focus on Mr. Franklin's goals for learning, his beliefs about teaching and assessment, and his knowledge of different ways to assess learning. Efforts to change his practice would be grounded in changing his individual thoughts and skills. A situative approach to understanding Mr. Franklin's assessment practice would begin by considering the activity systems within which he works. Mr. Franklin's 4th-period U.S. government class, for example, is an activity system (context) co-created by all of the people (Mr. Franklin and his students) interacting with each other and with things (desks, textbooks, computers, charts, whiteboards, curricula, original source materials, laptops, homework, exams). Even when the teacher, objects, and activities are the same (as might be the case for Mr. Franklin's 2nd-period U.S. government class), the students are different, with different personal histories, identities, relationships, resources. Therefore, the interactions in class are different; the opportunities to learn, develop, and engage are different. The opportunities to participate also differ for different individuals within the same context. From one day to the next, the absence or presence of particular individuals can change the context. Differences between sections of a government course might impact choices of assessment tasks and grading practices, as well as the particular instructional practices he chooses. And, of course,

Mr. Franklin's classes are embedded in a department, school, district, town, state, and country, all with histories and structures that have the power to influence what happens in classrooms. Mr. Franklin may know about and want to implement project-based assessments, for example, but feel constrained by the dominant quiz-and-test approach in his department, or the length of class periods, or the reactions of parents. The students in Mr. Franklin's classes are also members of other classrooms, homes, and community organizations. They bring those experiences with them to the U.S. government class and to the assessment tasks. Changes in systems outside the classroom can impact the activity within. As we write, the worldwide experience of the coronavirus pandemic and the effects of the Black Lives Matter movement have impacted students, families, and educators in ways we are only beginning to understand.

In typical methods courses in a teacher education program or in a typical professional development offering, these layers of context are mostly ignored. Assessment methods may be taught with attention to how assessment practices fit with a particular teacher's classroom, subject area, and instructional strategies; faculty or professional developers may emphasize assessment methods that fit the subject area discipline (e.g., Windschitl et al., 2011) or the learning goals. However, in practice, teachers' choices of assessment strategies are not made in isolation, and neither are the choices of districts or states. To understand teachers' assessment practices, it is important to work from the system to the individual rather than focus only on the individual teacher (Greeno, 1998, 2011). Teachers may learn about particular assessment methods in a workshop, professional development seminar, or college course; however, their implementation of the practice will be influenced by colleagues, the school culture, district policies, and state efforts to drive teaching (Horn et al., 2008; Nolen, 2011; Nolen et al., 2009).

One of the most striking examples of the embedded nature of classroom assessment practice can be seen in the changes following the passage of the Elementary and Secondary Education Act of 2001, also known as the No Child Left Behind Act (NCLB). At the time of this writing, each state and territory in the United States has convened educator committees to develop academic standards and state-level assessments to measure students' achievement of those standards. States have directly or indirectly pressured districts and schools to raise state test scores. State and district professional development activities have focused on teachers' understanding of state standards and, in some states, methods of teaching likely to help students achieve the standards. School districts have adopted "scripted" curricula wherein teachers are to follow the detailed teaching plans, including materials, scripts for their presentations, and conversations with students (Esposito & Swain, 2009; Howard & Rodriguez-Minkoff, 2017; Royal

& Gibson, 2017; Sleeter, 2012; Sleeter & Stillman, 2005). Thus, a federal mandate has led to state pressures on districts, district adoptions of instructional materials and interim assessments, teacher professional development, teacher evaluations during principal observations, daily conversations among teachers—all of which impacts teachers' daily pedagogical practices. Critics of NCLB have argued that the reification of the "achievement gap" and the resulting demands for increased test scores influence classroom assessment practice in ways that contribute to the oppression of students of color (Davis & Martin, 2018).

Teachers' assessment practices exist within institutional assumptions that drive how schools operate. For example, using an intelligence test to sort children into educational tracks is a practice situated in a cultural system that takes for granted individual differences in "intelligence" (a construct proposed by eugenicists in the late 1800s to explain differences in performance and reified by test developers for nearly a century). Ability testing exists in a system structured to separate "smart" or "gifted" students from those who are "less smart" or "less capable." Such systems reflect cultural beliefs in the immutability of intelligence and the desirability of freeing "top" students to progress without being held back by "lower ability" students. These beliefs have been shown to directly impact the performance of both high- and low-achieving students over time (Ferguson, 2003; Payne, 2004; Rheinberg, 1983; Tenenbaum & Ruck, 2007).

The fact that the language, topics, and contexts within ability tests are likely to be more familiar to upper-class White students (e.g., classification items based on classist concepts such as working-class versus professional-class jobs) has helped bolster racist beliefs about innate low abilities of immigrants, English learners, and low-income students (Gould, 1981). An implicit belief in intelligence has also led to bias in standardized achievement tests and classroom assessment practices (i.e., teacher grading and recommendations). This has contributed to suppressed performance for low-income, Black/African American, Latinx, and Indigenous students for many generations and has increased the placement of students of color in special education programs (Davis & Martin, 2018; Farkas, 2003). Even though emphasis on intelligence has waned in public conversations, teachers continue to create ability groups in classrooms, and schools continue to place students in different educational tracks based on achievement test scores and grades in school. Since the beginning of the standards-based educational movement, the purpose of standardized achievement tests has shifted from measuring students' relative abilities to assessing students' achievement of grade-level standards. Yet, the methodologies of achievement test development and score generation are still fully grounded in the methodologies of intelligence testing. Clearly, our collective belief systems and historical precedents still influence what counts as knowledge, what we assess, and how we assess.

IMPLICATIONS OF A SITUATIVE PERSPECTIVE ON CLASSROOM ASSESSMENT PRACTICES

Classroom assessment practices are *situated* in social systems. This situative approach to understanding how and why educators use assessment practices and assessment data in the ways that they do contrasts with narratives that suggest teachers have more choice and autonomy in their decisionmaking about assessment than they actually do. Despite the efficacy of formative assessment (Black & Wiliam, 2012; Brookhart, 2009; Heritage & Wylie, 2018; Taylor & Nolen, 2008), effective use of formative assessment requires changes in thinking and practice. Keeping the role of the system in view helps us understand historical and current practices of assessment for diverse students, as well as how to work for change. Assessment practices range from the institutional to the individual, but all are products of and function within social systems. Shepard et al. (2018) refer to sociocultural learning theory to describe the powerful role social systems have in learning:

> Participation in sociocultural activity necessarily involves more than simply acquiring knowledge; it involves processes of identification that, in turn, present opportunities for participants to become certain kinds of people in activity. (p. 23)

For educators to embrace culturally and socially responsible assessment practices, they must engage with systems that may or may not support new ways of thinking about assessment. Assessment practices produce boundary objects (Star & Griesemer, 1989)—grades, student work, portfolios, and course credits—that are used by others in and beyond the classroom and school to make decisions about students (Nolen, 2011; Nolen et al., 2011). As boundary objects, assessment results "have different meanings in different social worlds"; however, "their structure is common enough to more than one world to make them recognizable, a means of translation" (Star & Griesemer, 1989, p. 393). Specifically, relevant to the ideas in this book, Star and Griesemer (1989) state that "the creation and management of boundary objects is a key process in developing and maintaining coherence across intersecting social worlds" (p. 393). For teachers, this means that they must navigate the boundaries between their own interpretations and uses of assessment results and the meanings and purposes assigned to assessment results by different audiences within and beyond the teachers' communities of practice.

Within a high school mathematics department, for example, a passing grade in a lower-level math class is taken to indicate competence at a certain level and to predict performance in the next class. Poor performance in the standard mathematics class may result in students being placed in a lower track or remedial course, which has implications for graduating "college ready" and acceptance to colleges that require certain prerequisite mathematics courses (Farkas, 2003; Horn, 2008; Nieto, 2002–2003; Oakes, 1990; Oakes & Lipton, 2007).

Because of their ubiquitous nature, grades serve as very important boundary objects that can reinforce biases; drive teachers' assessment practices; and affect students, their families, and their futures. Research on biases in teachers' grading practices was presented in Chapter 2. Here we describe how grading practices are affected by communities of practice.

Teachers working together within communities of practice (e.g., departments, grade levels) can influence each other's assessment practices through collaborative norm setting (Should young children get grades? Should effort or "citizenship" be evaluated? Should a score of 70% on an exam be considered a "pass"? etc.). They can also influence each other through informal discussions of assignments or grading and through historical practices (i.e., "the way we do things here"). Students and their families can influence assessment practices, putting pressure on individual teachers or groups of teachers if they do not understand or do not approve of current assessment practice (or of the results of assessment of their students). For example, attempts to change methods of teaching (e.g., from lecture to group work), implement new grading practices (e.g., standards-based grading), or to give students feedback so they can all succeed (assessment for learning) may lead to backlash from students and parents who consider these practices unfair to students who receive high grades with current methods (Nolen, 2011; Nolen et al., 2011).

Hence, grades and other assessment results can take on very different meanings in different communities of practice and the systems within which these communities exist. In what follows, we provide an example of how two high school mathematics departments interpreted student performance based on their beliefs and assumptions about the meaning of grades and test scores, as well as how their actions impacted students.

How Communities of Practice Can Create Unintentional Biases: A Case Study

Horn's (2008) study of "turnaround kids" at two schools illustrates the situated nature of assessment and how educator responses to student performance can reify or challenge prevailing beliefs about student ability. Horn (2008) analyzed data on "turnaround kids" who, when they entered high school, were considered underprepared for college-preparatory mathematics based on relatively low pretest performance. Despite low pretest performance these students were successful in their 1st year of high school, ending the year with confidence in their identities as competent mathematics students, ready to continue in college-bound courses. Horn attributed their confidence to the teachers who employed a type of "reform mathematics" approach called complex instruction (Boaler, 2002; Boaler & Staples, 2008) aimed at equitable access to mathematics and competence. Horn (2008) stated, "Together they sought to make a multidimensional curriculum that would provide all students an entrée into the big ideas of mathematics" (p. 214). The teachers developed practices that built on students' initial ideas, explorations, and conjectures toward understanding the big mathematical ideas.

Horn compared "turnaround kids" at two schools, "Railside" and "Greendale" (psuedonyms for the schools in her study). Railside was significantly more diverse economically, racially, and linguistically than Greendale. Although teachers in both schools participated in and worked collaboratively on reform mathematics, the math departments at the two schools had different communities of practice and different curricular structures that provided students different resources for developing identities as competent, college-bound mathematics students.

Railside teachers collaborated regularly, meeting two to three times per week, looking at students' work and focusing on understanding students' ideas and how to support their growth in mathematics. Teachers worked together across the levels of the curriculum and emphasized similar practices and resources for students in all 4 years, emphasizing multiple pathways to mathematical competence. Greendale teachers met two to three times per semester and collaborated less. Teachers at both schools worked very hard to support all students.

Railside teachers employed a college-bound curriculum where all students were expected to progress through the same path (untracked). Prior to the time of Horn's study, Railside teachers had done an "experiment" where they taught the college prep course to "remedial" students and observed that their students' work was at about the same level as that of the traditional college prep students. Taking this as evidence that all Railside students could do college prep mathematics, they removed the remedial courses from the mathematics course offerings. This meant that, when students struggled, the teachers had to figure out how to support their success within the single curriculum. School scheduling allowed for students to take two math courses at a time, so struggling students stayed in their in-sequence college prep course and took a second math course focused on providing extra instruction. Horn attributed the success of the turnaround kids at Railside, in part, to this curricular structure; all completed or exceeded the college entrance requirement in math.

Greendale teachers worked in a curriculum with three tracks (integrated math [high track], regular college-bound math [algebra, geometry, trigonometry], and noncollege-bound or remedial mathematics). This structure reified ability differences by providing places to put students who were seen by teachers as less able in mathematics. Students who underperformed were placed in the noncollege-bound track for a year, then moved to the college-preparatory track. If they underperformed again, they were placed back in the noncollege-bound track. Beyond the 1st-year remedial course, teachers did not consistently emphasize multiple pathways to mathematical competence; because reform mathematics instructional practices had led to success in the remedial course, the students were positioned as less competent by college-prep mathematics teachers. These alternative practices were interpreted as indications of lack of mathematical ability and the need to go slower, to be sheltered from unfavorable comparisons to the "brighter" students. Placement in the remedial track limited students' opportunity to complete the three required courses for college entry before graduation; none of the turnaround kids at Greendale who started in the remedial track were college-ready by the time of graduation.

> The tracking system provided a mechanism for status maintenance, while Railside's common curriculum held the possibility of success for students with low prior achievement. (Horn, 2008, p. 223, internal citations omitted)

At Railside, both the belief that all students could complete the college-prep courses (which led to the de-tracking in the first place) and teacher collaboration meant that teachers worked collaboratively to understand students' thinking and support their learning throughout the college-prep curriculum. At Greendale, assessment data were interpreted as evidence of mathematical ability and led to tracking decisions that limited some students' opportunities. The bias in the system at Greendale was expressed in the curriculum, teachers' beliefs, and their teaching practices.

Horn's (2008) research shows how communities of practice (teacher beliefs and layers of structure) lead to different interpretations of assessment data. Railside teachers collectively focused on what they could learn from assessment data (formal and informal) about students' thinking, with the goal of supporting their growth in mathematics throughout the curriculum. All teachers in the department had a shared vision of what students could know and be able to do. Their shared vision was supported by their ongoing collaboration, planning, and reassessment.

Greendale teachers did not have a community of practice that featured collaborative interpretation of student work with the aim of understanding students' thinking and planning instruction to move all students' thinking forward toward achieving academic goals. Instead, students who did not perform well were seen as inherently less able to learn and in need of the protection of a sheltered track where there was less pressure to perform well compared to others with more ability. This led to bias by structure: Because of the curricular structure, placement in the remedial track made it nearly impossible to complete the precollege requirements by the time of graduation. Even if an individual teacher at Greendale chose to implement reform mathematics strategies and help students in remedial courses engage with college prep content, the curricular structure established by the teachers in the mathematics department prevented the students from moving on to college-prep courses.

In short, individual teachers' assessment practices are situated in social systems and are not purely up to the individual choices of teachers. Teachers in a school or department work within a school or district grading system that may define the kinds of assessment data teachers gather and how it is used across the system.

Changing Practice and Structure to Support Diverse Students

A situative perspective on classroom assessment recognizes teachers are *part of* their contexts. That is, teachers help to create their contexts through their participation in them. Thus, we can understand teachers' assessment practices as part of their participation in an activity system (e.g., students' needs, peer expectations, department-/grade-level policies, administrative expectations, parent pressures) while also understanding change in the activity system itself through the joint participation of its members (e.g., studying change in practice, shared values, power structure, tools: sometimes called *organizational learning*). If teachers wish to create student-centered, fair, and valid assessment and grading systems, they must work for change within their communities of practice, including peer teachers, school administrators, and the people in the communities they serve.

COMMUNITIES OF PRACTICE AND CULTURALLY RESPONSIVE ASSESSMENT

Research on culturally relevant and culturally responsive pedagogy shows that when instructional materials and practices honor the cultural and social backgrounds of students, when there is a commitment to students' success, and when teachers hold high expectations for all students, students from diverse cultural and social backgrounds succeed at higher rates than otherwise. Horn's (2008) study demonstrates how low expectations for students combined with rigid curricular structures can lead to failure for students. Horn's study also demonstrates how a schoolwide commitment to student success and understanding the needs of each student can lead to success for all students.

Many of the programs that have been successful for Black/African American, Latinx, and Indigenous American students were schoolwide programs (e.g., the Mexican American Studies program in Tucson, Arizona [Phippin & The National Journal, 2015]; Brooklyn Collegiate High School in Brooklyn, NY [Borck, 2019]; Railside School in California [Horn, 2008]).

As Palumbo and Kramer-Vida (2012) state, in a summary of their research on the characteristics of schools that are successful with students from low-income and racially diverse backgrounds:

> Successful educational programs . . . are school-wide programs, dedicated to meeting the academic and emotional needs of students. These schools try to be consistent, to give students a second home. . . . [providing] emotional support while teaching what all students need: academic success, basic skills, factual knowledge, a core curriculum, self-discipline, hope. (p. 119)

Resistance to Culturally Responsive Pedagogy

Although we know that schoolwide commitment to high expectations for all students does, indeed, lead to higher achievement for students from diverse cultural and social backgrounds, resistance to culturally responsive pedagogy can be striking. Given that teachers work in systems that include students, parents, peers, school administrators, district administrators, and so forth, efforts to change practices to make them more conducive to the needs of diverse learners can face significant opposition. Two examples of this resistance were shown in New York City and Tucson, Arizona.

Brooklyn Collegiate High School (BCHS) is a "transfer school" designed to serve low-income youth who are "over-age and undercredited" (Borck, 2019, p. 377). The teachers at BCHS are committed to helping their students achieve high standards and overcome barriers through awareness of the effects of racism and classism on their lives. This is a schoolwide commitment. Teachers in the school believe it is their job is to create a community where students have a sense of belonging. One teacher stated that a major goal for the principal and teachers was to

> [set] up our school so it's a place where young people of color from marginalized communities can come and be like, "Oh, I belong here," which then allows us to do other things, some of it pragmatic, some of it hopefully in touch with students' needs in terms of self-determining their lives and their communities. Without students being able to feel like they belong, so much of the other stuff that we need to accomplish academically, instructionally, is just spinning wheels if a student doesn't invest enough or feel that connection to the place as a school that sees them and allows them to belong. (Borck, 2019, p. 388)

The goals of the BCHS teachers were (1) to be honest with students about structural inequality and how it breaks down along race and class lines, (2) to help students understand that their experiences of failure are created by structural inequalities rather than their own innate shortcomings, (3) to help students see their cultural identities are valuable, worthwhile, and legitimate, and (4) to teach students how to survive in the dominant culture by "code switching" between their home/community cultures and the dominant culture.

BCHS teachers communicated their commitment to students through daily efforts (Borck, 2019) and students recognized that commitment. As one teacher stated,

> So when I think about my relationships with my students, I think about how I can communicate to every individual, 'I see you. I know you. I care about you. I got your back. And I've got your back to the extent that I'm gonna jump in your face when I see you screwing up.' (Borck, 2019, p. 387)

BCHS takes New York City students who are furthest behind academically. Principals of other transfer schools said they would not admit the students who went to BCHS because the students' performance would "skew their outcome data, thus affecting their teacher evaluations and school evaluations" (Borck, 2019, p. 379). If evaluations weren't at a certain level, these principals worried that their schools' policies and funding would be undermined.

During the time of Borck's study, a New York State regent visited the school to observe and meet with teachers. The regent did not understand the focus on community or the familial relationship between students and teachers. She suggested teachers spend more time preparing students for the regents exams. In 2017, New York City public schools threatened to close BCHS because of the students' poor performance. However, after giving the school more time to improve, graduation and college readiness rates rose to levels on par with the rest of the city's schools (Inside Schools, 2018).

Another example of external resistance to a culturally responsive community of practice was shown in the Arizona state legislature's reaction the Mexican American culture program in Tucson public schools. Students in the program had higher graduation and attendance rates and better test scores than students who did not participate in the program. Cultural beliefs about what should be taught in "America" and whose version of language, history, and culture were to be privileged led Arizona state legislators to pass a 2010 law prohibiting the program—indicating that it was causing students to disrespect mainstream culture. A federal judge declared the Arizona law unconstitutional and discriminatory in 2017 (Strauss, 2017b).

Each of these examples shows that teachers and schools do not act in bubbles; the programs, including assessment programs, are scrutinized by individuals and groups within and outside of these communities of practice. In both the BCHS and Tucson, Arizona, cases, students, parents, and community members who believed in the programs advocated on behalf of the schools. It is evident that if communities of practice are going to deviate from mainstream norms, they must communicate effectively with the parents and communities in which they serve about the goals of the programs and the degree to which the programs are effective for students.

Building Communities of Practice Within and Outside of Schools

Change, whether at the classroom level or the school level or the system level takes time. However, supporting students' learning is worth the time it takes to make sure assessment is part of the solution rather than a cause of the problems.

Creating communities that support culturally and socially diverse students' learning can begin with the classroom community. Successful teachers create a culture of caring wherein the purpose of schooling is to support students' high achievement (Gay, 2010; Ladson-Billings, 1995a, 1995b). Within the classroom, the assessment practices most effective in supporting student achievement include clarity about learning goals, engagement of students in setting goals and self- and peer evaluation, feedback, and opportunities for revision and growth. Not only can these practices help students reach high expectations, but they communicate to students that they are expected to achieve. Student-centered assessment and grading practices, however, cannot occur in isolation. Teachers must work with their colleagues, school administrators, students, and their families to make these changes possible.

As we discussed in Chapter 4, assessment tasks must be worth doing in order to engage students. To create tasks worth doing, teachers can work with colleagues to step back from teaching to the dizzying array of state standards and think about what matters most for their students—what students need to learn to be successful in school and life beyond school. Building assessments aligned with the learning goals requires developing a shared vision about what achievement looks like.

For example, reading, writing, vocabulary, and critical thinking are essential adult skills and are part of every state's academic standards for the language arts. There may be dozens of supporting skills within these important language arts areas; however, teaching and assessing these reading, writing, vocabulary, and critical thinking skills can happen in real-world contexts that connect with students' communities. As communities of practice, teachers can work together to identify the texts and contexts that will best prepare students to use the language arts skills in authentic ways.

Teachers are not alone in having goals for student learning. Although teachers need to be clear about what matters most to them and to their students, they also consider what might be important to parents and community members. Some schools have established partnerships with parents and the larger community that can provide a framework for discussing learning and assessment (Barajas-López & Ishimaru, 2020; Ishimaru & Galloway, 2020; Ishimaru & Takahashi, 2017). If teachers do not work in schools that already use culturally responsive teaching and assessment practices, individual teachers can still work with students, parents, and colleagues toward shared goals.

Educators can bring assessment expertise to conversations with parents and community members and learn from them about how school-relevant skills and knowledge might be used in the community. Local issues and concerns can form the basis for PBL and the like (Gonzalez et al., 2001; Smith, 2007). Convincing students, parents, and peers that students' work beyond test performance is important may take courage. Convincing others also takes examples of how authentic work can become the basis of productive assessments. If students, parents, and colleagues believe that they are valued and their ideas are welcome, they are more likely to engage in and help plan the assessment tasks—particularly if the tasks are relevant to students' own lives and communities.

Teachers, students, school leaders, and community members can collaborate to develop ideas for authentic work that connects students to their communities. Teachers can reach out to parents for feedback, describing projects as well as how involvement with families and communities is important to the success of the project (e.g., doing research on a local issue, interviewing a family member). As students work on the assignments, teachers can practice using formative assessment strategies (assessment for learning) to help all students learn the concepts and skills.

Change takes time—possibly one unit at a time (maybe one unit per term): thinking about the learning goals for a single unit, thinking about how the learning goals are shown in life beyond school, and constructing an assignment that has students engage with the concepts or skills to accomplish the assignment. Teachers can use "action research" to evaluate the success of their trials and then share the results with colleagues and school leaders. Teachers can also share the results with parents through parent–teacher–student conferences at school or during home visits.

If teachers already work in a community of practice that is oriented toward effective assessment practices, teachers can use the ideas in Chapters 2 and 7 to conduct bias and sensitivity reviews, language complexity reviews, and accessibility reviews of their existing assessments. They can use the ideas in Chapters 3 and 6 to develop culturally responsive assessment tools, try them out in their classrooms and work together to assess students' work—evaluating students' performances, evaluating the success of teaching, and evaluating clarity of directions for tasks and assignments. Teachers can use the ideas about fair grading practices in Appendix A to reflect on any schoolwide grading policies or other practices that may unintentionally create bias against low-income students, students with disabilities, and students from diverse cultural and social backgrounds.

Over time, teachers can work together with community members toward partnerships that help students engage with their communities as they accomplish important work (Smith, 2007). Wade (2000) recommends that educators work with communities to create service learning opportunities for students. Projects "must be mutually beneficial and equitably framed where both educator and the community share common goals" (Richardson & Dinkins, 2014, p. 61). Engagement with community means teachers have to be especially sensitive to the cultural values, primary languages, and relationship rules for family and community members (Gay, 2010). This is more likely when there is two-way communication between school and community, but it can be difficult to avoid power imbalances (Ishimaru & Galloway, 2020).

School leadership is essential in creating communities of practice that are focused on culturally responsive, unbiased, fair, and valid classroom assessments. Each example of schools and school districts that have been successful in helping students of color to be successful has had strong leadership—committed to the success of all students and willing to apply research-based practices known to support student learning.

SUMMARY

This chapter takes a situative view of assessment practices by examining how communities of practice influence teachers' classroom assessment practices. Throughout this book, we have described how assessment tools and practices are developed and implemented by communities of practice throughout the educational system (from the federal government to publishers of instructional materials and developers of standardized tests to school systems and classroom teachers). We have described how communities of practice can create biases in assessment tools and processes and prevent valid assessment of students with diverse cultural and social identities. We have described how these practices can not only interfere with valid assessment, but actually lead to long-term harm by suppressing performances of students of color and female students, contributing to students' lack of faith in their own abilities to learn and damaging students' future prospects.

We have also described how communities changed their practices in order to support the success of historically marginalized students. We have provided research that supports practices more appropriate for students from diverse cultural and social backgrounds—practices that can support student learning and provide fair and valid assessment of that learning. Implementation of fair and valid assessment practices will require individual teacher commitment and support from communities of practice. It may be necessary for communities of practice to work against the dominant paradigm or create new paradigms.

We have arrived at an ideal time in history to address invalidity in assessment and inequities in education. Since the emergence of the Black

Lives Matter movement and the deaths of many innocent African American children and adults at the hands of police, American citizens have become keenly aware of the injustices in our social systems. Because of school closures and online learning during the coronavirus pandemic, American citizens have become keenly aware of the inequities in our educational systems. Inequities in school funding, differences in support for teachers, disgraceful conditions of schools and textbooks, and low expectations for students have created contexts that entrench multigenerational disenfranchisement. Standardized testing practices that are replicated in classroom assessments have become instruments of oppression and reified beliefs about the low abilities of English learners, immigrants, low-income students, students with disabilities, and students of color. Ladson-Billings (2006) speaks of an "educational debt," wherein generations of insufficient educational opportunities have created a significant debt to people who have not been and are not now served by our educational system—particularly people of color. Educators at all levels of the educational system—especially those who have experienced the frustration of demands to raise test scores at the expense of student learning—may be ready to address these issues and to do so with practices grounded in research. Hopefully the information and ideas in this book can help teachers and other educators work together to create communities of practice dedicated to fair and valid assessment of all students, not just those from White middle- to upper middle-class backgrounds.

Valid assessment of students' learning depends on clarity about learning goals and clarity about what students will be able to do when they achieve those goals. Valid assessment requires educators to consider factors that interfere with or detract from students' opportunities to learn and to demonstrate what they know and can do. Valid assessment requires clarity about the purposes of assessments and how assessment results can serve those purposes. If the primary purpose of assessment practice is to generate scores and grades for gradebooks, assessment practices will be quite different than when the primary use for assessment results is to support student learning. Fair assessment practices require removing barriers and biases that influence students' learning and performances.

Removing barriers may require rethinking the literature, texts, topics, and contexts of assessment tasks to make them more culturally relevant. It may require making sure evaluation of students' work is not influenced by factors unrelated to learning goals such as pet peeves or personal biases. Valid assessment requires educators to become aware of how belief systems and biases drive practice and how implicit biases are expressed in grading policies, evaluations of students' work, and school policies (e.g., tracking) that limit students' opportunities to learn. It will require educators to look critically at instructional and assessment materials in terms of their inherent assumptions about the experiences and background knowledge of students. It will require viewing students as real partners with their own rich knowledge and experiences to contribute to the overall learning community.

In the end, validity is about truth—telling the truth about the students we serve and making sure they have as much opportunity to succeed as those the educational system was originally designed to serve.

CHAPTER 6

Developing Assessments for Diverse Classrooms

In this chapter, I explore how to address diversity in classroom assessment. My goal is to help educators take the next steps in making classroom assessment fair for students from diverse cultural and social backgrounds and to optimize students' opportunities to show what they know and can do. The chapter offers strategies for thinking about how to develop assessments in four core subject areas—reading, science, social studies, and mathematics. The validity of claims about student learning begins with clarity about what students are to know and be able to do. Therefore, as a starting point, I anchored the ideas presented here in national academic standards in those subject areas. Most states have adopted or adapted these standards; therefore, they are the standards that drive the content of large-scale tests—the tests used to evaluate the success of schools. These are the standards that drive district curriculum adoptions, classroom instruction, and assessment at the state, district, school, and classroom levels. Teachers need to be able to examine these standards critically in order to plan culturally and socially relevant instruction and assessment. Teachers can apply the strategies described here as they work to make their own state's academic standards relevant to their students.

Following the subject area strategies, I provide links to online recommendations for developmentally appropriate literature and nonfiction texts by authors with diverse social and cultural backgrounds and about social issues. Teachers can use these texts for reading and social studies in the development of their own classroom assessments.

DEVELOPMENT OF CULTURALLY AND SOCIALLY RESPONSIVE ASSESSMENT TOOLS

Chapter 1 introduces the concept of validity and the ideas of validity theory—a theory about how we can know whether the assessment results (e.g., scores on tests and other assignments, grades in school) can be trusted to represent what students know and can do related to learning goals. The only way to ensure that classroom scores and grades reflect student learning of targeted learning goals is for teachers to be clear about their learning goals and to make certain that instruction and assessment are focused on students' achievement of those goals.

Until recently, the fundamental model of educational assessment was based on the scientific method. Students receive a "treatment" (instruction), and tests indicate how well students benefited from the treatment. Teachers then move on to the next "treatment." Unfortunately, the long-term impact of this model is that students' performances on tests have been attributed to students' abilities rather than the quality of instruction and the cumulative effects of an inequitable educational system (Ladson-Billings, 2006).

The testing methodology used in large-scale achievement tests and generally adopted in most classrooms is based on two assumptions. The first assumption is that student learning in each subject area can be measured on a scale from no understanding to exceptional understanding. This assumption is seriously limited. A single score on a test or performance task will provide no meaningful information to students about how to improve, nor can a single score give teachers information they need to support students or evaluate their own instruction (Shepard et al., 2018).

The second assumption of the traditional model of testing is that a particular assessment tool or assessment process will be appropriate for all students. Standardization in educational testing, at the state, district, or classroom level is accomplished by following routines that have developed over a century. These routines define everything from how tests are designed to the types of questions and prompts given to students, and to the ways that scores are analyzed and reported. Similarly, typical routines for summarizing end-of-term or end-of-course grades have developed over many decades—often passed from one generation of teachers to the next by example.

Many of these routines grew out of a factory model of schooling that requires educators to process large numbers of students quickly and to move quickly from subject area to subject area. These assessment routines are definitely not designed to yield information that supports students' learning or that helps students take ownership for their own learning. The routines are designed to move students through lessons, instructional units, terms, and school years efficiently. Assessments serve as pause points in the trajectory of schooling. In short, the focus of most instructional and assessment routines is on efficiency rather than student learning. Few of these routines benefit or are intended to benefit students.

Most educators would prefer to focus on student learning rather than doing a 180-day dash from the beginning to the end of the school year—where some students fall behind and others move ahead. This relentless push is driven, in part, by local expectations for content coverage and in part by pressure to raise accountability test scores. With support and better understanding, educators can confront the routines of education and work toward more responsible and responsive classroom assessments that support student learning.

Effective assessment is tied to focused teaching. To make assessment relevant and responsive to students with diverse social and cultural identities, teachers must focus instruction and assessment on what matters most. Rather than trying to "teach everything of importance" (Wiggins, 1989, p. 44), teachers must step back from the broad array of knowledge, skills, and strategies represented in textbooks and state standards and focus instruction and assessment on the "super-significant" learning goals most likely to support students' continued growth and development (Popham, 2005). Grant Wiggins, a well-known advocate for the use of performance-based assessments to anchor education in authentic work, wrote in his 1989 paper, "The Futility of Trying to Teach Everything of Importance":

> [Teaching] has been reduced to the . . . equivalent of TV news soundbites. . . . Content is reducible to soundbites only when curricular lobbyists (and an alarming number of educators) believe that learning occurs merely by hearing or seeing the 'truth.' . . . . The pejorative simile of the school as factory could only have taken hold in a culture which already believed that knowledge is facts passively received. (p. 45)

Later in this chapter, I describe how I examined academic standards in four core subject areas for relevance as well as for whether the standards are amenable to culturally relevant and responsive assessment. My goal is to model for teachers how to make thoughtful choices about what matters most. I then show how to think about the assessment of those standards in a way that is culturally and socially relevant to students. I also provide examples of how to frame test items and tasks to elicit valid responses from students.

In Chapter 3, I recommended the use of performance-based assessments as the most effective tools for representing the intent of learning goals and for eliciting valid student work relevant to standards. Performance-based assessments can be the most effective way to make sure that classroom assessment helps students make sense of learning goals and the most viable way to develop culturally relevant and responsive assessments. Samuel Messick (1989a), an assessment expert who had a profound effect on our thinking about validity and validation, wrote that performance-based assessments are

> less stigmatizing, more adaptable to individual student needs, less narrow and more faithful to the richness and complexity of real-world problem solving, more instructionally relevant, more useful for public and parental reporting, and more reflective of the actual quality of student understanding. (p. 21)

In this chapter, I describe performance tasks that can elicit students' learning in ways that address state academic standards and allow educators to adapt assessment to the needs of students. I also provide a step-by-step guide for developing effective performance assessments, including task directions and scoring guides, in Appendix B.

I recognize that educators may want to use tests or quizzes to efficiently assess specific skills or knowledge. I have also provided examples of how to approach traditional tests and quizzes so that they honor the diversity of students in classrooms today. For tests and quizzes, I provide guidance on how to do the following:

1. Select stimulus materials responsive to specific students' cultural and social identities. Stimulus materials (e.g., reading passages, historical events, real-world data) are especially important. Students need to see themselves and their communities in the stimulus materials they encounter on tests (Linn, 1994; Schraw et al., 2001; Olivier et al., 2020).
2. Write "generic" item stems (the prompts or questions given to students) aligned with the most relevant standards that can be adapted to different stimulus materials.
3. Adapt item stems and task directions, as appropriate, for selected stimulus materials (e.g., reading passages, science scenarios, social studies contexts).
4. Ensure that evaluations of students' responses are focused on students' demonstrations of learning goals rather than unrelated features of their responses (e.g., evaluating students' social studies responses for demonstration of a particular concept rather than for spelling or neatness).

For the sample test items I provide in this chapter, I created short-answer or essay items rather than multiple-choice items. Multiple-choice items are the most difficult to construct. Multiple-choice item stems can include complexities (e.g., odd syntactic structures designed for multiple-choice items) that affect how students comprehend the intent of the item. The reading load for multiple-choice items includes not only the item stem (prompt or question) and the correct answer but also the incorrect answers. Incorrect responses must be *viable* for students who do not understand a concept or lack a skill, and they also must be *absolutely incorrect*. The most effective incorrect responses in multiple-choice items reflect common misconceptions or common errors so that teachers can look at students' responses and diagnose the causes of wrong answers. Teacher knowledge of common misconceptions grows over time. So, although it is possible to write multiple-choice items that address these misconceptions or common errors, misconceptions are just as likely to be shown in short-answer items or extended-response tasks.

Finally, background variables can influence how students interpret stimulus materials and the intent of test items. Since students bring their own interpretations to information provided, multiple-choice items tend to be especially problematic if the items target anything beyond factual knowledge. There are very few learning goals worth achieving that involve indisputable facts. Multiple-choice items that require interpretation, reasoning, and inferences about data or text (a major focus in current national standards) are the most likely to be biased against students with knowledge and life experiences that differ from the item writers who are predominantly White, middle-class educators (Taylor & Lee, 2011, 2012).

UNPACKING STANDARDS FOR RELEVANT
AND RESPONSIVE ASSESSMENT

Given that most states have adopted (and adapted) some version of national standards in language arts, mathematics, science, and social studies, I reviewed national standards as resources for possible learning goals. Until now, my experience with these national standards has been to take them on faith and write items and tasks that align with the standards. However, as I reviewed these standards from a culturally and socially responsive perspective, I became more critical of them. As Cumming (2000) has asked: Are these universal standards? Do the standards prioritize the perspectives of White, middle- to upper middle-class culture over or even counter to the perspectives of individuals from other cultural and social groups?

In the four sections that follow, I discuss issues related to culturally and socially responsive assessment in different core subject areas (reading, social studies, science, and mathematics). I begin with reading, because it is the easiest area to make relevant and responsive to students. Reading naturally lends itself to culturally and socially responsive pedagogy. Most of the national reading standards have value regardless of what students read. Most reading skills and strategies also apply to other contexts such as television, radio, music, oral presentations, social media, and the Internet.

Next, I deal with assessment in social studies and science. These subject areas can naturally lend themselves to culturally and socially responsive teaching and assessment. Concepts and skills in social studies can be taught and assessed through the histories, cultures, life experiences, and economic realities of any cultural or social group. In addition, scientific phenomena impact the daily lives of all students; therefore, science concepts and skills can be taught and assessed in ways that help students think about how they and their communities are affected by science and technology. Science and social studies projects can be designed to engage with and support students' own communities (see Chapter 3 for suggested community-based projects). Finally, I address mathematics. Mathematics is the gateway to well-paying jobs and higher education. However, current national standards in mathematics present significant challenges in terms of making instruction and assessment relevant to students.

MODELS FOR CULTURALLY AND SOCIALLY RESPONSIBLE READING ASSESSMENT

In this section, I focus on how to create a culturally and socially responsible reading assessments related to the Common Core State Standards for Language Arts and Literacy (CCSS, 2010a). I describe how to develop both tests and performance tasks. It is important to recognize the political context for the CCSS standards. Dianne Ravitch (Strauss, 2014), a well-known historian and cultural commentator, described the development of the CCSS as follows:

> The Common Core standards were written in 2009 under the aegis of several D.C.-based organizations: the National Governors Association, the Council of Chief State School Officers, and Achieve. The development process was led behind closed doors by a small organization called Student Achievement Partners, headed by David Coleman. The writing group of 27 contained few educators, but a significant number of representatives of the testing industry. From the outset, the Common Core standards were marked by the absence of public participation, transparency, or educator participation (Strauss, 2014).

Although I acknowledge concerns about the relevance of the CCSS, the CCSS for Language Arts and Literacy are the foundation of testing and curriculum adoptions in most states. It is important to look at them critically and make judicious decisions about which standards are most important for the success of students with diverse cultural and social identities. In what follows, I address culturally and socially responsive reading tests and performance assessments separately.

Culturally and Socially Relevant Reading Tests

There are two aspects teachers must consider when developing culturally and socially responsible reading tests: passages and items/questions. The basic structure of a reading test is to have students read a text and answer questions related to comprehension, analysis, and interpretation of the text (and possibly embedded graphic information). Too often, teacher-developed reading assessments ask students to analyze or interpret texts that were read and discussed as part of instruction; therefore, students' responses to items or questions may reflect what they learned from class discussions or lectures rather than their own abilities to read and understand texts. Yet, when students encounter district- or state-level tests, they must apply those reading skills to new text. Therefore, to assess students' reading skills and strategies, teachers should select culturally relevant texts specifically for assessment purposes and ask students to apply their skills and strategies to these new texts.

The most straightforward strategy for creating culturally and socially responsive reading tests is to select texts and passages that are relevant to the backgrounds of students in the classroom. Many resources are available for selecting expository and literary texts (see the online resources section of this chapter for ideas). Teachers can select whole texts, chapters, or excerpts as passages. It is important to include both literary texts and nonfiction texts. Where possible, literature should be written by individuals with cultural backgrounds similar to the students in a class. Nonfiction texts should focus on culturally relevant issues, ideas, and people. As indicated in Chapter 2, fair use laws allow educators to copy published materials so long as they acknowledge the source and the use the materials for educational purposes (i.e., not for profit) (U.S. Copyright Office, 2021). Therefore, teachers have a wide range of print material available to choose from for assessment purposes.

Questioning the Standards. The first task of an educator, when confronted with standards in any subject area, is to ask the question: What do I want students to learn? Are all these standards important for my students? James Popham (2005) talks about focusing instruction and assessment on a "modest number of supersignificant curricular aims":

> To avoid overwhelming teachers and students with daunting lists of curricular targets, an instructionally supportive . . . test should measure students' mastery of only an intellectually manageable number of curricular aims, more like a half-dozen than the 50 or so a teacher may encounter today. However, because fewer curricular benchmarks are to be measured, they must be truly significant. (Popham, 2005)

To identify the "manageable number of curricular aims," educators must decide what matters most for the long-term success of their students. Table 6.1 gives a list of the "anchor" reading skills and strategies included in the CCSS for Language Arts and Literacy (p. 10). Overall, the CCSS for Language Arts and Literacy include what are considered fundamental reading skills and strategies as well as skills and strategies related to literacy in history, social studies, science, and other technical content. The anchor standards are adjusted and refined by grade level and by type of text. A careful look at the CCSS for language arts at each grade level can help teachers focus reading instruction and assessment on the skills most relevant to the age of students and the types of text.

As I read through these anchor standards to write generic item stems (prompts or questions), I paused at various points to ask myself: Are these

Table 6.1. CCSS Reading Anchor Standards

Key ideas and details	1. Read closely to determine what the text says explicitly and to make logical inferences from it; cite specific textual evidence when writing or speaking to support conclusions drawn from the text. 2. Determine central ideas or themes of a text and analyze their development; summarize the key supporting details and ideas. 3. Analyze how and why individuals, events, and ideas develop and interact over the course of a text.
Craft and structure	1. Interpret words and phrases as they are used in a text, including determining technical, connotative, and figurative meanings, and analyze how specific word choices shape meaning or tone. 2. Analyze the structure of texts, including how specific sentences, paragraphs, and larger portions of the text (e.g., a section, chapter, scene, or stanza) relate to each other and the whole. 3. Assess how point of view or purpose shapes the content and style of a text.
Integration of knowledge and ideas	1. Integrate and evaluate content presented in diverse media and formats, including visually and quantitatively, as well as in words (including print and nonprint media). 2. Delineate and evaluate the argument and specific claims in a text, including the validity of the reasoning as well as the relevance and sufficiency of the evidence. 3. Analyze how two or more texts address similar themes or topics in order to build knowledge or to compare the approaches the authors take.

Source: CCSS for Language Arts and Literacy (2010), p. 10

skills and strategies relevant to all students? Can I make them more relevant and responsive to students with diverse cultural, social, and personal identities?

Consider Reading Anchor Standard 5 "Analyze the structure of texts, including how specific sentences, paragraphs, and larger portions of the text (e.g., a section, chapter, scene, or stanza) relate to each other and the whole" (p. 10). Teachers have limited time with students. Should they spend time teaching students how to unpack the interconnected structure of texts? Although examining text from this perspective may help students learn how to be more effective writers, is it worth spending instruction and assessment time on teaching students to analyze "how specific sentences, paragraphs, and larger portions of the text . . . relate to each other and the whole" for a reading test? How would this skill occur in real life? Is this what average readers do? Or is this one of the reading skills that has relevance primarily to literary scholars?

I also looked hard at Standard 4, "Interpret words and phrases as they are used in a text, including determining technical, connotative, and figurative meanings, and analyze how specific word choices shape meaning or tone" (p. 10). At first, this standard looked like one that is about literary criticism or the ability to write literary analyses. However, this standard could be focused on helping students be alert to the types of strategies writers (and speakers) use to manipulate and indoctrinate. How teachers frame teaching and assessment of a standard like Standard 4 can make all the difference between esoteric activity relevant to a privileged few academics or helping students become critical readers of texts. Teachers can use assessment to find out whether students are learning to examine language and how it is used to create images, messages, and tone, particularly when language is used to manipulate readers or shape individuals' beliefs and attitudes about marginalized groups.

The second question educators can ask is, "Are all of these standards important at every grade level?" Again, in order to pare down that which is taught and assessed to super-significant learning goals, culturally and socially responsive teachers can focus on the reading skills and strategies that will give their students the greatest amount of autonomy and personal power at their age. Elementary students certainly need to comprehend the main ideas of a text but may not need to "integrate content across diverse media," "evaluate the argument and specific claims," or evaluate the "validity of reasoning." However, as students mature, particularly if a primary learning goal is that students develop an understanding of sexism, racism, and classism and how these biases have affected students' own lives, educators will want students to critically question the ideas in text, whether the "text" is a television news program, lyrics to a song, memes on a social media site, or history textbooks. The CCSS grade-level reading standards are intended to support teachers in creating developmentally appropriate instruction; however, teachers still must ask themselves which standards will give their students the greatest independence and personal power.

Selecting Texts. The next task for developing reading assessments is to select the literary and expository (nonfiction[1]) texts students will read and apply their skills to. For culturally relevant and responsive reading assessments, literary texts should be written by authors with cultural/social backgrounds similar to the students in a class. Nonfiction texts should be about topics and issues relevant to students' personal lives. Students are more likely to engage with texts that have meaning for them and their lives—texts that allow them to draw on their own background knowledge and experiences. The CCSS for language arts include literacy skills in history, social studies, science, and technical fields. Nonfiction texts selected for an assessment can be focused on history and social studies topics relevant to the histories of students' families and communities. Social studies and science texts can be focused on how social studies and science concepts apply to the communities in which students live. Technology texts can be focused on how technology affects students' daily lives.

The selection of texts requires consideration of the difficulty and complexity of text. The truth is that, in learning reading skills, reading level is not as important as being able to use the skills and strategies to support comprehension, analysis, and interpretation. The anchor reading standards for the CCSS clearly apply to all grade levels; what changes by grade level is the complexity of text and nuances in the reading skills. Many of the skills defined in the grade-level standards are intended to ensure that students can read and comprehend more and more complex text as they grow and develop. Teachers can focus assessment on whether students are developing the grade-level reading skills and strategies as they apply to texts at the appropriate reading levels for each student. If students are reading literature and nonfiction texts relevant to their own lives, they are more likely to be motivated to develop the reading skills and strategies that will give them access to more complex texts.

Much of the literature and nonfiction text that has been "leveled" for instructional and testing purposes is primarily relevant to students with White, middle- to upper middle-class backgrounds. Literature by authors from much of the world may not be available at reading levels appropriate for young children or struggling readers. Similarly, literature by African American, Latinx, Indigenous American, and Asian American, LGBTQ+ authors, or authors with disabilities may not be readily available in locally available curriculum materials.

Educators can consider some of recommended literature in the online resources section of this chapter to obtain texts relevant to their students. In choosing the type of text for each standard, a teacher may want students to read texts related to issues of justice, equity, gender, race, and class. That teacher might select nonfiction passages more than literary passages unless the focus of a literary work is on justice, equity, gender, race, or class (e.g., "I, Too" by Langston Hughes). As students grow older and develop greater vocabulary and more sophisticated reading skills, nonfiction texts can be selected from primary documents relevant to students' own lives and communities.

Generic Item Stems. Item stems are the questions or prompts in tests. Teachers can use generic item stems that apply across different texts by different authors and on different topics. Generic item stems allow teachers to target reading skills via a test but give students options of choosing passages that are relevant to their own lives (Linn, 1994). Table 6.2 provides sample

Table 6.2. Item Stems for Reading Comprehension, Analysis, and Interpretation

Anchor Standard[1]	Type of Text	Generic Stems That Could be Adjusted for Almost Any Passage
2. Determine central ideas or themes of a text and analyze their development; summarize the key supporting details and ideas.	Literary	Identify one main theme in this story and describe how [the author[2]] communicated the theme. Explain your thinking using two details or ideas from the story.
	Informational	What is the main idea of this passage? Explain your thinking using information from the passage.
		What is the main idea of this passage? Describe three important points the author used to support the main idea.
3. Analyze how and why individuals, events, and ideas develop and interact over the course of a text.	Literary	Describe [character name]'s main conflict. Use two ideas from the story to explain the conflict.
		OR
		Describe how [character name] changed from the beginning to the end of the story.
		OR
		Describe how [character name] solved [his/her/their[3]] problem in the story.
4. Interpret words and phrases as they are used in a text, including determining technical, connotative, and figurative meanings, and analyze how specific word choices shape meaning or tone.	Literary	Give [two/three] examples of how the author used language (words or phrases) to help you imagine the [scene/character].
	Informational	Identify the author's point of view and give [two/three] examples of how the author used language (words or phrases) to convince you to take [her/his/their] point of view.
6. Assess how point of view or purpose shapes the content and style of a text.	Informational	What is the author's primary purpose in writing this passage? List two ideas [she/he/they] used to support her/his/their purpose.
		What is the author's [point of view/perspective] on the issue? Describe how the author used language, style, or voice to show [her/his/their] point of view/perspective.

8. Delineate and evaluate the argument and specific claims in a text, including the validity of the reasoning as well as the relevance and sufficiency of the evidence.	Informational	What is the main issue in this passage and what is the author's position on the issue? Describe the author's reasons for the position and the examples [she/he/they] use to justify reasons.
9. Analyze how two or more texts address similar themes or topics in order to build knowledge or to compare the approaches the authors take.	Informational	Both passages give information about [topic]. Explain whether or not the two passages give the same message. Use ideas from both passages to explain your thinking. OR What is a theme found in both passages? Compare/contrast how each author communicated the theme. Use at least two examples from each passage in your explanation.

[1] Anchor Standard 1, "Read closely to determine what the text says explicitly and to make logical inferences from it; cite specific textual evidence when writing or speaking to support conclusions drawn from the text," applies to all of the remaining anchor standards and to all types of text (print or otherwise). Stems to target "cite specific textual evidence when writing or speaking to support conclusions drawn from text" are given in each of the examples.

[2] Words in brackets can be adjusted based on specific topics, characters, issues, genders, and so on in the passage as appropriate. Teachers may or may not wish to reference specific author names in the items.

[3] In recognition of current practice of allowing individuals to identify their own self-referring pronouns, I have provided "they" and "their" as options.

131

item stems related to the CCSS language arts anchor reading standards listed in Table 6.1. Some of the CCSS language arts anchor standards are quite complex; therefore, I wrote more than one generic item for complex standards.

Writing effective item stems involves ensuring that the demands of the item fit the language of the standard—keeping the language of the item as closely aligned to the language of the standard as possible. The language of the standards is the language of the academy; however, the primary audience for academic standards should be students. As is evident in the stems in Table 6.3, I used different wording at times to make the language of the stem more student friendly. Since standards are slightly different at each grade level, teachers should use the grade-level standards as the basis for the generic stems.

Evaluating Student Responses. As discussed in Chapter 1, the validity of scores from a test does not reside in the items or the tests but in the degree to which students' responses demonstrate learning goals and how responses are evaluated. Any item or task can appear to target a particular learning goal, but responses depend on students' interpretation of the items or task directions and whether there are factors in the item or task that interfere with students' ability to show what they know and can do related to learning goals.

When students construct their own responses, validity depends on whether students are clear about the expectations in the question or prompt and on the validity of the evaluation of students' responses, whether by teachers, peers, or students themselves. Evaluation of student work can be in the form of a narrative description, checks on a list of criteria, a score, or a grade. When evaluations are scores or grades, the numbers or letters *represent* an underlying narrative about students' performance in relation to criteria.

Research has shown that when scoring rules are vague, teachers are more likely to insert overt or implicit biases into the evaluation process; however, when criteria are clear, evaluation is more consistent and reliable (Tenenbaum & Ruck, 2007; Uhlmann & Cohen, 2005). Therefore, scoring rules are a critical aspect of validity. When scoring rules (rubrics) guide the evaluation process, scores, grades, and and other forms of evaluation are more likely to allow for valid inferences about students' accomplishments. When students do peer or self-evaluations, they also can incorporate their biases into the evaluation process. However, when the scoring rules have clear criteria related to the targeted learning goals, students can learn from peer and self-evaluations.

Generic rules can guide evaluation of students' responses to the generic item stems. Scores can be words, numbers, or pictures. Scoring rules can be *checklists*, *rating scales*, or *rubrics*. If an item simply asks students to state one or more important facts given in a passage, a *scoring guide* can simply list the facts that answer the question.

Table 6.3. Generic Scoring Rules for Anchor Reading Standards

Anchor Standard[1]	Generic Stems That Could Apply to Any Passage	Checklist	Rubric
2. Determine central ideas or themes of a text and analyze their development; summarize the key supporting details and ideas.	Identify one main theme in this story and describe how the author communicated the theme. Explain your thinking using two details or ideas from the story.	☐ Theme is viable or understandable. ☐ All details or ideas from story support theme. ☐ Explanation makes a connection between theme and evidence from story.	3[2]. Theme is viable, and student provides solid examples from the story with explanation that supports claims. 2. Theme is viable, and student provides one example from the story with explanation that supports claim. 1. Theme is viable or expected.
	What is the main idea of this passage? Explain your thinking using information from the passage.	☐ Main idea is viable based on information provided. ☐ Information supports main idea. ☐ Explanation makes connection between main idea and evidence from passage.	3. Main idea is viable, and student provides solid examples from the passage with explanation that supports claims. 2. Main idea is viable, and student provides one example from the passage with explanation that supports claim. 1. Main idea is viable or expected.
	What is the main idea of this passage? Describe three important points the author used to support the main idea.	☐ Main idea makes sense in relation to information provided. ☐ All points support main idea. ☐ Two points support main idea. ☐ One point supports main idea.	3. Main idea is viable, and all points support main idea. 2. Main idea is viable, and two points support main idea. 1. Main idea is viable, and one point supports main idea.
3. Analyze how and why individuals, events, and ideas develop and interact over the course of a text.	Describe [character name]'s main conflict. Use two ideas from the story to explain the conflict.	☐ Conflict makes sense based on the story. ☐ Ideas from the story support claim about conflict.	3. Conflict is viable, and student provides solid examples from the story to support claim about conflict. 2. Conflict is viable, and student provides one solid example from the story to support claim about conflict. 1. Conflict is viable or expected.

(continued)

Table 6.3. (continued)

Anchor Standard[1]	Generic Stems That Could Apply to Any Passage	Checklist	Rubric
	Describe how [character name] changed from the beginning to the end of the story. Use details from the story in your description.	☐ Description of character changes is accurate. ☐ Details support claims about character change.	3. Description of character changes is accurate and well supported by details from the story. 2. Description of character changes is reasonable and supported by one detail from the story. 1. Description of character is based on events in the story.
	Describe how [character name] solved [his/her/their] problem in the story.	☐ Problem is identified. ☐ Description of solution is accurate.	2. Character's problem is identified, and description of solution is based on events in story. 1. Character's problem is accurately identified.
4. Interpret words and phrases as they are used in a text, including determining technical, connotative, and figurative meanings, and analyze how specific word choices shape meaning or tone.	Give [two/three] examples of how the author used language (words or phrases) to help you imagine the [scene/character].	☐ All examples focus on descriptive language. ☐ Descriptive language is relevant to scene/character. ☐ Descriptive language is from the story.	2. All examples of descriptive language are from the story and relevant to the scene/character. 1. One example of descriptive language is from the story and relevant to the scene/character.
	Identify the author's point of view and give [two/three] examples of how the author used language (words or phrases) to convince you to take [her/his/their] point of view.	☐ Interpretation of point of view is viable. ☐ All examples focus on persuasive language. ☐ Persuasive language is relevant to author's point of view. ☐ Persuasive language is from the passage.	3. Interpretation of point of view is viable and supported by all examples of persuasive language from the passage. 2. Interpretation of point of view is viable and supported by one example of persuasive language from the passage. 1. Interpretation of point of view is viable; persuasive language, if given, is related to the passage.

[1] Anchor Standard 1, "Read closely to determine what the text says explicitly and to make logical inferences from it; cite specific textual evidence when writing or speaking to support conclusions drawn from the text," applies to all the remaining anchor standards and to all types of text (print or otherwise). Scoring criteria to target "cite specific textual evidence when writing or speaking to support conclusions drawn from text" are given in each of the scoring rubrics.

[2] Note that scoring rubrics give descriptions of the highest scores first and then descriptions of less proficient or less complete work follows. Therefore, the rubrics shown here list scores from highest to lowest.

The items given in Table 6.2 ask for fairly complex short-answer or extended interpretations, inferences, or conclusions; therefore, student responses may vary in quality. Table 6.3 provides example checklists and rubrics for several of the generic item stems given in Table 6.2. All the scoring rules use language that is very similar to the language of the standards.

Figure 6.1 shows examples of checklists and rating scales for the example generic items related to Reading Anchor Standard 9. Figure 6.2 shows examples of two rubrics for the items assessing Reading Anchor Standard 9. Because of the complexity of CCSS Reading Anchor Standard 9, more than one generic item stem is given in Table 6.2, and more than one checklist, rating scale, and rubric are given in Figures 6.1 and 6.2. As with the scoring rules in Table 6.3, all the scoring rules are tightly tied to the language of the standards.

Three important features can be seen in these scoring rules:

1. The language of all three types of scoring rules is tightly tied to the language of the standard. There are no statements like "partially correct" or "somewhat accurate"—language that can lead to biased evaluations.
2. There is no reference to the content of specific reading passages in any of the scoring rules. The generic item stems and associated scoring rules can be used with any paired passages. Teachers can create many different pairs of literary passages representing different cultures or pairs of nonfiction passages representing a range of culturally relevant topics. Students could select the passage pairs they want to read, or teachers could assign the passage pairs based on students' cultural or social identities.
3. Not only are the generic items and stems flexible in terms of passage content, generic items and associated scoring rules could be used more than once in a school year. Comparison of texts for themes, topics, and authors' approaches may be a recurring learning goal, particularly when the themes and topics students are reading about have to do with culturally important issues such as equity, racism, classism, sexism, and so forth.

A very important feature of the scoring rules in Figures 6.1 and 6.1 and in Table 6.3 has to do with the *viability* of responses. Recall, from Chapter 2, that when students are asked to go beyond recall of facts given in the text (i.e., when they make inferences, develop interpretations, or draw conclusions), multiple-choice items tend to favor White students and boys; items that require students to provide their own responses tend to favor non-White students and girls (Henderson, 2001; Taylor & Lee, 2011, 2012). Therefore, it is essential that reading items or tasks that require reasoning about texts give students an opportunity to develop their own ideas. Scoring

Figure 6.1. Generic Checklists and Rating Scales for CCSS Reading Anchor Standard 9

CCSS Reading Anchor Standard 9. Analyze how two or more texts address similar themes or topics in order to build knowledge or to compare the approaches the authors take.

Item Stem 1

Both passages give information about [topic].

Explain whether or not the two passages give the same message. Use ideas from both passages to explain your thinking.

Checklist	☐ Makes claim about whether the topic is the same for both passages ☐ Gives at least one idea from each passage to support claim about topic ☐ Explanation presents viable comparison or contrast of passages
Rating scale	2 1 Makes claim about whether the topic is the same for both passages 3 2 1 Gives at least two ideas from each passage to support claim about topics 3 2 1 Explanation presents viable comparison of passages

Item Stem 2

What is a theme in both passages?

Compare how each author communicated the theme. Use at least two examples from each passage in your comparison.

Checklist	☐ Names a theme common to both passages ☐ Describes at least one important idea or event in each passage that communicates the common theme ☐ Explanation effectively compares/contrasts how the authors used ideas or events to communicate the theme
Rating scale	1 Names a theme common to both passages 3 2 1 Describes at least two important ideas or events in each passage that communicate the common theme 3 2 1 Explanation effectively compares/contrasts how the authors used ideas or events to communicate the theme

rules must allow for students to develop their own interpretations, conclusions, inferences—ones that may be different from their teachers or other students. The key to applying the scoring rules is to evaluate whether the students' reasoning is justified through their explanations and examples. This approach to scoring allows students with diverse lived experiences to show their own thinking rather than searching through answer choices to figure out someone else's interpretation, conclusion, or inference.

Figure 6.2. Generic Rubrics for CCSS Reading Anchor Standard 9

CCSS Reading Anchor Standard 9. Analyze how two or more texts address similar themes or topics in order to build knowledge or to compare the approaches the authors take.

Item Stem 1

Both passages give information about [topic].

Explain whether or not the two passages give the same message. Use ideas from both passages to explain your thinking.

Rubric	4	Makes a claim about whether theme or topic is the same for both passages. Explanation presents a viable comparison or contrast of themes in both passages using at least two ideas from each passage.
	3	Makes a claim about whether theme or topic is the same for both passages. Explanation presents a viable comparison or contrast of themes in both passages using at least one idea from each passage.
	2	Makes a claim about whether theme or topic is the same for both passages. Explanation presents a comparison or contrast of themes in both passages using ideas from each passage.
	1	Makes a claim about whether theme or topic is the same for both passages. Explanation includes ideas from both passages.

Item Stem 2

What is a theme in both passages?

Compare how each author communicated the theme. Use at least two examples from each passage in your comparison.

Rubric	4	Makes viable claim about a theme common to both passages. Explanation compares or contrasts how author communicated the common theme using at least two ideas from each passage.
	3	Makes viable claim about a theme common to both passages. Explanation compares or contrasts how author communicated the common theme using at least one idea from each passage.
	2	Makes viable claim about a theme common to both passages. Explanation describes how author communicated the theme in both passages.
	1	Response includes information from both passages.

Assessing Students' Ability to Compare Ideas Across Texts. CCSS Reading Anchor Standard 9, "Analyze how two or more texts address similar themes or topics in order to build knowledge or to compare the approaches the authors take," is complex. It includes themes (literary text) or topics (non-fiction text) and comparison and contrasting of ideas in two or more passages. The standard indicates the point of the goal is to learn new information from multiple texts or to compare the ideas and approaches of multiple authors. This standard is one that would typically apply to research papers (e.g., writing a report on the causes of an historical event) and comparative literature. Both of these are performances that occur primarily in school (or academia); therefore, may be considered, by some, to be inauthentic and irrelevant to nonacademic contexts.

One aspect of culturally and socially responsive teaching is to help students develop critical consciousness (Freire, 2000; Gay & Kirkland, 2003; Jemal, 2017). Martin (2003) states that critical consciousness requires "the act of intellection . . . questioning fundamental assumptions and constantly reconstructing ever new interpretations of the world" (p. 414). Teachers can help students use critical reading skills to unpack "systemic, institutionalized forms of discrimination associated with racism, classism, and heterosexism" (Shin et al., 2016, p. 210), as represented in the texts of multiple authors. Hence, the skills related to comparing the themes and ideas across multiple authors has value beyond typical school-based tasks.

CCSS Reading Anchor Standard 9 is represented in the CCSS for Reading at all grade levels. The skill of comparing ideas across multiple texts becomes more sophisticated over time; therefore, teachers may want younger students to compare brief passages through test items similar to those in Table 6.3 and have older students do more authentic performances related to Reading Anchor Standard 9.

Culturally and Socially Relevant Reading Performance Assessment

Traditional tests of reading don't usually reflect authentic acts of reading. The language arts, in general, are performance oriented. To develop high-quality, culturally, and socially responsible performance tasks for reading, teachers need to think about authentic contexts for reading and identify texts that are relevant to students. Teachers can interview their students to talk about where they see people reading and how people use text in their daily lives.

If students cannot think of real-world contexts in their own families and communities, teachers can share examples of real-world performances done by individuals with the same cultural and social identities as the students. For example, in the world beyond school, some readers join book clubs to share thoughts about the books or poetry they have read. Some readers integrate ideas from multiple sources to write newspaper articles about important issues, to write a proposal for a neighborhood grant, to prepare a presentation about a community issue, to create a documentary, and so forth. Readers might write book reviews for journals, newspapers, or literary magazines. Readers might turn a book or short story into a play or screen.

Students and teachers can look at real-world examples and work together to identify the features that make the performances effective. Whenever possible, students should have opportunities to see what a good performance looks like before they begin their own work.

Constructing an effective performance task requires a clear idea of what the performance will look like, clear directions to students so they know what is expected, and scoring rules (aligned with the targeted learning goals) to evaluate students' performances. Appendix A provides guidelines for how to construct effective performance assessments along with an example of how performance tasks in reading and social studies might look.

As teachers write performance tasks, they will find that the more tightly they tie requirements of the performance to the standards, the more likely students will demonstrate what they know and can do related to the standards. Students should know the expectations for the performance and apply the scoring rules to their own work. Once teachers have used the task directions and scoring rules with students, they should reflect on the clarity of the directions, the effectiveness of the scoring rules, and whether instruction prepared students for doing the performance and use their analyses to improve future instruction and assessment tools.

Some educators may worry that teaching to and assessing a state's academic standards will prevent them from teaching important goals about cultural awareness and pride and critical consciousness about how systemic racism, classism, sexism, and xenophobia affect their own lives. Any performance task can be grounded in the language, literature, and culture of students and help students develop critical consciousness and learn about their own histories through the choice of stimulus materials (e.g., print or online texts, videos, interviews with family and community members) and the demands of performance tasks. As students read historical documents or literature, criteria for performance tasks can include evaluation of an author's messages about race, class, culture, immigration, and so forth.

Incorporating Nonacademic Skills Into Reading Assessment

Teachers also want students to learn nonacademic skills such as timeliness, organization, group work skills, and so forth. Helping students plan their pathway from idea to performance can help them develop important nonacademic skills. Projects and performances become ideal situations in which students can develop those skills in a purposeful way.

Finally, when students can work together on aspects of a performance, they can learn group work skills and communication skills. These skills will not develop without support and guidance from teachers. Teachers can work with students to develop group work "norms" that help to define effective group work and communication skills. Appendix A describes an effective strategy for developing self- and peer evaluation checklists that students can use to assess their own communication and group work skills. The CCSS for Language Arts and Literacy include listening and speaking standards relevant to group work and discussions (e.g., coming to discussions prepared, following agreed-on rules for discussion, listening carefully,

Figure 6.3. Sample Self-Evaluation Checklist for Group Projects

Use this checklist to assess your own communication skills and your contributions to the group project.

☐ I came to class prepared to work on the project.

☐ I shared my ideas as we planned the project.

☐ I shared my ideas while we worked on the project.

☐ I listened respectfully to other students' ideas while we worked on the project.

☐ I did my share of the work for the project.

☐ I asked other members of the group for help before asking the teacher.

☐ When I got stuck, I asked for help.

☐ When I disagreed, I was respectful of others.

☐ I made sure everyone had a chance to share ideas when we planned the project.

Figure 6.4. Sample Self-Evaluation Checklist for Group Discussion

Use this checklist to assess your own communication skills and your contributions to the group discussion.

☐ I completed any work I needed to do before the discussion.

☐ I came to the group prepared for the discussion.

☐ I contributed ideas to the discussion.

☐ I listened to other students' ideas during the discussion.

☐ I shared ideas from readings and other sources during the discussion.

☐ I made sure that everyone had a chance to share ideas during the discussion.

☐ I asked questions if I needed to understand another student's ideas.

respectfully asking and responding to questions, contributing ideas and adding to others' ideas) (CCSS, 2010a, pp. 23–24, 49). An example of a group project and group discussion checklists are given in Figures 6.3 and 6.4. When developing checklists like these, be sure that students contribute to criteria for effective communication skills and group work skills. This type of assessment must respect students' cultural norms and traditions about communication styles and relationship norms.

CULTURALLY AND SOCIALLY RELEVANT ASSESSMENT IN SOCIAL STUDIES

The study of the social sciences is the study of history, economics, geography, and civics—all of which are relevant to students with diverse cultural and social identities. Social studies issues are relevant to the oppression of people of color, immigrants, women, LGBTQ+, and people with disabilities. Social studies concepts of culture, themes in geography, historical themes, civics, and economics concepts can guide development of culturally relevant and culturally and socially responsive assessment.

Throughout this book, I have recommended the use of performance-based assessments as the most effective way to create culturally and socially responsive assessments. History and social studies are no exception to that recommendation. Tests of facts that are soon forgotten may be easy to grade, but they don't reinforce lasting conceptual and factual understanding. In addition, "facts" are generally debated by individuals with diverse perspectives about a time in history, an economic phenomenon, or the roots of civic ideas and human behaviors.

Framing Social Studies Performance Assessments

Much of what students learn in social studies focuses on issues relevant to a Eurocentric culture—minimizing the histories, geographies, economics, and political contexts for the rest of the world. The human race has a very long history; there are too many eras, events, ideas, people, and locations for students to learn all the details teachers might want them to learn, or all that students may need to learn to be able to function in the reality of global interdependence. However, social studies' concepts and skills apply across the world and to all cultures. To make social studies performance assessments culturally and socially responsive, teachers must think about authentic work in the social sciences and how students' projects and performances can be connected to the students' lives, languages, literatures, and cultures. For example, if the learning goals include geography concepts, projects can give students opportunities to show their understanding of place and location, regions, movement of ideas, people, and things, and human-environmental interactions as they investigate the ways these themes have influenced the histories of their own families and communities.[2] When students learn how to apply themes of geography to their own histories and cultures, they will have the perspectives and skills to apply geographic themes to the histories and cultures of others.

If learning goals involve knowledge of particular historical eras or events, students can investigate how particular historical events impacted their families and ancestors and/or how their ancestors contributed to and influenced historical ideas and events. When projects allow students to anchor historic eras, events, ideas, and phenomena to students' own lives, students can learn concepts and skills in a way that allows them to make sense of histories, cultures, events, and the ideas of others.

The range of possible performances in social studies is large. One way to focus social studies performance tasks is through investigations. Research suggests that students are more engaged when they have opportunities to

Table 6.4. Themes in History–Social Studies from National Standards' Documents Mapped Onto Traditional Social Sciences Topics

Social Studies Themes	Geography	History	Economics	Civics and Government
Culture	X	X		
Time, continuity, and change	X	X		
Individual development and identity	X	X		
Individuals, groups, and institutions	X			X
Production, distribution, and consumption			X	
Power, authority, and governance		X		X
Science, technology, and society	X	X	X	

use inquiry and to construct new knowledge (Chang & Mao, 1999; Murray & Summerlee 2007; Schwartz et al., 2004; Summerlee & Murray, 2010). Students can generate research questions about how the big ideas and important themes in geography, economics, history, and civics are connected to their own lives, families, and communities.

Table 6.4 gives important social studies themes established by the National Council of Social Studies. Teachers can use these themes to focus students' research questions. Then, as students investigate their questions, they will develop new knowledge as well as gain knowledge and conceptual understanding related to the content of their courses.

The Intersection of Social Studies Domains

Because geography, history, economics, and civics are so interdependent, any of the social sciences can be the entry point for students' investigations. For example, students can act as geographers investigating human movement through the push-and-pull factors that brought their families to where they live now. Push-and-pull factors may include sociocultural issues (e.g., oppression, pogroms, genocide, war, religious freedom), economic demands (e.g., poverty, lack of economic opportunity, potential for resources), and environmental pressures (drought, population pressures, toxic environmental conditions). Digging deeply into one of these dimensions can help students develop conceptual and historical understanding.

Alternately, students could act as political scientists and policymakers and investigate the intersection of laws, government, individual rights, and court rulings connected to students' own lives and that of their families and communities. In doing so, they will encounter economic and historical factors that have influenced laws, regulations, and rights. Students might act as historians and investigate the causes and effects of particular historical events or eras, tracing the effects of these events or eras on themselves, their families and communities or investigating how their families and cultures contributed to these events or eras. All historical events or eras are affected by economic, geographic, and sociopolitical factors.

Clearly, the possibilities for authentic investigations of any historical event, geographic phenomenon, economic issue, or sociopolitical event or issue are so rich that teachers will have difficulty making choices in how to focus their efforts. Teachers will also have to make sure tasks are not overwhelming by demanding demonstration of too many social studies concepts and skills in a single performance.

The primary purpose of the social studies performance tasks should be for students to develop and show understanding of important social studies concepts (e.g., social justice, balance of powers, causes of human movement, interplay of supply and demand). Tasks must be designed so that students apply relevant concepts in their projects or performances. Directions for students' performances or projects must clearly identify the focuses of the inquiry (e.g., causes of human movement during the late 20th century) and what students must demonstrate in their work (e.g., writing skills; evaluation of the credibility of sources; integration of information from multiple credible sources; economic, social, and geographic causes of human movement; etc.). Scoring rules must focus on the central concepts and skills rather than on recall of facts, definitions, and details.

Creating a Safe Space for Controversial Issues

The foci of students' social studies investigations are likely to lead students to controversial issues and sources that involve subtle or explicit examples of racism, classism, sexism, and other forms of injustice. Teachers must be certain to create a classroom context that allows all students to safely express their own opinions and interpretations and to draw their own conclusions. Teachers can work with students to create class norms for discussion and debate. As mentioned earlier in this chapter, the CCSS for Language Arts and Literacy include listening and speaking standards relevant to group work and discussions (CCSS, 2010a, pp. 23–24, 49).

Figures 6.3 and 6.4 show simple self-evaluation checklists for group work and group discussion skills.

Assessing Social Studies Research Skills

Because of the Internet, students have infinite primary and secondary resources available for their investigations. For younger students, teachers can select resources for students that best fit with the targeted social studies concepts. Older students can access the sources most useful for answering their research questions.

Whether teachers provide resources or students find their own sources, teachers can create projects that give students opportunities to learn how to critically read or listen to information, access credible sources, cross-validate information, look for bias, ask questions of sources, and look for and interpret multiple perspectives. The CCSS for Language Arts and Literacy includes literacy standards for reading and writing in history and social studies (CCSS, 2010a, p. 61). Some of these standards include corroborating or challenging claims, determining authors' purposes and arguments, evaluating the strategies authors use to convince others of their opinions (e.g., persuasive language, selective inclusion or omission of information, biased language), and comparing ideas across authors and between primary and secondary sources. These skills are particularly important as teachers help students develop critical consciousness about social, political, economic, and environmental issues related to their personal worlds. The checklist in Figure 6.5 could be used as a self-evaluation tool for students as they develop critical reading and listening/viewing skills.

Teachers may also need to teach interview skills so students can gather information from primary sources such as family and community members.

Figure 6.5. Self-Evaluation Checklist for Critical Reading Skills (Grades 6-12)

☐ I chose sources that are trustworthy.

☐ I looked for evidence of claims and ideas in more than one source.

☐ I looked for multiple perspectives on the topic or issue.

☐ I used more than one source for each perspective.

☐ I double-checked "facts" provided in sources.

☐ I looked for manipulative strategies in the sources (unsupported claims, one-sided arguments, extreme statements).

☐ I looked to see if quotes and images were taken out of context to support a claim.

☐ I looked for main ideas and ignored trivial details.

Authentic Presentations of Learning

Performance tasks in social studies can mirror the work that historians, social scientists, political scientists, policymakers, economists, geographers, and active citizens do to investigate events and phenomena and present their work to important audiences. Students and teachers can work together to identify the authentic ways for students to demonstrate conceptual understanding and the connections to their own lives. Performances, through which students demonstrate their learning, should be authentic (e.g., biographies, historical narratives, informed debates, documentaries, demonstrations, policy proposals, and other authentic types of work).[3]

Performances can be presented to the larger community, and the larger community can be involved in defining the focus of investigations and serve as a resource for investigations. Appendix B provides guidelines for how to develop effective performance assessment tools, including how to write directions for students and scoring rules.

Social Studies Summary

The social studies provide rich opportunities for students to connect school learning to their own lives. They can generate research questions about how major ideas, themes, and events in the social studies relate to their own histories, cultures, communities, and social identities. Through their investigations, students can develop conceptual understanding; historical, sociopolitical knowledge; and critical thinking, reading, writing, and presenting skills. Importantly, their presentations of what they have learned can be in forms that are authentic to the world beyond school. Social studies performance assessments can be opportunities for students to investigate oppression and injustice as well as opportunities to develop new knowledge about their own histories, cultures, and social identities. Social studies performance assessment provides an ideal context for assessment *as* learning—where students learn and demonstrate their learning via authentic intellectual work that is connected to their own lives.

CULTURALLY AND SOCIALLY RELEVANT ASSESSMENT IN THE SCIENCES

The study of science is the study of natural phenomena as well has how human behavior affects natural phenomena, and vice versa. Physical sciences (chemistry, physics), life sciences, and earth/space science have immediate relevance in the lives of students. Although science concepts are often taught and investigated in isolation, any science concept can be investigated in terms of its connections to the cultural and social realities of students.

As with other academic subject areas, I recommend the use of performance-based assessments as the most effective way to create culturally and socially responsive assessments in science. Tests of facts, principles, and abstract applications of formulas (e.g., balancing a chemical equation) will soon be forgotten unless these facts and principles are grounded in real-world contexts so that students understand the relevance of these concepts to their own lives. Facts and principles in science change as humans construct more precise tools, consider new avenues for investigation, and develop new knowledge.

The most obvious performances in the sciences are laboratory and field investigations of scientific phenomena. However, authentic scientific work also involves the synthesis of the research of scientists to investigate issues that arise due to the intersection between scientific phenomena, technology, and society. Scientists, concerned citizens, and policymakers may synthesize scientific research to look at how technology has contributed directly to the oppression of low-income people, people of color, and other marginalized groups (e.g., disposal of toxic chemicals near low-income communities, fracking for natural gas in poor rural areas) or of the impacts of human behavior on environmental health, the viability of farming, the availability of natural resources, and so forth.

Next Generation Science Standards

The Next Generation Science Standards (NGSS, 2013b) represent the latest thinking about what students should know and be able to do in science. These standards were largely written by academics, practicing scientists, and engineers. The initial framework of NGSS was developed by a committee. The NGSS (2013a) development overview states that the committee was:

> composed of practicing scientists, including two Nobel laureates, cognitive scientists, science education researchers, and science education standards and policy experts. In addition, the [National Research Council] used four design teams to develop the Framework [for K–12 Science Education]. These design teams, in physical science, life science, earthy/space science, and engineering, developed the framework for their respective disciplinary area.

Next, in a process coordinated by Achieve (a nonprofit organization created by College Board and American College Teaching Program), science educators, academics, industry representatives, and other stakeholders drafted the academic standards (learning goals) for science. Given the preponderance of White men in the sciences, engineering, and technology industries, these standards reflect the academic and economic aims of the dominant culture. As of May 2019, all but nine states in the United States had adopted or adapted the NGSS.

The NGSS are organized in three dimensions: science and engineering practices (e.g., planning and carrying out investigations, analyzing and interpreting data, arguing from evidence), cross-cutting concepts (e.g., patterns, cause and effect, stability and change), and disciplinary core ideas (e.g., forces, ecosystems). Each page of the NGSS lists "performance expectations" (PEs)—descriptions of performances students will be able to do if they learn the disciplinary core ideas, understand cross-cutting concepts, and can apply science and engineering practices. These PEs are very specific and are provided for each grade level.

A close look shows PEs (see Table 6.5 for examples) reflect specific ways of showing the disciplinary core ideas. No new knowledge is constructed via these performances; the performance expectations simply define how students will show their knowledge. Educators can download the NGSS organized either by disciplinary core ideas (e.g., biological evolution, ecosystems) or by topics (e.g., interdependent relationships in ecosystems).

Table 6.5. NGSS Grade 5 Conceptual and Practice Performance Expectations and Grade 3–5 Engineering Design Performance Expectations

Structure and Properties of Matter	5-PS1-1.	Develop a model to describe that matter is made of particles too small to be seen.
	5-PS1-2.	Measure and graph quantities to provide evidence that regardless of the type of change that occurs when heating, cooling, or mixing substances, the total weight of matter is conserved.
	5-PS1-3.	Make observations and measurements to identify materials based on their properties.
	5-PS1-4.	Conduct an investigation to determine whether the mixing of two or more substances results in new substances.
Matter and Its Interactions	5-PS3-1.	Use models to describe that energy in animals' food (used for body repair, growth, motion, and to maintain body warmth) was once energy from the sun.
	5-LS1-1.	Support an argument that plants get the materials they need for growth chiefly from air and water.
	5-LS2-1.	Develop a model to describe the movement of matter among plants, animals, decomposers, and the environment.

(continued)

Table 6.5. (continued)

Earth's Systems	5-ESS2-1.	Develop a model using an example to describe ways the geosphere, biosphere, hydrosphere, and/or atmosphere interact.
	5-ESS2-2.	Describe and graph the amounts of salt water and fresh water in various reservoirs to provide evidence about the distribution of water on Earth.
	5-ESS3-1.	Obtain and combine information about ways individual communities use science ideas to protect the Earth's resources and environment.
Space Systems: Stars and the Solar System	5-PS2-1.	Support an argument that the gravitational force exerted by Earth on objects is directed down.
	5-ESS1-1.	Support an argument that differences in the apparent brightness of the sun compared to other stars is due to their relative distances from Earth.
	5-ESS1-2.	Represent data in graphical displays to reveal patterns of daily changes in length and direction of shadows, day and night, and the seasonal appearance of some stars in the night sky.
Engineering Design	3-5-ETS1-1.	Define a simple design problem reflecting a need or a want that includes specified criteria for success and constraints on materials, time, or cost.
	3–5-ETS1-2.	Generate and compare multiple possible solutions to a problem based on how well each is likely to meet the criteria and constraints of the problem.
	3–5-ETS1-3.	Plan and carry out fair tests in which variables are controlled and failure points are considered to identify aspects of a model or prototype that can be improved.

Source: Next Generation Science Standards, 2013b, pp. 27–32.

Disciplinary core ideas and topics are simply different ways to organize the same PEs.

In the typical classroom, conceptual understanding in science is the goal of instruction. Most classroom science investigations are focused on students' learning of these concepts—rediscovering what scientists have already discovered. Performance assessment in this context would focus on students' abilities to apply scientific and technology practices while more traditional tests would focus on students' learning of the scientific concepts.

Framing Culturally and Socially Responsive Performance Assessments in the Sciences

Probably the most effective way to break from the knowledge-driven NGSS and to frame culturally and socially relevant and responsive performance assessments in science is through the performance expectations. The framers of the NGSS wanted to make sure teachers used hands-on activities in their teaching and assessed students' learning through performances. Table 6.5 lists the performance expectations for Grade 5 NGSS. It is evident from these performance expectations that culturally relevant connections to life beyond school were not considered in the development of the standards. The learning goals reflect science understanding for the sake of science. It is interesting to note that the Engineering Design performance expectations given in the table (intended to apply to grades 3 through 5) are disconnected from any particular conceptual understanding.

To develop culturally and socially responsive science assessments, the performance expectations must be vehicles through which teachers can connect science to the lives of students from diverse cultural and social backgrounds as well to issues of racism, classism, sexism, and social justice. The performance task in Figure 6.6 combines several of the performance expectations from Table 6.5 into a semester-long investigation allowing students to connect the performance expectations to community health.

This example shows one strategy for making science assessment relevant to students through an authentic community-based project: (1) identify performance expectations most likely to relate to each other and to students' lives and (2) create a performance task that requires application of the selected performance expectations. The performance described in Figure 6.6 is an example of assessment *as* learning where students learn science concepts and demonstrate their learning at the same time through authentic intellectual work (Newman, 1996; Newman et al., 2001). This type of performance lends itself well to effective formative assessment practices. Students can work through stages of the project with guidance from teachers and work through iterations of the final performance with feedback and opportunities for improvement.

Although not all the 5th-grade standards and performance expectations can be demonstrated in a single project, once students have had opportunities to connect their science concepts to their own lives, they can brainstorm ways that other science concepts may be relevant to their lives. Students might use the results of their science investigations to generate research questions about the connections between particular scientific phenomena and

Figure 6.6. Sample Science Performance Tasks Incorporating Performance Expectations from NGSS: Connecting NGSS to Community

This is a semester-long project that involves a two-part investigation. Part 1 of the investigation involves research from online sources. Part 2 of the investigation involves data collection and analysis. During part 1, students will work in teams to gather information from credible online sources about

- the chemical compositions of healthy air and soil,
- how soil and air quality affect each other, and
- how soil and air quality affect food and water.

They will create three models:

- One showing compositions of healthy air, soil, and water (5-PS1—Develop a model to describe that matter is made of particles too small to be seen) and how toxins in air, soil, and water can be invisible.
- One showing how toxins in soil, air, and water affect each other (5-ESS2-1—Develop a model using an example to describe ways the geosphere, biosphere, hydrosphere, and/or atmosphere interact).
- One showing how toxins in soil, air, and water can move through the food chain to humans through the transfer of energy from plants and animals to humans (5-LS2-1—Develop a model to describe the movement of matter among plants, animals, decomposers, and the environment).

During part 2, students will collect several soil samples from their local communities. Students will use soil test kits to test soil samples for nutrients and toxins and then organize the results of their research into a presentation (e.g., posters, documentary, written report). The presentation will include the models they developed during part 1 and the results of their soil investigations.

In their presentations, they will do the following:

- Use the models developed in part 1 to explain
  - ✓ how soil health influences the health of water and air (5-ESS2-1—Develop a model using an example to describe ways the geosphere, biosphere, hydrosphere, and/or atmosphere interact);
  - ✓ how soil health influences plant health (5-LS1-1—Support an argument that plants get the materials they need for growth chiefly from air and water);
  - ✓ how plant health affects the entire food chain (5-LS2-1—Develop a model to describe the movement of matter among plants, animals, decomposers, and the environment).
- Present their data and analyses of the soil samples (5-PS1-3—Make observations and measurements to identify materials based on their properties).
- Describe how they used the models in part 1 to draw conclusions about the environmental health of their communities (5-LS2-1—Develop a model to describe the movement of matter among plants, animals, decomposers, and the environment).
- Make recommendations for what is needed to improve the environmental health of their community.

their own lives and communities. With teacher support, students can then design new investigations to answer their research questions. Investigations might require text-based research and/or data collection and synthesis.

For example, 5th-grade students might combine their understanding of the "properties of substances" and their knowledge about the "movement of matter among plants, animals, decomposers, and the environment" to generate research questions about how environmental toxins can be identified in their communities and how toxins might move through the food chain. Based on their research, they could construct a visual model showing the possible impacts of environmental toxins on their themselves, their families, and their communities.

It is unlikely that teachers can orchestrate projects like the one described in the previous paragraph or the one given in Figure 6.6 without involvement of the local community and their school's community of practice as well as parents and school administrators. Successful culturally and socially responsive teachers see teaching as a school community partnership and the work they do as a way to give back to the communities they serve (Foster, 1997; Ladson-Billings, 1995b). Communities of practice that create rich projects similar to the one described in Figure 6.5 and similar to the mathematics projects described in *Rethinking Mathematics: Teaching Social Justice by the Numbers* (Gutstein & Peterson, 2005) come to believe that the benefits for students are worth the efforts of collaboration and community connections.

THE CHALLENGE FOR CULTURALLY AND SOCIALLY RELEVANT AND RESPONSIVE MATHEMATICS ASSESSMENT

In this section, I focus on creating culturally and socially relevant and responsive mathematics assessments. Mathematics presents a particular challenge because the subject area is often viewed (and taught) as rigid, abstract, and disconnected from life. Yet, many educators have focused on teaching mathematics in ways that help students make connections between mathematics, social justice, and equity (e.g., Adair, 2008; Brantlinger, 2005; Frankenstein, 1990; Gutstein & Peterson, 2005; Moses & Cobb, 2001). Gutstein (2006) recommends project-based learning wherein students learn concepts and skills while engaged in projects grounded in their communities. For example, in Gutstein and Peterson's 2005 book, *Rethinking Mathematics: Teaching Social Justice by the Numbers*, Brantlinger (2005) describes how students learned geometric principles while learning about inequities in resources by comparing communities north of Chicago to communities in South Los Angeles. Steele (2005) describes a unit where students explored the mathematics of sweatshops. To make these connections, teachers had to know their subject areas and social justice issues well and be able to combine these areas of knowledge to create learning experiences for students.

> To balance academics and social justice issues, a deep knowledge of both is critical to avoid an oppositional binary between the two, as can happen in a standards-dominated environment. (Adair, 2008, p. 411)

Grappling With Mathematics Standards

To make mathematics assessment relevant to students and make sure that scores from tests and other assessments validly reflect students' learning, teachers must begin by closely reading mathematics standards, understanding them, and then developing instruction and assessment relevant for students in their classrooms. In this section, rather than describe how to construct culturally and socially relevant mathematics assessment tools, I show how to examine mathematics standards and reframe them from culturally and socially relevant perspectives.

The Common Core State Standards (CCSS) for Mathematics (CCSS, 2010b) have been adopted or adapted in most of the states and territories in the United States. I recognize that choosing the CCSS for Mathematics as the focus of this analysis is a political act. In considering mathematics standards, the question of cultural responsiveness must address two fundamental questions raised by Cumming (2000). First, do academic standards reflect knowledge that is really needed? Second, do the academic standards represent and help to maintain the dominant culture? These questions are particularly relevant to mathematics. How often do adults, even engineers and computer scientists, use the types of mathematics taught in school? These professionals may face problems that require mathematical reasoning, but rarely as abstractions outside the context of real-world problems. Mathematics for the sake of mathematics (also known as *pure* math) is the domain of mathematicians. Needless to say, a very small percent of the student population will become mathematicians.

The CCSS Standards for Mathematics were primarily developed by White men, most of whom are mathematicians (e.g., David Coleman of College Board; Jason Zimba of Student Achievement Partners, William McCallum, chair of mathematics at Arizona State University; James Milgram, Department of Mathematics at Stanford University; and individuals from a nonprofit organization, Achieve, founded by College Board and the American College Testing Program) (Garland, 2014). These men had an agenda—to prepare more students for college mathematics.

As Ravitch (Strauss, 2014) indicated, educators were not well represented in the drafting of these standards. Nevertheless, I focused on the CCSS for Mathematics because most states have adopted or adapted them, and they drive much of what is taught and assessed in schools.

Considering the large number of mathematics standards at each grade level, and the largely abstract wording of the mathematics standards, teachers may wish to avoid thinking about culturally and socially relevant or responsive mathematics instruction and assessment—particularly at the elementary level where many teachers lack subject matter knowledge in mathematics (Ball et al., 2005; Ma, 1999). However, mathematics has become a powerful gateway to successful completion of high school as well as entry into postsecondary education and technology careers. Gutstein and Peterson (2005) note that teachers need help from communities of practice who work together to develop materials that support culturally and socially responsive teaching in mathematics. Communities of educators that wish to create culturally and socially responsive classrooms have to figure out how to help students achieve these standards while making mathematics instruction and assessment relevant to their students. In what follows, I consider how to make the standards relevant to students with diverse cultural and social backgrounds.

The CCSS for Mathematics include both concepts and procedures. The overarching goals of the CCSS for Mathematics include helping students do the following:

1. Develop deep understanding of mathematical *concepts* (e.g., not only to apply ratios and solve rate and proportion problems but to understand what rate, ratio, and proportion actually mean).
2. Understand the number system (e.g., the properties of whole numbers, rational numbers, negative numbers, number patterns, and so forth), "operate" on numbers (adding, subtracting, multiplying, dividing, factoring), and represent numbers, numeric relationships, and numeric ideas (e.g., ratios, linear functions).
3. Apply mathematical concepts, operations, problem-solving strategies, and reasoning as appropriate in real-world situations (e.g., solving real-world problems involving mathematics; describing real-world phenomena using mathematical models, symbols, and language; using mathematical tools to construct, create, and invent).
4. Solve (pure) mathematical problems and reason mathematically (e.g., being able to find the factors of a whole number or a polynomial equation; being able to identify the flaw in a particular mathematical solution).

As is evident from the overarching goals, the purpose of the CCSS Standards for Mathematics is for students to become mathematically proficient individuals who understand and can use mathematics. Much of the focus of pure mathematics in the standards derives from a belief that, if students understand the underlying principles of mathematical concepts and procedures, they will be able to think mathematically and apply mathematics more effectively in real-world problems.

Given the many mathematics standards within and across grade levels, I have limited my analysis to the 6th-grade standards in two domains from the CCSS for Mathematics: Ratio and Proportional Relationships and Number Systems. In Tables 6.6a and 6.6b, I list the standards for these two domains (CCSS, 2010b, p. 42) and show how they relate to the overarching goals described. As is evident in these tables, there are a large number of mathematics standards for these two domains.

Table 6.6a. CCSS Ratio and Proportional Relationships Domain—Grade 6 (6.RP)

Understand ratio concepts and use ratio reasoning to solve problems.	
CCSS Mathematics Standard	**Primary Goal**
1. Understand the concept of a ratio and use ratio language to describe a ratio relationship between two quantities. For example, "The ratio of wings to beaks in the bird house at the zoo was 2:1, because for every 2 wings there was 1 beak." "For every vote candidate A received, candidate C received nearly three votes."	Conceptual understanding
2. Understand the concept of a unit rate a/b associated with a ratio a:b with b ≠ 0, and use rate language in the context of a ratio relationship.	Number representations
3. Use ratio and rate reasoning to solve real-world and mathematical problems, e.g., by reasoning about tables of equivalent ratios, tape diagrams, double number line diagrams, or equations.	Real-world and mathematical problem solving
a. Make tables of equivalent ratios relating quantities with whole number measurements, find missing values in the tables, and plot the pairs of values on the coordinate plane. Use tables to compare ratios.	Mathematical problem solving
b. Solve unit rate problems including those involving unit pricing and constant speed.	Real-world problem solving
c. Find a percent of a quantity as a rate per 100 (e.g., 30% of a quantity means 30/100 times the quantity); solve problems involving finding the whole, given a part and the percent.	Mathematical problem solving
d. Use ratio reasoning to convert measurement units; manipulate and transform units appropriately when multiplying or dividing quantities.	Real-world problem solving

Source: Common Core State Standards (CCSS) for Mathematics, 2010, p. 42, http://www.corestandards.org/Math/.

Table 6.6b. CCSS Number System Domain—Grade 6 (6.NS)

Apply and extend previous understandings of multiplication and division to divide fractions by fractions.	
CCSS Mathematics Standard	**Primary Goal**
1. Interpret and compute quotients of fractions, and solve word problems involving division of fractions by fractions, e.g., by using visual fraction models and equations to represent the problem. *For example, create a story context for (2/3) ÷ (3/4) and use a visual fraction model to show the quotient; use the relationship between multiplication and division to explain that (2/3) ÷ (3/4) = 8/9 because 3/4 of 8/9 is 2/3. (In general, (a/b) ÷ (c/d) = ad/bc.) How much chocolate will each person get if 3 people share 1/2 lb of chocolate equally? How many 3/4-cup servings are in 2/3 of a cup of yogurt? How wide is a rectangular strip of land with length 3/4 mi and area 1/2 square mi?*	Understanding number operations
Compute fluently with multi-digit numbers and find common factors and multiples.	
2. Fluently divide multi-digit numbers using the standard algorithm.	Mathematical problem solving
3. Fluently add, subtract, multiply, and divide multi-digit decimals using the standard algorithm for each operation.	Mathematical problem solving
4. Find the greatest common factor of two whole numbers less than or equal to 100 and the least common multiple of two whole numbers less than or equal to 12. Use the distributive property to express a sum of two whole numbers 1–100 with a common factor as a multiple of a sum of two whole numbers with no common factor. *For example, express 36 + 8 as 4 (9 + 2).*	Real-world problem solving
Apply and extend previous understandings of numbers to the system of rational numbers.	
5. Understand that positive and negative numbers are used together to describe quantities having opposite directions or values (e.g., temperature above/below zero, elevation above/below sea level, credits/debits, positive/negative electric charge); use positive and negative numbers to represent quantities in real-world contexts, explaining the meaning of 0 in each situation.	Real-world problem solving
6. Understand a rational number as a point on the number line. Extend number line diagrams and coordinate axes familiar from previous grades to represent points on the line and in the plane with negative number coordinates.	Understanding the number system

(continued)

Table 6.6b. (continued)

a. Recognize opposite signs of numbers as indicating locations on opposite sides of 0 on the number line; recognize that the opposite of the opposite of a number is the number itself, e.g., –(–3) = 3, and that 0 is its own opposite.	Conceptual understanding
b. Understand signs of numbers in ordered pairs as indicating locations in quadrants of the coordinate plane; recognize that when two ordered pairs differ only by signs, the locations of the points are related by reflections across one or both axes.	Conceptual understanding
c. Find and position integers and other rational numbers on a horizontal or vertical number line diagram; find and position pairs of integers and other rational numbers on a coordinate plane.	Representing number relationships
7. Understand ordering and absolute value of rational numbers.	Conceptual understanding
a. Interpret statements of inequality as statements about the relative position of two numbers on a number line diagram. *For example, interpret –3 > –7 as a statement that –3 is located to the right of –7 on a number line oriented from left to right.*	Conceptual understanding
b. Write, interpret, and explain statements of order for rational numbers in real-world contexts. *For example, write –3 C° > –7 C° to express the fact that –3 C° is warmer than –7 C°.*	Real-world problem solving
c. Understand the absolute value of a rational number as its distance from 0 on the number line; interpret absolute value as magnitude for a positive or negative quantity in a real-world situation. *For example, for an account balance of –$30, write |–30| = 30 to describe the size of the debt in dollars.*	Conceptual understanding
d. Distinguish comparisons of absolute value from statements about order. *For example, recognize that an account balance less than –$30 represents a debt greater than $30.*	Conceptual understanding
8. Solve real-world and mathematical problems by graphing points in all four quadrants of the coordinate plane. Include use of coordinates and absolute value to find distances between points with the same first coordinate or the same second coordinate.	Solving real-world and mathematical problems

Source: CCSS for Mathematics, 2010, pp. 42–43, http://www.corestandards.org /Math/.

Omitted from these tables are 6th-grade standards for the domains Expressions and Equations, Geometry, and Statistics and Probability. The large number of standards (and subcategories for standards) define mathematics with very fine detail—which creates a dizzying array of concepts and skills students are expected to learn (e.g., there are between 40 and 45 standards for 6th-grade alone). As Wiggins (1989) noted,

> [Much] of what [educators and policymakers] wish to be taught is now taught. The problem is that it isn't learned. . . . The inescapable dilemma at the heart of curriculum and instruction must, once and for all, be made clear: either teaching everything of importance reduces it to trivial, forgettable verbalisms or lists; or schooling is a necessarily inadequate apprenticeship. (p. 45)

In short, with this large array of standards, teachers may "cover" the concepts and procedures during lessons, but students may not learn them. If standards are taught as isolated algorithms, procedures, and concepts, students are highly unlikely to integrate the standards and make sense of them—much less learn how to apply them in real-world situations. Given the significant disenfranchisement of people of color in science, technology, engineering, and mathematics (STEM) careers, significant efforts should be made to help students see the connections between mathematical concepts and procedures and their own lives.

The CCSS for Mathematics represent progressions within each domain. Therefore, success at each grade level depends on a solid understanding of the concepts and procedures from previous grade levels. Unfortunately, mathematics is the subject area wherein teachers are most likely to move on to the next lesson (and associated assessments), regardless of whether students have actually learned the concepts and procedures.

How do teachers prioritize the super-significant standards? One way to prioritize is to recognize that many of the subcategories for a standard are simply different ways to show understanding of a concept. Another way to prioritize is to construct performance tasks wherein students learn concepts and skills while engaged in authentic work (PBL). This strategy requires teachers to understand enough about mathematics to know how and when mathematics concepts and skills are used in the real world. A third strategy is to focus on students' deep understanding of the mathematical concepts and procedures that will give them the most benefit in developing further understanding of and ability to use mathematics in future years.

A close look at the CCSS for Mathematics makes it clear that the social context of mathematics has been given little consideration. The authors of the standards give examples to help teachers understand the meaning of the standards; however, these examples are often out of touch with the realities of children. Clearly no effort was made to ensure that examples have relevance to students from diverse cultural and social backgrounds.

To build culturally and socially relevant and responsive mathematics assessment tools, teachers must critically analyze standards and help students bridge the gap between how mathematics standards are written and students' own lives. In what follows, I have identified some of the challenges teachers face and selected a few of the standards from Tables 6.6a and 6.6b to demonstrate these challenges. I then suggest strategies for making mathematics concepts and procedures more relevant to students.

Standards That Present Contrived Problems as Examples. Contrived problems are common in mathematics instruction and assessment. The examples given with Standard 1 of Ratio and Proportional Relationships, "Understand the concept of a ratio and use ratio language to describe a ratio relationship between two quantities," show this. The first example is the ratio of birds' beaks to birds' wings. The second is the ratio of candidate C's votes to candidate A's votes. While these two examples reflect the intent of the standards, they set the stage for the development of test items that have neither authenticity nor relevance. In what context would people write the ratio of birds' beaks to birds' wings? Why would the ratio of candidates' votes be important to 6th-grade students? To make assessment of this standard more authentic and relevant to students, a teacher might show students an example that has relevance to students, such as the one in Figure 6.7, and ask students to brainstorm other relevant situations. Asking students to generate examples is an effective form of assessment; students give teachers information about their understanding of the concept and students are involved in the assessment process.

Standard 3 of Ratio and Proportional Reasoning has a subcategory, "Find a percent of a quantity as a rate per 100 (e.g., 30% of a quantity means 30/100 times the quantity); solve problems involving finding the whole, given a part and the percent." Figure 6.8 shows two problems that are modified versions of ones I found on the Internet. The first problem is contrived. It is unlikely that someone buying a bicycle will not know the total cost of the bicycle. The second problem is more reasonable; however,

Figure 6.7. Example of a Student-Relevant Item Assessing Concept of Ratio

Jamal will bring 50 cookies to school for a class party. There are 25 students in his class. What is the ratio of students to cookies?

Figure 6.8. Examples of Items Intended to Assess Ability to Find Whole Amount From a Percent

1. $25 is 20% of the cost of a bicycle. How much is the bicycle?
2. Barbara hiked 3 miles on a trail before stopping for a break. Three miles is 25% of the entire trail. How many miles long is the trail?

most hikers know the length of a trail when they begin their hike. Again, students, with guidance from teachers and viable examples, can brainstorm other situations in which people have partial information and must work from a percent to find the whole.

Standards That Involve Multimeaning Mathematical Words and Symbols. One mathematical issue that is rarely addressed in textbooks is the phenomenon of multimeaning words and symbols. Someone who is quite familiar with mathematics may be able to figure out the appropriate connotation of a word or symbol from a context; however, when students are learning new concepts, teachers need to help students make sense of words and symbols. Standard 2 of Ratios and Proportional Reasoning is "Understand the concept of a unit rate a/b associated with a ratio $a:b$ with $b \neq 0$, and use rate language in the context of a ratio relationship." This standard is focused on students' abilities to represent ratios in three (abstract) ways: with conventional representation ($a:b$), using fraction representation (a/b), and in language. Sixth-grade students have been learning about fractions, so this is a new meaning for the a/b representation that can cause confusion for any student.

There are many multimeaning symbols and terms in mathematics. For example, decimal numbers may represent a fractional amount, a proportion, the slope of a line, or money. Teachers need to recognize when students encounter symbols and terms that have multiple meanings in mathematics and explicitly address multimeaning representations when they occur, just as multimeaning words are addressed directly in language arts. In fact, teachers could challenge students to find other examples of multimeaning words and symbols and terms in their instructional materials.

Standards That Lead to a Focus on Examples Rather Than the Standard. Standard 3 of Ratios and Proportional Relationships states "Use ratio and rate reasoning to *solve real-world and mathematical problems*, e.g., by reasoning about tables of equivalent ratios, tape diagrams, double number line diagrams, or equations" (emphasis added). The focus of this standard is on using ratio and rate reasoning to solve real-world and mathematical problems involving ratio and rate. The danger with standards such as this is how examples given with the standard are interpreted in instructional materials and standardized assessments. The examples (tables of equivalent ratios, tape diagrams, double–number line diagrams, or equations) are intended to show teachers some strategies students could use to think about ratios so that they can solve real-world problems. If textbook materials teach double–number line diagrams, tape diagrams, and tables of equivalent ratios, and then textbook assessments include items to assess whether students have learned these strategies or can interpret these representations, teachers and students may come to believe that double number line diagrams, tape diagrams, and tables of equivalent ratios are the learning goals rather than strategies for thinking about or representing ratios when solving real-world problems.

When I searched on the Internet for "What is a tape diagram?" I found an item similar to the one in Figure 6.9. The task involves a tape diagram and a table of equivalent ratios. No reason is given for the table and why it is incomplete. What is the problem students are to solve with the data in the table? Does Kim have 10 gray beads and wants to know how many white beads she will need for a necklace? Does she have 60 white beads and needs to know how many gray beads she will need for a necklace? As written, the situation is contrived to include a tape diagram and a table of equivalent ratios, likely because the mathematics standard uses tape diagrams and tables of equivalent ratios as examples of problem-solving strategies. In situations such as this one, the focus of learning and assessment drifts away from the primary learning target; assessment results will not reflect the intent of the standard, making assessment results invalid. Although the value of the strategies given with the standard may have made sense to those who wrote the standards (e.g., tables of equivalent ratios are precursors to later understanding of linear functions), they are very abstract and may not make sense to students as ways to think about ratios, causing even more confusion about the concepts in the first place. When the focus of an item misses the intent of a standard, teachers can adjust items and tasks to make them more authentic.

Completion of the item given in Figure 6.9 reflects willingness to engage with a fairly meaningless context. When students feel marginalized in school, they are much less likely to engage with content that has no meaning for them. Research suggests that students from White, middle-class backgrounds are more able to compartmentalize and carry out decontextualized, obscure tasks than students from culturally diverse backgrounds

Figure 6.9. Example Item Using Tape Diagram and Table of Equivalent Ratios

This figure shows the ratio of gray beads to white beads for a necklace.

The table shows the number of beads Kim uses in necklaces of different lengths.

Gray Beads	White Beads
10	
	60

Complete the table to show the number of beads of different colors Kim uses.

Figure 6.10. Ratio Item Adjusted to Be Less Contrived

Kim is planning to make bead necklaces. This figure shows the ratio of gray beads to white beads for each necklace.

What is the ratio of gray beads to white beads shown in the diagram? _____

Use the ratio to make a table to help Kim plan necklaces of three different lengths.

Necklace	Gray Beads	White Beads	Total Beads in the Necklace
1			
2			
3			

(Darling-Hammond et al., 2008). One possible explanation for this is that White, middle-class students are willing to engage with inauthentic tasks because they see the value of school for themselves and their lives.

Culturally and socially responsive teachers must consider their students' real-world contexts wherein mathematics concepts have relevance. Teachers must ask themselves, what real-world scenario would be relevant to my students? Kim might be making necklaces for a street fair. She may want to use a ratio to plan necklaces of different lengths so that she can buy enough beads for her necklaces. Kim might use the ratio and the table to make a plan for how many beads of each color are needed for different necklaces (see revised item in Figure 6.10). Making contexts meaningful is essential for engaging students.

Standards That Represent Purely Abstract Mathematics. As students get older, mathematics becomes more and more abstract, making mathematics difficult for many students—particularly for those who are disaffected by school. However, even standards that represent abstract mathematics can be made relevant to students through real-world problems and by helping students see the long-term value of particularly abstract knowledge or skill.

For example, Standard 3 of Ratios and Proportional Relationships ("Use ratio and rate reasoning to solve real-world and mathematical problems") has a subcategory: "Make tables of equivalent ratios relating quantities with whole number measurements, find missing values in the tables, and *plot the pairs of values on the coordinate plane.* Use tables to compare ratios" (emphasis added). This standard is framed as a disconnected, abstract exercise with no attempt to create meaningful context. However, this standard doesn't have to be abstract and lack context.

All the steps in this statement are precursors to representations of linear functions—an important algebra concept that is introduced in grade 7 and is a significant focus of grade 8 CCSS for Mathematics. Teachers can help students understand why they would plot points on a coordinate plane rather than take them through an abstract activity that lacks purpose. For example, teachers can give students relevant, real-world examples of linear functions (represented as ratios) and have students create tables showing the relationship between variables, plot data related to those real-world examples on coordinate grids, and draw conclusions from data in the real-world context. Figure 6.11 shows a performance task that gives meaning to this particular set of skills in ratios and proportional relationships. Teachers can also help students understand how this type of work is central to much of the mathematics they will learn in 8th grade, showing them that they are on a learning progression that will help them be successful in high school and beyond.

This brief performance task helps to anchor a fairly abstract standard in a real-world situation.

Another example of abstract mathematics is shown in Standard 4 of the Number System domain: "find the greatest common factor of two whole numbers less than or equal to 100 and the least common multiple of two whole numbers less than or equal to 12." This standard is written as abstract mathematics. Students should know when greatest common factor and least common multiple are useful in real life. For example, hot dogs are often sold in packages of 5 or 10 while hot dog buns are sold in packages of 8. This presents an interesting mathematical problem for a school picnic or a family reunion.

Standards That Strain Credibility. Standard 1 of the grade 6 Number System domain deserves particular attention. The standard "interpret and compute quotients of fractions, and solve word problems involving division of fractions by fractions" represents *mathematics that is almost never used in real life.* Division of fractions by fractions should raise eyebrows for any mathematics educator. This is a mathematical operation that becomes relevant when older students solve abstract algebra problems involving fractional terms. In 6th-grade, students are simply learning an algorithm (a trick) to divide a fraction by a fraction. Unless handled well, this standard will have no relevance to any students and further marginalize those who do not find their own worlds represented in the examples provided with instructional materials.

The first example given with the standard places a huge burden on students: "create a story context for $(\frac{2}{3}) \div (\frac{3}{4})$ and use a visual fraction model to show the quotient; use the relationship between multiplication and division to explain that $(\frac{2}{3}) \div (\frac{3}{4}) = \frac{8}{9}$ because $\frac{3}{4}$ of 8/9 is $\frac{2}{3}$. (In

Figure 6.11. Performance Task for Ratios and Proportional Relationships

Tamika is helping to prepare for a spaghetti dinner at the community center. She needs to figure out how to buy enough spaghetti for any number of people who come to the dinner.

These are the facts she can use to decide how much spaghetti they will need. Tamika doesn't know how many people will come to the spaghetti dinner.

- Each box of spaghetti has 16 ounces of spaghetti.
- Each person will probably eat 2 ounces of spaghetti.

You can help Tamika plan for how much spaghetti to buy.

- What is a ratio that shows the number of people for each box of spaghetti?

_____

- Use the ratio to complete the table to show the relationship between the number of boxes of spaghetti and the number of people who can be fed.

Number of boxes of spaghetti	1	2	3	4	5	6	7	8
Number of people who can be fed								

Now, use the numbers in your table to plot points on the grid below. This will show the relationship between the number of boxes of spaghetti and the number of people who can be fed.

The table shows the relationship between people and boxes of spaghetti for 1 to 8 boxes of spaghetti. Draw a line through your points on the graph. Then use the graph to estimate how many boxes of spaghetti you will need if 80 people come to the spaghetti dinner.

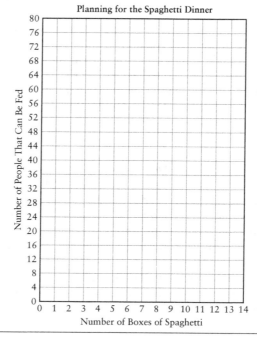
Planning for the Spaghetti Dinner

general, (a/b) ÷ (c/d) = ad/bc.)" In what real-world situation would students divide $\frac{2}{3}$ by $\frac{3}{4}$? A visual fraction model would likely be another abstraction. In addition, the parenthetical statement "In general (a/b) ÷ (c/d) = ad/bc," simply shows the trick used to figure out the quotient.

The remaining examples for this standard highlight the challenge of creating relevant real-world contexts for mathematical ideas that have few real-world applications. The first example could be a real-world situation if there were a reason to know the weight of each person's share. The standards writers have assumed that students know 3 is equivalent to $\frac{3}{1}$ or that sharing $\frac{1}{2}$ pound of chocolate among 3 people means each person gets $\frac{1}{3}$ of the available chocolate, or $\frac{1}{6}$ of a pound of chocolate. However, in the real world students are more likely to treat $\frac{1}{2}$ pound of chocolate as a whole and divide it into thirds. If the context were more authentic (such as dividing a recipe in thirds), students could see that the "invert and multiply" strategy gives them a quick way to figure out that $\frac{1}{2}$ divided by 3 equals $\frac{1}{6}$.

The second example, "How many $\frac{3}{4}$-cup servings are in $\frac{2}{3}$ of a cup of yogurt?" is a perfect representation of a failed effort to show how this particular mathematical idea applies to a real-world situation. In the real world, it is impossible to find $\frac{3}{4}$ cup of yogurt in a $\frac{2}{3}$ cup container of yogurt. Eleven- and 12-year-old students should not be asked to stretch their thinking to figure out something that is outside the realm of direct experience. The final example is "How wide is a rectangular strip of land with length $\frac{3}{4}$ mi and area $\frac{1}{2}$ square mi?" How likely is it that 6th-graders, particularly urban, suburban, or low-income students, will need to figure out the width of a piece of property based on its length and area?

Unfortunately, these examples will drive teachers, curriculum developers, and test developers, and students will inevitably be asked to find quotients of fractions divided by fractions in unrealistic situations. If relevance is essential to engagement, teachers face a major challenge if they attempt to make this standard relevant. However, if students understand that they are learning an algorithm that will help them later in school, they might be willing to engage with purely computational problems that ask them to divide fractions by fractions.

Fluency and Standard Algorithms. Standards 2 and 3 in Number Systems (i.e., Compute fluently with multi-digit numbers and compute with decimal numbers) are examples of mathematics standards that are familiar to teachers. Teachers should be able to figure out real-world contexts for these standards. Because the focus is on fluency and "standard algorithms," Standards 2 and 3 are too often the focus of classroom instruction at the expense of opportunities to use mathematics in authentic ways to solve real problems. Although students may benefit from learning how to fluently compute with whole numbers and decimal numbers, students need to know when (and whether) fluency and standard algorithms will be needed for their success in life beyond school.

The previous examples vividly demonstrate the dilemmas of working with the CCSS for Mathematics as currently written. While the standards may represent important mathematical concepts and procedures, the way the standards are written and the examples provided make these standards nearly impossible to connect to the lives of students. The remaining Number System Standards given in Table 6.6b demonstrate some of the same challenges shown in the previous examples.

Making Mathematics Real for Students

Throughout these examples, there are many ways that teachers can make mathematics culturally relevant. One way to make mathematics relevant to students is to be honest with them about what is really going on with mathematics they learn in school. Relevance may help students understand why learning a particular concept or procedure can help them in their futures. Teachers need to look closely at standards and think about whether the items and tasks they have in the classroom are realistic or contrived. If realistic, are they relevant to students? If contrived, they can create contexts to make them more realistic or have students think of more authentic contexts where particular concepts apply. Teachers may have to help students understand that a particular mathematical procedure will apply to higher levels of mathematics so students can see they are moving along a mathematical learning progression. As students get older, and mathematics becomes even more abstract, teachers need to be honest about the real-world applications of many mathematical algorithms (e.g., doing mathematical proofs, representing patterns in nature, solving problems in physics), giving students opportunities to see the mathematics occur in real-life or academic settings.

Using Performance Assessment to Make Mathematics Real for Students

Where possible, rather than creating separate items for each standard, teachers can think about performance tasks that could be focused on students demonstrating their understanding of several the standards within or across domains. The example performance task given in Figure 6.11 is fairly simple and only addresses two standards within grade 6, Ratios and Proportional Relationship. Teachers can work with colleagues to brainstorm performances that involve more than one standard within a domain or across domains. Standard 9 of the Expressions and Equations Domain (Use variables to represent two quantities in a real-world problem that change in relationship to one another; write an equation to express one quantity, thought of as the dependent variable, in terms of the other quantity, thought of as the independent variable. Analyze the relationship between the dependent and independent variables using graphs and tables, and relate these to the equation, CCSS, 2010b, p. 44) is related to the standards in the Ratios and Proportional Relationship Domain.

The standards targeted in the performance task shown in Figure 6.11 could be integrated with Standard 9 of Expressions and Equations to construct a richer problem situation grounded in a real-world context such as a science investigation, sales, or other contexts involving dependent and independent variables. Standard 9 of Expressions and Equations expands the types of representations to include equations as well as tables and graphs.

Just as teachers in Gutstein's and Peterson's 2005 book connected mathematics to social justice issues, teachers can look for ways to make key concepts and skills real for students through projects that allow them to investigate issues in their own communities.

As described in Chapter 3, projects can become assessment as learning—wherein students learn concepts and demonstrate their learning while engaged in meaningful work. For example, when learning ratio and proportion, students could work on projects that involve ratios (e.g., cooking for a community center event, making jewelry, doing an art display), create ratios to represent what materials they will need to complete the project, and then carry out the project using the ratios. The more standards that are integrated into the project the better and richer the project. In short, mathematics could be made relevant to students if teachers step back from standards and think about when and how mathematics standards are used in life. When the true application of a standard is in higher level mathematics, teachers should help students understand how higher level mathematics serves as a gateway for their progress through high school and beyond.

Mathematics Summary

Adopted mathematics instruction or assessment materials are unlikely to be culturally and socially relevant. Teachers must examine mathematics standards and textbook exercises to decide what matters most for their students. Teachers can create honest classrooms where students are allowed to question the purpose of mathematics standards and learning goals.

It is unlikely that teachers will be able to rewrite their mathematics textbooks to make them more culturally relevant. However, educators can work together in communities of practice to do the following:

1. Sift through standards to identify the conceptual focus for each standard.
2. Look at lesson activities, as well as related exercises and assessments, and consider how to ensure that the focus of lessons is on primary concepts or skills.
3. Brainstorm and engage students in brainstorming authentic contexts in which students are likely to use concepts.

4. Help students connect concepts to their own lives either through real-world problems or their future academic progressions in school.

Teachers can ask students to generate their own examples as part of the assessment process. When students create their own examples, they not only demonstrate their understanding, but they deepen their understanding. Creating their own examples, relevant to their own lives, also helps teachers learn about students' lives.

As teachers learn how to make assessments real for their students, they are more likely to make valid inferences about students' learning. Deborah Ball, a well-known mathematics educator, tells a story of how, after she took a course on number theory, she began to hear what her students were saying and realizing how much mathematics they really understood. Instead of focusing on whether they were getting right answers, she began to focus on their mathematical thinking:

> I realized that the kids were doing all kinds of mathematical things that teachers were missing, which, to me, had everything to do with kids' failure in math. Kids would say interesting things and their teachers would say, "No, don't do it that way" or "We're not talking about that" or "That has nothing to do with what we're talking about." Then, it would be pretty easy to explain why lots of kids would end up thinking, "This is a dumb subject and I'm checking out of this," because they were thinking things that were mathematically viable but most primary teachers couldn't hear it. (Richardson et al., 2009, p. 56)

The more students engage with mathematics in meaningful ways, the more they will understand mathematical concepts and operations, and the more they will care about learning.

BOOKS BY AUTHORS WITH DIVERSE CULTURAL AND SOCIAL IDENTITIES TO SUPPORT READING AND SOCIAL STUDIES ASSESSMENT

In this section of the chapter, I have identified websites that are intended to help parents and educators locate rich, culturally and socially responsive reading materials for teachers and students.

Students need to see themselves in the literature they read—particularly when they are being assessed on their reading skills and strategies, learning important social studies concepts, and so forth. Many websites provide recommendations for books by authors of color and authors with diverse cultural, racial, and social identities. Research suggests that students bring their own background knowledge and experiences to the reading process (Brooks & Browne, 2016; Copenhaver, 1999; Rosenblat, 1976; Sloan, 2002). Their prior knowledge and life experiences affect how well they comprehend ideas in text as well as their analyses and interpretations of texts. Culturally and socially responsive teachers can use culturally relevant literature and non-fiction texts in authentic performances to give students optimal opportunities to show their reading skills. Teachers can also use excerpts from these stories and nonfiction texts along with the generic item stems like those in Table 6.2 and the generic scoring rules in Table 6.3 and Figures 6.1 and 6.2 as resources for more traditional assessments of students' comprehension, analysis, and interpretation skills. In what follows, I provide the titles of different website pages as well as the URLs.

Multicultural Stories

The focus of these books is on diversity and culture—including both literary and nonfiction texts:

- A Multicultural Bibliography of Short Stories, https://jccc.libguides .com/c.php?g=511276
- Must-Read Story Collections by People of Color, https://www .readitforward.com/essay/article/must-read-short-stories-by-poc/
- 17 New Authors of Color Writing Much-Needed Stories for Kids, https://www.readbrightly.com/new-authors-of-color-writing-for -kids/
- Books About Diversity and Culture for Children (Nonfiction), https://dbrl.bibliocommons.com/list/share/72113334/1120001737
- "Kids and Parents Plead for Diversity in Children's Books. 8 Great Titles That Deliver," https://www.usatoday.com/story/life /allthemoms/2019/03/20/childrens-books-diversity-multicultural -read-kids/3205449002/

Books for Children and Teens About Racism, Oppression, and Social Justice

Several websites provide book lists for children and teens addressing issues of racism, classism, and other forms of social injustice. Some books are nonfiction; others are fictional stories or novels. If teachers want to incorporate themes of social justice into their teaching and assessment, these books or excerpts from these books could be used for classroom assessments in either language arts or social studies. In what follows, I provide the titles of different website pages and the URLs.

- Best Social Justice Books for Teens, https://parentinghighschoolers .com/social-justice-books-for-teens/
- Social Justice Books for Teens, https://seattle.bibliocommons.com /list/share/200121216/675212937

- Anti-Racist Books for Middle and High School Students, https://colorfulpages.org/2020/07/26/anti-racist-books-for-middle-and-high-school-students/
- Books About Racism and Social Justice, https://www.commonsensemedia.org/lists/books-about-racism-and-social-justice
- Children's Picture Books on Oppression, https://diversebookfinder.org/book-category/oppression/
- 37 Children's Books to Help Talk About Racism & Discrimination, https://coloursofus.com/37-childrens-books-to-help-talk-about-racism-discrimination/
- "These Books Can Help You Explain Racism and Protest to Your Kids," https://www.nytimes.com/2020/06/02/parenting/kids-books-racism-protest.html
- "14 Antiracist Books for Kids and Teens Recommended by BIPOC Teachers and Librarians," https://www.nytimes.com/wirecutter/reviews/antiracist-books-for-kids-and-teens/
- Social Justice: Poems for Kids, https://poets.org/text/social-justice-poems-kids

CONCLUDING REMARKS

The purpose of this chapter was to give teachers ways to think about assessment that are responsive to the cultural and social identities of students with diverse backgrounds. The diversity of schools will only continue to increase. The time for one-size-fits-all assessment has passed—if it was ever appropriate in the first place. Large-scale testing models and the "teach-test-grade" models used in classrooms were never intended to support student learning. A model of testing as a common (standardized) dipstick that is supposed to provide appropriate assessment of all students is neither valid nor useful. One-size-fits-all assessment has failed to meet the needs of students from diverse cultural and social backgrounds and has suppressed evidence of achievement for students of color, English learners, and female students for generations.

The purpose of schooling for nearly a century has been to rank students and select the best for higher education. This model is socially and economically unwise. Those who have been forced to the bottom by such an educational system are marginalized in every possible way throughout schooling and beyond. Unless we deal with the ways that assessment supports oppression, no one can proposer.

Standards that decompose learning goals into testable bits distract educators from teaching what matters. Even if classroom and large-scale assessment weren't biased in favor of the dominant society, performances on these tests do not generalize beyond testing. Hence, performances on traditional tests are inherently invalid for all students. As Asa Hilliard (2003), a renowned educational psychologist, noted:

> [The] acceptance of the reality of diversity will undermine the possibility for standardized, mass produced, universally applicable measurement instruments. It must be recognized that cultural pluralism is a reality, and not rhetoric. Cultural salience seems to be a taboo topic in testing, but it is one that cannot be ignored. (p. 1)

The purpose of schooling should be to support student learning so that all students can be successful throughout school and in life beyond school. Current assessment models, tools, and processes should serve those goals rather than work against them. Extensive research, much of it described in these chapters, shows us what works and how assessment can play a significant role in improving outcomes for students. Transformation from our current models of assessment to more effective models will require communities of practice to work together for change. Educators must refocus learning goals on what matters most for students' success rather than the dizzying array of standards that drive education today. Transformation will also require educators to recognize their power in coming together to try new practices and reject old, failed practices. Finally, transformation will require teachers to create classrooms that communicate respect for students and a belief in their capacity to succeed.

CHAPTER 7

Resources and Tools

In this chapter, I provide tools and resources to help improve assessment for students from diverse racial, cultural, and social identities. Part 1 and Appendices C, D, and E provide tools educators can use to conduct bias and sensitivity reviews processes, language complexity reviews, and accessibility reviews for their current and future classroom assessments. These reviews can improve the quality of assessment tools so that they are more likely to result in valid performances by students from diverse cultural and social backgrounds. These tools can also be used by school and district leadership as they think about curriculum adoptions and adoptions of interim and benchmark assessments. The tools can be used with traditional tests or performance assessments.

The materials given here are intended to help communities of practices create better assessment tools and to evaluate the quality of the tools already in place. My assumption is that educators care about the success of their students and want to know how to make their assessment practices supportive of student learning. Valid inferences about student learning are only possible when barriers to student performance are removed—whether those barriers are from teacher biases that impact grading practices, features of assessment tools that favor some students over others (e.g., the familiarity of assessment materials and contexts), the cultural appropriateness of assessment materials, or students' engagement with assessment tasks.

Part 2 provides a list of books that can help teachers think about validity, effective formative assessment practices, performance-based assessment, effective grading practices, and culturally and socially responsive assessment. I provide descriptions of each book and the URL. These books only scratch the surface of the literature available to help communities of teachers reflect on and improve their practices.

PART 1: WORKING IN COMMUNITIES OF PRACTICE TO EXAMINE PUBLISHED AND TEACHER-DEVELOPED CLASSROOM ASSESSMENTS

Chapter 2 describes some of the subtle biasing issues discovered by bias and sensitivity reviewers in a Pacific Northwest state. Developers of large-scale tests use several review processes to evaluate test items and stimulus materials for several important issues that can cause invalid assessment results for students with diverse cultural and social backgrounds:

1. Possible bias and sensitivity issues
2. Language complexity issues
3. Accessibility issues for students with disabilities

In this section, I provide guidance on how to conduct these three types of reviews. Appendices C and D provide tools for bias and sensitivity reviews and language complexity reviews. Appendix E provides guidance for accessibility reviews. Communities of practice can use, whether at the school, district, or state level, these and similar tools to guide reviewers and to capture reviewer input.

Bias and Sensitivity Reviews

It is highly likely that conscious efforts were applied to published instructional materials to minimize potential sources of bias. However, published and teacher-developed classroom assessments rarely go through formal bias and sensitivity reviews (Beck, 2009). The primary goal of bias and sensitivity reviews is to identify any factors within items, passages, or stimulus materials that can interfere with students' ability to show their knowledge and skills during an assessment event. Local educators in communities of practice work together to review published assessment materials in interim or benchmark tests as well as assessment materials included in published instructional materials. Individual teachers can look at the assessment tools they develop using the same criteria shown here and in Appendix C.

Bias and sensitivity reviewers should be individuals who represent students from diverse cultural and social backgrounds—particularly the families and the local community. Although conscientious educators and assessment developers work hard to make sure that instructional and assessment materials are appropriate for their students, it is difficult to step outside of one's own experiences and see what might affect those who have backgrounds and life experiences different from one's own. A bias and sensitivity panel should have at least one person representing each significant demographic group in the community (e.g., African Americans, Latinx, Indigenous Americans, Asian Americans, females, low-income families, nontraditional families, LGBTQ+ students and families, students with special needs, etc.). A neutral person with no connection to the assessments under review and with good facilitation skills should be chosen to manage the review process. The primary issues bias and sensitivity reviewers look for are given in Table 7.1. The review process involves systematically examining assessment materials with an eye to issues that may interfere with the validity of students' performances: distressing content, stereotyping,

Table 7.1. Categories for Bias and Sensitivity Reviews

Categories	Subcategories	Comments
Involves respectful and balanced treatment of individuals and groups	Language Images Roles Problems Values	Are all individuals and groups represented in a respectful manner? Are any stereotypes reinforced by word choices, images, social roles, socioeconomic backgrounds, personality characteristics, physical appearances, types of problems, daily activities, careers, behaviors, and values?
Avoids the unfamiliar	Linguistic structures Culture or social class Obscure or specialized vocabulary Regional vocabulary Social contexts Culture-specific knowledge	Are there any challenging linguistic demands (e.g., complex sentence structures, formal English phrasing, acronyms, idioms, and multimeaning words)? Are there any everyday or professional terms, irrelevant to the task, that may be unfamiliar to some students? Are there any social contexts and activities that would be familiar only to those who are part of a particular cultural group or social class?
Avoids controversial issues	Social controversies Health issues and problems Sexuality Religion Abuse and violence Death and dying	Are there topics in reading passages, items, or stimulus materials that could upset students and distract them from the main purpose of an assessment? Note: In courses where these topics are the focus (e.g., natural selection in a biology course), they would, of course, be part of the assessments.
Uses appropriate labels	Disabilities Ethnic groups Genders Sexual orientation	Publishers provide lists of terms that are appropriate and inappropriate when discussing people in particular socially defined categories. Teachers can ask the students for their ideas about appropriate and inappropriate ways to refer to people from different groups.

negative representations of any individuals or groups, misrepresentations of individuals or groups, factors that influence the familiarity of vocabulary and idiomatic phrases, contexts for items, required background knowledge that may not be available to all students, and so forth.

Once reviewer input is gathered, educational communities must decide how to handle the input. It is critical that input from reviewers be respected—even if educators are not in a position to change anything about items, tasks, passages, or stimulus materials. Educators should conduct bias and sensitivity reviews prior to the adoption of instructional programs using the assessment materials provided by the publishers. Publishers of interim and benchmark assessments may be willing to allow school or district personnel to review representative samples of items and stimulus materials prior to adoptions. Once adoptions are made, educators can conduct bias and sensitivity reviews of published classroom assessment materials and decide whether to use the existing materials, eliminate and replace assessment materials, or develop their own.

The general protocol and sample tools for conducting bias and sensitivity reviews is given in Appendix C.

Language Complexity Reviews

Language complexity issues can interfere with valid assessment of students who are English learners and students with limited English proficiency. Teachers and school leaders may want to review published assessments to evaluate the impact of language complexity on their students' abilities to show their knowledge and skills. The primary goal of language complexity reviews is to identify issues that might interfere with students' ability to understand assessment items and tasks due to limited English proficiency.

Language proficiency reviewers should be individuals who work with students who are developing English proficiency (ELL teachers, bilingual educators). Educators and assessment developers work hard to make sure that instructional and assessment materials are appropriate for students. However, as with issues of bias, it is difficult to step outside of one's own language proficiency and see what might affect those who are developing English proficiency. English learners may be officially designated as English language learners, or they may have limited English proficiency for other reasons. Minimizing language complexity has been shown to benefit students with limited English without having any impact on students with strong English skills (Abedi & Lord, 2000; Abedi & Sato, 2008). Recent statistics suggest that many urban areas work with students from many language groups. Table 7.2 provides examples of the language challenges faced by schools. Although assessment tools cannot be adapted to the language needs of all students, educators can minimize the impact of language complexity, a primary problem in large-scale, interim, published, and teacher-developed classroom assessment tools.

A language complexity review panel should have at least one person representing each of the most common language groups found in local schools. (Some common examples include Alaska Native, Arabic,

Table 7.2. Number of Languages Spoken in Major U.S. Cities as of January 2020

City	Number of Language
Atlanta	146
Houston	113
Los Angeles	92
San Francisco Bay Area	112
Seattle	154
New York City	176

Cambodian, Chinese, Farsi, Hindi, Korean, Russian/Ukrainian, Spanish, Urdu, and Vietnamese). These individuals do not have to be educators; however, their primary role is in identifying language complexity issues (e.g., unfamiliar language, complex syntactic structures) that may interfere with students' abilities to show their knowledge and skills.

Examples of language complexity issues were given in Table 2.1, along with example items and recommendations for how to remove complexities. The general protocol and samples tools for conducting bias and sensitivity reviews is given in Appendix D.

Accessibility Reviews

Accessibility is a major validity issue in assessment. Many accessibility issues arise due to visual, auditory, and motor disabilities. For example, as schools move toward more computer-based testing, some online items require motor skills that are difficult if not impossible for students with motor disabilities (e.g., drag and drop, drawing a line of best fit on a graph, sorting text, highlighting). Subjects that are highly visual, such as mathematics and science, require students to comprehend and interpret visual models such as graphs, charts, and diagrams. Even social studies tests often require interpretation of images, timelines, and graphs. Students with visual disabilities often need what is called "alternate text"—text that describes the particular visual stimulus. Students with visual and auditory disabilities may not be able to comprehend a reading passage or a test item that involves visual imagery or words referring to sounds. The item shown in Figure 7.1 shows an item that would make no sense to a deaf student.

For the most part, students with disabilities have access to a variety of assistive devices to help them during instruction. For example, speech-to-text software allows students to write essays and respond to short-answer and extended-response test items. Students with disabilities must also have access to these same assistive devices during assessment events. Students may have special devices that allow them to choose correct answers without having to use their hands. Aides may be able to help students complete

Figure 7.1. Item Biased Against Students With Auditory Disabilities

In the poem "The Bells," what is the effect of phrases such as *the jingling and the tinkling* and *the moaning and the groaning*?

☐ A. They describe the actual sounds of bells.

☐ B. They reflect the beauty of the sounds made by the bells.

☐ C. They provide the correct number of syllables in each line of the poem.

☐ D. They show that the speaker is distracted by the bells.

online tests by handling motor demands for them. Online testing may provide alternate text for images and visual representations.

However, teachers must be alert to more subtle issues such as that shown in Figure 7.1. Not only will students with auditory disabilities have difficulty correctly responding to the item, they may not even comprehend the main ideas in the poem. In large-scale testing, students with disabilities may have what are called "twin" items to allow them to show their conceptual understanding in a way that bypasses their disability. For example, if a classroom test is assessing students' understanding of linear relationships, students with visual disabilities could show that knowledge through an equation rather than a visual model.

All U.S. states and territories have accessibility guidelines as part of their testing programs. These guidelines show the allowable accommodations for students with different disabilities. These guidelines are available to all educators on state education agency websites.

Only recently have testing companies begun to include accessibility reviews as part of their test development processes. Some questions that are asked during these reviews are given in Appendix E. Schools and districts can use questions like these to conduct accessibility reviews for the published assessment they use at the classroom and district level. As with other reviews, teachers, schools, and districts may not be able to alter published assessments to make them more accessible to their students with disabilities. Making assessment tools fairer to students with disabilities may require local communities of practice to develop their own assessment tools with guidance from educators who specialize in serving students with disabilities.

PART 2: RESOURCES FOR TEACHER LEARNING THROUGH BOOKS ABOUT ASSESSMENT, CULTURALLY RESPONSIVE PEDAGOGY, AND MULTICULTURAL EDUCATION

Throughout this book, I have referenced books that focus on different aspects of assessment—from validity to formative assessment, to grading, to culturally responsive pedagogy. In what follows, I list these books and provide a brief summary about each book.

Formative Assessment

Formative Assessment: Making it Happen in the Classroom, Margaret Heritage, 2010, Corwin Press (https://us.corwin.com/en-us/nam/formative -assessment/book272852)

> This research-based book helps educators develop the knowledge and skills necessary to successfully implement formative assessment in the classroom. . . . This book explains how to: (1) Clearly articulate learning progressions, learning goals, and success criteria; (2) Select strategies for assessment and provide quality feedback; (3) Engage students in self-assessment and self-management; and (4) Create a classroom environment that values feedback as part of the learning process. (https://eric.ed.gov/?id=ED579802)

How to Create and Use Rubrics for Formative Assessment and Grading, Susan M. Brookhart, 2013, Association for Supervision and Curriculum Development (https://www.ascd.org/books/how-to-create-and-use-rubrics-for -formative-assessment-and-grading)

> In this guide, author Susan M. Brookhart identifies two essential components of effective rubrics: (1) criteria that relate to the learning (not the "tasks") that students are being asked to demonstrate and (2) clear descriptions of performance across a continuum of quality. Brookhart outlines the difference between various kinds of rubrics (for example, general versus task-specific, and analytic versus holistic), explains when using each type of rubric is appropriate, and highlights examples from all grade levels and assorted content areas. (http:// www.ascd.org/Publications/Books/Overview/How-to-Create-and-Use-Rubrics -for-Formative-Assessment-and-Grading.aspx)

Embedding Formative Assessment: Practical Techniques for K-12 Classrooms, Dylan Wiliam and Siobhan Leahy, 2011, Solution Tree (https:// www.solutiontree.com/embedded-formative-assessment-second-ed.html)

> This book outlines what formative assessment is, and what it is not, and presents the five key strategies of formative assessment:
>
> 1. Clarifying, sharing, and understanding learning intentions and criteria for success
> 2. Engineering effective classroom discussions, activities, and learning tasks that elicit evidence of learning
> 3. Providing feedback that moves learning forward
> 4. Activating learners as instructional resources for one another
> 5. Activating learners as owners of their own learning
>
> The book presents a summary of the research evidence that shows the impact of each strategy and offers a number of practical techniques that teachers have

used to incorporate the strategy into their regular classroom practice. (https://eric.ed.gov/?id=ED591904)

Assessment and Learning, John Gardner, 2005, Sage Books (https://uk.sagepub.com/en-gb/eur/assessment-and-learning/book235374)

> This book provides a comprehensive overview of assessment used to support learning, and it makes this area accessible and understandable for a wide range of users. This unique text is a major source of practice-based theory on assessment for learning, a formative assessment to support individual development and motivate learners. (https://eric.ed.gov/?id=ED500378)

Grading Practices

What We Know About Grading: What Works, What Doesn't, and What's Next, Thomas Guskey and Susan Brookhart, 2019, Association for Supervision and Curriculum Development (https://www.ascd.org/books/what-we-know-about-grading)

> Edited by Thomas R. Guskey and Susan M. Brookhart, this indispensable guide features thoughtful, thorough dives into the research from a distinguished team of scholars, geared to a broad range of stakeholders, including teachers, school leaders, policymakers, and researchers. Each chapter addresses a different area of grading research and describes how the major findings in that area might be leveraged to improve grading policy and practice. (https://eric.ed.gov/?id=ED592082)

How to Use Grading to Improve Learning, Susan Brookhart, 2017, Association for Supervision and Curriculum Development (https://www.ascd.org/books/how-to-use-grading-to-improve-learning)

> Brookhart explores topics that are fundamental to effective grading and learning practices:
>
> - Acknowledging that all students can learn
> - Supporting and motivating student effort and learning
> - Designing and grading appropriate assessments
> - Creating policies for report card grading
> - Implementing learning-focused grading policies
> - Communicating with students and parents
> - Assessing school or district readiness for grading reform
>
> The book is grounded in research and resonates with the real lessons learned in the classroom. Although grading is a necessary part of schooling, Brookhart reminds us that children are sent to school to learn, not to get grades. This highly

practical book will help you put grading and learning into proper perspective, offering strategies you can use right away to ensure that your grading practices actually support student learning.

Culturally Responsive Pedagogy

Crossing Over to Caanan: The Journey of New Teachers in Diverse Classrooms, Gloria Ladson-Billings, 2001, Wiley (https://www.wiley.com/en-us /search?pq=crossing over to canaan)

> Gloria Ladson-Billings provides a perceptive and interesting account of what is needed to prepare novice teachers to be successful with all students in our multicultural society. This book is must reading for all those entering the profession of teaching today and for those who prepare them for this important work. (Blurb from, Ken Zeichner, Professor Emeritus, College of Education, University of Washington and former Associate Dean and Professor of Curriculum and Instruction, School of Education, University of Wisconsin-Madison)

The Dreamkeepers: Successful Teachers of African American Children, third edition, Gloria Ladson-Billings, 2022, Jossey-Bass (https://www.wiley .com/en-us/The+Dreamkeepers%3A+Successful+Teachers+of+African +American+Children%2C+3rd+Edition-p-9781119791935)

> In this mixture of scholarship and storytelling, you'll learn how to create intellectually rigorous and culturally relevant classrooms that have the power to improve the lives of all children. This important book teaches:
>
> - What successful teachers do, don't do, and what we can learn from them
> - Why it's so important for teachers to work with the unique strengths each student brings to the classroom
> - How to improve educational outcomes for African American children across the country
>
> Perfect for teachers, parents, school leaders, and administrators, *The Dreamkeepers* will also earn a place in the libraries of school boards, professors of education, urban sociologists, and casual readers with an interest in issues of race and education.

Black Teachers on Teaching, Michele E. Foster, 1997, The New Press (https: //thenewpress.com/books/black-teachers-on-teaching)

> The stories of 20 black [*sic*] teachers, born between 1905 and 1973, are told in their own voices. These 20 life interviews collect the experiences of black teachers and document the constraints and supports in their professional lives,

as well as how their experiences have changed over their careers and over the years. All interviews covered the social, economic, and cultural milieus of the teachers' families and communities, their schooling and teaching experiences, and other aspects of their personal and professional lives. (https://eric .ed.gov/?id=ED413407)

Culturally Responsive Teaching: Theory, Research, and Practice, third edition, Geneva Gay, 2018, Teachers College Press (https://www.tcpress.com /culturally-responsive-teaching-9780807758762)

Combining insights from multicultural education theory with real-life classroom stories, this book demonstrates that "all" students will perform better on multiple measures of achievement when teaching is filtered through students' own cultural experiences. The Third Edition [*sic*] features new research that validates the positive effects of culturally responsive teaching. (https://eric .ed.gov/?id=ED581130)

Culturally Sustaining Pedagogies: Teaching and Learning for Justice in a Changing World, Django Paris and H. Samy Alim, 2017, Teachers College Press (https://www.tcpress.com/culturally-sustaining-pedagogies-9780807758335)

"Culturally Sustaining Pedagogies" [*sic*] raises fundamental questions about the purpose of schooling in changing societies. Bringing together an intergenerational group of prominent educators and researchers, this volume engages and extends the concept of culturally sustaining pedagogy (CSP)—teaching that perpetuates and fosters linguistic, literate, and cultural pluralism as part of schooling for positive social transformation. The authors propose that schooling should be a site for sustaining the cultural practices of communities of color, rather than eradicating them. (https://eric.ed.gov/?id=ED580787)

Transforming the Culture of Schools: Yup'ik Eskimo Examples, Jerry Lipka with Gerald V. Mohatt and the Ciulistet Group, 1998, Routledge (https:// www.routledge.com/Transforming-the-Culture-of-Schools-Yupk-Eskimo -Examples/Lipka-Mohatt-Ilutsik/p/book/9780805828214)

This book speaks directly to issues of equity and school transformation and shows how one indigenous minority teachers group engaged in a process of transforming schooling in their community. Documented in one small locale, far removed from mainstream America, the personal narratives by Yup'ik Eskimo teachers address the very heart of school reform.

Radical Equations: Civil Rights From Mississippi to the Algebra Project, Robert P. Moses and Charles E. Cobb, Jr., 2001, Penguin Random House (https://www .penguinrandomhouse.com/books/206027/radical-equations-by-robert-p-moses/)

At a time when popular solutions to the educational plight of poor children of color are imposed from the outside—national standards, high-stakes tests, charismatic individual saviors—the acclaimed Algebra Project and its founder, Robert Moses, offer a vision of school reform based in the power of communities. Begun in 1982, the Algebra Project is transforming math education in 25 cities. Founded on the belief that math-science literacy is a prerequisite for full citizenship in society, the Project works with entire communities—parents, teachers, and especially students—to create a culture of literacy around algebra, a crucial stepping-stone to college math and opportunity.

Rethinking Mathematics: Teaching Social Justice by the Numbers, second edition, Eric Gutstein and Bob Peterson, 2005, Rethinking Schools (https:// rethinkingschools.org/books/rethinking-mathematics-second-edition/)

More than 50 articles show how to weave social justice issues throughout the mathematics curriculum, as well as how to integrate mathematics into other curricular areas.

Rethinking Mathematics offers teaching ideas, lesson plans, and reflections by practitioners and mathematics educators. This is real-world math–math that helps students analyze social problems as they gain essential academic skills.

This book offers hope and guidance for teachers to enliven and strengthen their math teaching. It will deepen students' understanding of society and help prepare them to be critical, active participants in a democracy. Blending theory and practice, this is the only resource of its kind.

Multicultural Education

An Introduction to Multicultural Education, sixth edition, James A. Banks, 2019, Pearson (https://www.pearson.com/us/higher-education/program/Banks -An-Introduction-to-Multicultural-Education-6th-Edition/PGM1794312.html)

Banks includes the widely used concepts and paradigms that he has developed, such as the dimensions of multicultural education; approaches to multicultural curriculum reform; types of knowledge; and how to teach students to know, to care, and to act. In addition, the text covers the characteristics of effective multicultural lessons and units, the major benchmarks educators can use to determine sound multicultural education implementation, and benchmarks to reform. (https://eric.ed.gov/?id=ED372129)

Cultural Diversity and Education: Foundations, Curriculum and Teaching, James A. Banks, 2016, Routledge (https://www.routledge.com/Cultural -Diversity-and-Education-Foundations-Curriculum-and-Teaching/Banks/p /book/9781138654150)

In the opening chapter author Banks presents his well-known and widely used concept of Dimensions of Multicultural Education to help build an understanding of how the various components of multicultural education are interrelated. He then provides an overview on preparing students to function as effective citizens in a global world; discusses the dimensions, history, and goals of multicultural education; presents the conceptual, philosophical, and research issues related to education and diversity; examines the issues involved in curriculum and teaching; looks at gender equity, disability, giftedness, and language diversity; and focuses on intergroup relations and principles for teaching and learning. (https://www.routledge.com/Cultural -Diversity-and-Education-Foundations-Curriculum-and-Teaching/Banks/p /book/9781138654150)

Multicultural Education, 10th edition, James A. Banks and Cherry A. McGee Banks (Eds.), 2019, Wiley (https://www.wiley.com/en-us/Multicultural +Education %3A+Issues+and+Perspectives%2C+10th +Edition-p-9781119511564)

Multicultural Education helps current and future educators fully understand sophisticated concepts of culture; become more effective practitioners in diverse classrooms; and view race, class, gender, social class, and exceptionality as intersectional concepts.

Now in its tenth edition, this bestselling textbook assists educators to effectively respond to the ways race, social class, and gender interact to influence student behavior and learning. Contributions from leading authorities in multicultural education discuss the effects of class and religion on education; differences in educational opportunities for male, female, and LGBTQ students; and issues surrounding non-native English speakers, students of color, and students with disabilities. . . . Practical advice helps teachers increase student academic achievement, work effectively with parents, improve classroom assessment, and benefit from diversity. (https://www.wiley.com/en-us /Multicultural+Education%3A+Issues+and+Perspectives%2C+10th+Edition-p -9781119511564)

Other People's Children: Cultural Conflict in the Classroom, Lisa Delpit, 2006, The New Press (https://thenewpress.com/books/other-peoples-children)

In this groundbreaking, radical analysis of contemporary classrooms, MacArthur Award–winning author Lisa Delpit develops the theory that teachers must be effective "cultural transmitters" in the classroom, where prejudice, stereotypes, and assumptions often breed ineffective education. Delpit suggests that many academic problems attributed to children of color are actually the result of miscommunication, as primarily white teachers educate "other people's children" and perpetuate the imbalanced power dynamics that plague our system.

Raising Black Students' Achievement through Culturally Responsive Teaching, Johnnie McKinley, 2010, Association for Supervision and Curriculum Development (https://www.ascd.org/books/raising-black-students-achievement -through-culturally-responsive-teaching)

> In this book, Johnnie McKinley reveals the depth of her caring about black [*sic*] students' learning and describes the beliefs and values that exceptional teachers and their students follow as they grow and learn together. By sharing educators' stories, Johnnie introduces readers to classrooms where learning is continuous, where teachers and students respect each other, and where principals and teachers alike approach teaching students of color from a position of efficacy and confidence. (http://www.ascd.org/publications/books/110004.aspx)

Classroom Assessment Textbooks

An Introduction to Student Involved Classroom Assessment for Learning, seventh edition, Jan Chapuis and Richard Stiggins, 2016, Pearson (https:// www.pearson.com/us/higher-education/program/Chappuis-Introduction -to-Student-Involved-Assessment-FOR-Learning-An-with-My-Lab-Education -with-Enhanced-Pearson-e-Text-Access-Card-Package-7th-Edition/PGM334667 .html)

> This book is best known for its focus on teaching pre-service teachers how to involve students in the assessment process and how to use assessment as a tool to advance learning. (https://www.amazon.com/Introduction-Student -Involved-Assessment-Learning-7th/dp/0134450264)

Classroom Assessment: Supporting Teaching and Learning in Real Classrooms, second edition, Catherine Taylor and Susan B. Nolen, 2008, Pearson (https:// www.pearson.com/us/higher-education/program/Taylor-Classroom -Assessment-Supporting-Teaching-and-Learning-in-Real-Classrooms-2nd -Edition/PGM162583.html)

> The second edition of this exceptionally lucid and practical assessment text provides a wealth of powerful concrete examples that help students to understand assessment concepts and to effectively use assessment to support learning. The book offers unique coverage of ways to use assessment to support student learning across the developmental span from Kindergarten through high school. Rather than treat assessment separately from instruction, this book's unique approach treats assessment as a central factor in the life of a teacher every day. . . . The book also provides more coverage than any other classroom assessment text of how to adapt assessment to the needs of students with disabilities and students whose first language is not English. (https://www.pearson.com/

us/higher-education/program/Taylor-Classroom-Assessment-Supporting
-Teaching-and-Learning-in-Real-Classrooms-2nd-Edition/PGM162583.html)

Validity and Validation

Validity: An Integrated Approach to Test Score Meaning and Use, Gregory
Cizek, 2020, Routledge (https://www.routledge.com/Validity-An-Integrated
-Approach-to-Test-Score-Meaning-and-Use-1st-Edition/Cizek/p/book
/9780367261382#)

> *Validity* is a clear, substantive introduction to the two most fundamental aspects
> of defensible testing practice: understanding test score meaning and justifying
> test score use. Driven by evidence-based and consensus-grounded measurement
> theory, principles, and terminology, this book addresses the most common
> questions of applied validation, the quality of test information, and the useful-
> ness of test results. Concise yet comprehensive, this volume's integrated frame-
> work is ideal for graduate courses on assessment, testing, psychometrics, and
> research methods as well as for credentialing organizations, licensure and certi-
> fication entities, education agencies, and test publishers. (https://www.amazon
> .com/Validity-Integrated-Approach-Score-Meaning/dp/0367261375)

Avoiding Bias in Grading Practices

The following are specific strategies teachers can use to address their concerns about effort, behavior, attitude, and homework.

Consider cultural norms for students when establishing behavioral expectations. There was a time when a class visitor would expect to find students seated in separate desks in rows facing the teacher. Today, visitors are more likely to find students around tables working together on tasks, sharing resources, discussing ideas, or moving around the classroom during activities and as they transition between activities (e.g., gallery walks, workstations, jigsaws). Active classrooms require explicit efforts to teach students how to be active while being productive. Often the behavioral expectations in schools are based on the social norms of White, middle-class culture. Chapter 3 of this book provides an extensive discussion about the importance of getting to know students and their cultural backgrounds, behavioral norms, and communication styles. When setting behavioral expectations for classrooms, for whole-class, small-group, and individual work time, students can contribute their own ideas to setting those expectations.

Work with students to create a self-evaluation tool related to behavioral expectations. In our teaching, we begin each term giving students a task that requires group discussion and cooperation. At the end of the task, we have each student list two to three behaviors they did to make the group work successful. If there is sufficient time, we have each group generate a group list of effective communication and group work behaviors. We use their lists to create a brief checklist (no more than 10 behaviors) students can use to assess their own behaviors in class. In the next class, we have students engage in another group activity and then self-assess using the checklist. We debrief with students and adjust the checklist as needed. Once the checklist is done, we use it in our observations of students, and students can use it for both peer and self-assessment. Students have ownership of the behavioral criteria, and we have a systematic way to observe classroom behaviors and provide feedback to students. Research suggests that when teachers have clear and specific criteria for evaluating students, the likelihood of biased evaluation decreases (Quinn, 2020; Tenenbaum & Ruck, 2007; Uhlmann &

Cohen, 2005). This also applies to behavior during whole-class and group discussion and behaviors. We find that student self-evaluations give students a chance to reflect on and learn from their classroom behaviors. If used as a teaching tool, peer evaluations can help students understand how others see them. Even young children can use simply worded checklists with icons (☺☺☹) in self- and peer evaluations.

Make sure homework assignments can be completed by all students. Many students from low-income families and homes where English is not spoken in the home cannot do schoolwork at home. Students may not have access to computers or, if they do, their homes may lack sufficient broadband to access resources needed for homework.[1] Students may not have anyone at home to help them if they are confused about requirements of an assignment, if their parents do not speak English, or if their parents are working. Students may be responsible for caring for younger siblings while parents are working. Avoid homework that requires going to libraries or visiting specific places that require access to transportation. Any of these factors can prevent students from completing homework. Teachers should interview their students at the beginning of the year or semester to learn about the feasibility of homework. If students do not have the time and resources they need, teachers should create homework time in class to make sure all students have time to complete homework and have access to resources and support.

Make sure homework is worthwhile. Whether done in class as seatwork or at home, homework should add to students' learning. If students can do well on class projects, tests, and quizzes without completing homework, the homework is not serving an educative purpose. For example, if teachers assign a chapter to be read before the next day and then spend the class time giving a lecture over the content of the chapter, students do not need to read the chapter to learn its contents. If teachers use class discussion to go over the content of a story, poem, or chapter from a novel, students do not need to read before the discussion. If homework is not necessary for what students do in class, it is not worthwhile. Students should be asked to use the ideas in a reading assignment in a classroom activity so that their experience goes beyond rehashing what they were to read. Almost any assignment given as homework should have immediate applicability so that students can build on the work done independently.

Students may not understand the value of homework based on past experiences. In our teaching, we recommend that teachers *teach* students the value of homework. Teachers can give students a small assignment that must be completed in order to successfully participate in the next day's activities. Students who do not do the homework will not know how to participate. Teachers can then debrief the lesson so students learn how homework could improve their in-class experiences.

Avoid using pop quizzes as a way to "motivate" students to do their homework. Pop quizzes create a "gotcha" environment in school and can harm relationships between students and teachers. When pop quizzes are graded, they further punish students who were not able to complete preparatory work. Quizzes can be announced ahead of time. Quizzes can have value as a "pause" in a unit, giving students a chance to think about ideas in a course or subject area and assess their own understanding. After completing a quiz, students can work together to go over their answers and explain their responses. Focusing on the learning value of quizzes adds to the learning climate in a classroom rather than creating an adversarial relationship between teachers and students.

Teach study skills and organizational skills, if needed. Teachers cannot assume that students know how to study, how to capture ideas in texts, and how to organize tasks so that larger projects are completed on time. If timeliness is to be part of grading policies, teachers may have to teach study skills so that students learn how to organize their time and tasks. Teachers will spend less time in the long run and lower their own overall frustration of dealing with late work, incomplete assignments, and disorganization if they start a term learning about their students' study skills and teaching what is needed. The most effective teachers scaffold the learning, starting with small tasks and moving to larger, more complex tasks.

Have students self-evaluate their own effort on assignments and during group work. Don't assume students' level of effort. Some students will be able to complete assignments with little effort while others will have to give the same task a great deal of effort. Some students will get significant help at home while others will not have any home support. If students see the classroom climate as one focused on learning rather than punishment, they are more likely to be honest about their own efforts. If students were not able to give the effort a task needed, ask them to talk about why. Was the assignment boring? Did students understand the requirements of the task? Did the students pace themselves so that they could complete the task on time? Did the students have conflicting responsibilities such as childcare, an after-school job, a sports tournament, or homework in other classes?

Make sure that all assignment directions are clear so that students can successfully complete any tasks. This may seem like an obvious recommendation. Unfortunately, teachers give assignments without sufficient explanation of requirements.[2] If an assignment is large and complex, give students check-in points as they progress through the work. Give students brief checklists to guide different stages of the work. If there is a long list of requirements, teachers should check to be sure that they have taught students how to do all the requirements.[3]

Provide students with a simple, clear grading policy. The grading policy should indicate what percent of a grade is associated with each aspect of the grade (e.g., tests = 20%, essays = 20%, projects = 20%, homework = 10%, group work = 20%, class discussion = 10%). If required to use grading software, know these types of software are designed to provide weights for different aspects of a grade. Discuss the components of the grade with students and incorporate students' self-assessments into the grade. When teachers use points without weights, they must look carefully at where the points come from. It may be that very few points are associated with the most important assignments and the most points are associated with small, more trivial assignments.

Use caution with grading software. A typo, a missing assignment, or inappropriate conversion of a scoring rubric can have a huge effect on grades. For example, writing rubrics are generally on a 4-, 5-, or 6-point scale. These scales do not fit well within a percentage-based grading system. A score of 3 on a 5-point writing rubric might mean the written piece is adequate but needs work in developing ideas or strengthening voice. Within a percentage-based grading system, a score of 3 will translate to 60%, which is typically a borderline D/F in a percentage-based grading system. Giving students a 0 for missing assignments will have a devastating effect on overall averages. Suppose scores for one student are 10, 8, 8, 10, 10, 0, with 10 being full credit for an assignment. By simply averaging the scores, the student would have an average of 7, which does not represent the student's typical performance.

Developing Culturally Relevant Performance Tasks

The following are the key tasks teachers should do to construct well-developed performance tasks that can be adapted to the cultural and social backgrounds of students. Whether simple or complex, well-developed performance tasks have meaning and value beyond school and are worth learning how to do. They can be tasks completed at the end of an instructional unit or as projects students work on over short or long periods of time. The best performance tasks will allow students at all proficiency levels to complete the performance successfully and will help students learn and grow while doing them. Important work beyond school often requires the input of many people. Performance tasks need not be individual tasks; students might need to work together to complete important work.[1]

Well-developed performance tasks will be usable more than once and can be used with different, culturally responsive stimulus materials (reading passages, historical documents, social studies texts, videos, etc.). To ensure that performance tasks can be adapted to the specific cultural and social identities of students, the task directions should be flexible and, if possible, allow students to make choices. Teachers may offer stimulus materials or students may select the materials themselves. If students are to select their own stimulus materials, they may need guidance on selecting topics and texts that are at an appropriate developmental and difficulty level. All aspects of the performance task (targeted learning goals or standards, expectations, and scoring rules) should be written in language students will understand at their developmental level.

Teachers should consider the specific needs of students by doing the following:

- Making sure performance tasks are accessible and doable by students with disabilities. If authentic work is not accessible by students with particular disabilities, consider how to adapt the tasks to make them accessible. Remember that individuals with disabilities are successful in life and careers (e.g., Stephen Hawking, Franklin Roosevelt, Greta Thunberg).

- Considering how to make tasks accessible for English learners by managing language complexity in performance descriptions, student directions, and scoring rules (see Chapter 2 about features of language complexity).
- Making sure that performances will not violate any relationship norms, cultural values, or beliefs. Interview students to find out what cultural issues might prevent them from completing tasks.
- Provide any tools and resources students need in order to complete performances. Performance tasks should not rely on parents to provide materials, take students to particular places, or oversee completion of the work.

The complexity of performances must be appropriate to the developmental level of students. Students at all developmental levels can write stories, communicate opinions, and read and describe what they've read. One trap many educators can fall into is the idea that high achievement means that items, tasks, and performances must be difficult. Authentic work is complex and requires thoughtful application of knowledge and skills. However, any task assigned to students must be doable by students. It should be possible for students at all proficiency levels to learn how to do a valued performance. Initial levels of performance should lead to better, more knowledgeable, more skilled performances as students learn more.

Aim for performance tasks where peer and self-evaluation will lead to further or deeper understanding and skill related to the targeted learning goals or academic standards. This applies to any project or performance in any subject area. Students learn how to play basketball by playing basketball. It is not sufficient to teach them the rules and give them practice with the skills.

STEPS IN PERFORMANCE TASK DEVELOPMENT

The following steps can be used with many different types of performance tasks. The key idea is to be systematic in development so that the tasks are effective, authentic, and well aligned with targeted standards. Avoid cramming too much into a given performance task. Performance tasks can be brief or can be week-long, month-long, or even year-long efforts. For longer efforts, break tasks down into meaningful stages and support students as they work through the stages:

1. Select a performance that has meaning to students, has value beyond school, and is relevant to students.
2. Choose performances that are worth doing and that will allow students to learn while doing them. Start with performances adults actually

do (in careers, home activities, academic work) in the students' communities; consider how to simplify the performances to make achievable by students.

3. Select performances that are authentic to subject areas and through which students can develop new knowledge just as the adults who engage in those performance learn while doing. It is through the real work of adults that new knowledge is constructed or unearthed. Adults develop new historical knowledge by engaging with historical information in authentic ways. Adults develop new knowledge about the causes and effects of economic conditions by applying economic concepts to real-world situations. Adults develop and expand science concepts when they engage in investigations related to those concepts. Students can participate in the development of new knowledge through their performances.

4. Involve students in selecting valued performances to do and learn how to do. Ask students to brainstorm about what the people in their communities do or have done related to the concepts, skills, or subject area. Ask students for suggestions about authentic performances.

5. Describe the performance in some detail so the teacher and students can envision it. The description should include sufficient detail that it is clear how students will demonstrate targeted learning goals or standards. Use language appropriate for students. Students should be able to read the description and see examples of the task before they embark on their work.

6. Identify the standards to be shown (and learned) through the performance. List the learning goals or academic standards students will demonstrate. Review the performance description to ensure that students can demonstrate the learning goals in performance. Plan to work iteratively between the performance description and the learning goals to make sure that targeted standards will be demonstrated through the performance. Don't force standards into a performance if they don't naturally fit. The goal is to make the performance authentic.

7. Write directions for students. Directions should give students a clear picture of what they are to do and the expectations for their work. Include in the directions any processes students are to demonstrate as they complete the performance (e.g., skill with writing processes, application of scientific skills during an investigation).

8. Write a scoring rule (rubric, rating scale, or checklist) that you and students can use to assess whether students have achieved the targeted standards. Scoring rules should be tightly tied to the learning goals students are to demonstrate via the performance. If students are to demonstrate certain skills, the scoring rules should be designed to evaluate their application of skills. If students are to demonstrate important knowledge or conceptual understanding, the scoring

rules should be designed to evaluate their conceptual or factual knowledge. Scoring rules for young children can be as simple as words with pictures. Scoring rules for older students can include levels of performance that are discernable in examples that students examine during instruction.

- Begin with performance criteria (specific knowledge or skills to be shown in the work), which may be listed within the task directions (as in the reading example in this appendix).
- Decide whether to use a checklist, rating scale, or one or more focused rubrics. Research on teachers' application of scoring rules suggests that teachers are most reliable, least biased, and most likely to agree with scores given by other teachers when scoring rules are detailed and focused (Taylor, 1998; Tenenbaum & Ruck, 2007; Uhlmann & Cohen, 2005).

EXAMPLE READING PERFORMANCE TASK

Description of the Performance

The performance is a review of a fiction or nonfiction book. Students will read a book or select a book they have already read. The book can be one they choose from among several offered by the teacher. Students will then describe the book (brief summary, key ideas and details) and make a claim about the author's primary message or an important theme. They will discuss the quality of the text, including their views about how well the author communicated messages, developed ideas or characters, and used ideas or images to help the reader understand the setting and characters (literature) or main ideas and important details (informational text). The students will end the book review with a recommendation about whether they recommend the book and explain why.

Standards to Be Shown and Learned Through the Performance

Grade 5 Reading Standards (CCSS, 2010a, p. 14)

R1. Quote accurately from a text when explaining what the text says explicitly and when drawing inferences from the text.

R2. Determine a theme of a story, drama, poem from details in the text, including how characters in a story respond to challenges; summarize the text (Literary Text)

R3. Describe how a narrator's or speaker's point of view influences how events are described (Literary Text)

R4. Determine two or more main ideas of a text and explain how they are supported by key details; summarize the text (Informational Text)

R5. Explain how the author uses reasons and evidence to support particular points in a text (Informational Text)

Grade 5 Writing Standards (CCSS, 2010a, p. 21)

W1. Write opinion pieces on topics or texts, supporting a point of view with reasons and information.

W2. Introduce a topic or text clearly, state an opinion, and create an organizational structure in which ideas are logically grouped to support the writer's purpose.

W3. Provide logically ordered reasons that are supported by facts and details.

W4. Provide a concluding statement or section related to the opinion presented.

Directions for Students

We're going to create a magazine to publish short stories, poems, essays, and movie and book reviews you write. We'll publish the magazine so you can share it with your family, friends, and community members. We'll publish at least three editions of the magazine this year so that everyone publishes their work. The first piece you will write is a book review. We'll spend the next couple of weeks learning how to write a good book review.

Task Directions

Choose a book to review. It can be nonfiction or a novel. Make sure it is a book you read and not a movie about a book. We will do movie reviews later this year. It doesn't matter when you read it. In the book review, you will give your opinion about the book. You may want to recommend it. You may like some things about the book and dislike others. Or you may want to tell people "Don't bother reading this book!"

The book review will have these characteristics:

☐ Title of the book and the author or authors (R1)
☐ Your opinion of the book (W2)
☐ A two-paragraph summary of the main events or ideas in the book (R2 or R4, W2)
☐ The two most important messages in the book or one theme in the book (R2 or R4)
☐ Characteristics of the book that stood out to you (good or bad) and why they stood out. Give examples from the book to support your ideas (R1, R3, W3)
☐ Whether you think the author did a good job of using events in the story to communicate the theme (R3)

OR

☐ Whether you think the author did a good job of supporting their message with evidence (R5)
☐ Give examples from the book to support your opinion of about the effectiveness of the author (W3)
☐ Write a conclusion that includes whether you recommend the book and why (W4)

SCORING RUBRICS FOR BOOK REVIEW

Reading Rubric

4 Student gives the title of the book and the name of the author and provides a thorough and accurate summary of the main ideas or events in the book. Student's claim about important messages or theme is viable based on the information provided to support the claim. Student's claim about the effectiveness of the author's work is viable and well supported by examples from the text. Specific examples and details used to support claim are text-based and accurate.

3 Student gives the title of the book and the name of the author and provides an accurate summary of the main ideas or events in the book. Claim about important messages or theme is viable based on the information provided to support the claim. Claim about the effectiveness of the author's work is viable and supported by information from the text. Information or ideas from the book support claim. Review needs more details or examples.

2 Student named the title and author of the book and provided a mostly accurate summary of the main ideas or events in the book. Claim about important messages or theme is viable based on the information provided to support the claim *or* claim about the effectiveness of the author's work is viable and supported by information from the text. Information or ideas from the book, if given, support claim.

1 Student named the title and author of the book and provided an accurate summary of the main ideas or events in the book. Student identified an important message or theme. Information or ideas from the book support claim about message or theme.

Writing Rubric

4 Review has a clear introduction and a solid conclusion that give student's opinion. Student presents ideas in a logical and organized way. Student presents claims about the text and explains how specific and detailed, text-based evidence supports the claims.

3 Review has an introduction and a conclusion that give student's opinion. Student presents ideas in an organized way. Student presents claims about the text and explains how information from the text supports the claims.

2 Review has an introduction or conclusion that gives student's opinion. Student presents ideas in an organized way. Student includes information from the text.

1 Student gives opinion about the book and gives reasons for their opinion.

Bias and Sensitivity Reviews

Appendix C provides several documents useful in conducting bias and sensitivity reviews. I begin with typical protocol for the bias and sensitivity review process. The remaining documents include the following:

- Group norms that review panelists are asked to honor during the review
- A sample of slides that could be used for training PowerPoint
- A sample passage for training purposes
- Sample items for training purposes
- Sample record sheet for passage and stimulus reviews
- Sample record sheet for item reviews
- Participant evaluation form

PROTOCOL FOR BIAS AND SENSITIVITY REVIEW

Materials are prepared for the review ahead of time—packets of passages and other stimulus materials; packets of items, reviewer record sheets, group norms, evaluation forms, sample items, passages, and other stimuli. All items should be numbered consecutively. All passages and stimulus materials should be numbered consecutively. Reviewers will record their comments on the record sheet next to the item, passage, or stimulus.

It is best to decide how to divide up passages or items into batches (5–10 passages; 20–30 items) prior to beginning so that record sheets are prepared based on batches.

The process requires a facilitator and a recorder who captures the input from reviewers.

The facilitator greets reviewers and introduces themself and the recorder. Facilitator briefly explains the purpose of the review process. It is important for the facilitator to explain that the purpose of the review is not to judge the content or measure the quality of items and tasks but rather to look for features of items and tasks that might interfere with students' performances.

The facilitator asks panelists to introduce themselves and briefly describe their backgrounds.

The facilitator goes over group norms for discussion (see example in this appendix).

The facilitator goes over a record sheet where reviewers record their observations and concerns (see example in this appendix).

The facilitator then goes through a brief training process (about 30 minutes; see example slides for PowerPoint in this appendix).

- The facilitator describes different potential sources of bias.
- The facilitator lists sensitive issues and topics that should be avoided.
- The facilitator explains that reviewers should identify any other bias or sensitivity issues they find.
- If reviewers will be reviewing reading passages, the facilitator asks reviewers to read a brief passage that includes sensitive or biasing content (see example in this appendix).
- If reviewers review a passage, the facilitator asks reviewers to discuss any issues they see in the passage; the recorder notes reviewers' ideas on a master record sheet visible on a whiteboard or projector.
- The facilitator walks reviewers through three to four test example items that have minor issues with bias and/or sensitivity (see sample items in slides for PowerPoint).
- The facilitator gives reviewers three to four sample items and asks reviewers to read each item independently and note any issues on their record sheets.
- The facilitator leads a discussion of reviewers' observations and captures reviewer input on a master record sheet visible on whiteboard or projector.
- The facilitator asks reviewers if they have any questions about the process or how to complete the review form. The facilitator clarifies, as needed.

Once training is completed, the facilitator takes reviewers through an actual review.

- The facilitator assigns batches, has reviewers review passages or items in each batch, and then leads a discussion of observations for each batch.
- Although all record sheets are retained, discussion is focused on items or passages that have raised the most concerns.
- The facilitator captures reviewers' input on a master record sheet.

- The facilitator works to ensure that all reviewers have opportunities to add ideas and that all points of view are accepted and attempts to bring the group to consensus on any items for which there is significant disagreement.

The facilitator gives reviewers periodic breaks (after one or two batches) so that reviewers can rest, eat or snack, get a drink, and so forth.

Once reviews are completed, the facilitator collects all review forms and distributes an evaluation form.

The facilitator collects evaluations, thanks all reviewers for their contributions, and adjourns the meeting.

The facilitator collates review forms and provides any remaining comments or notes on the master review sheet.

NORMS FOR BIAS AND SENSITIVITY REVIEW

☐ Share your own ideas and experience.
☐ Listen alertly to others' ideas and contributions.
☐ Ask questions for clarification.
☐ Ask about others' ideas and thinking.
☐ Encourage others to participate.
☐ Acknowledge others' perspectives.
☐ Be prompt after breaks.
☐ Keep the discussions focused on the purpose of the meeting.
☐ Help bring others back to the task if the conversation drifts.

EXAMPLE SLIDES FOR BIAS REVIEW TRAINING POWERPOINT

Bias and Sensitivity Review of Passages, Scenarios, and Items

Date
Location

What Is Test Bias?

Language or content in the item that prevents members of a group from demonstrating their knowledge and skills in a content area

Principles of Universal Design

- Assessments should be designed to be accessible to the widest possible range of students.
- Test results should not be influenced by disability, ethnicity, culture, gender, or English language ability.

Potential Sources of Bias and Stereotyping

- Regional and geographic differences in language usage and topic familiarity
- Linguistic issues (e.g., idiomatic expressions or figurative language)
- Gender and age stereotypes
- Ethnic, cultural, and religious stereotypes
- Socioeconomic and occupational stereotypes

Sensitivity Issues

Any reference or language in an item or passage that might cause a student to have a reaction that prevents the student from demonstrating knowledge and skills.

- Passage about abuse or struggles of an individual or group because of minority status
- Change of meaning or structure in a culture's legend or folk tale
- Competitive context in passages or items
- Controversial issue unrelated to the content standards
- Use of patronizing language to describe an individual or group

Purpose of Bias and Sensitivity Review

Review test items and stimulus materials for potential sources of bias, sensitive issues, and gender or cultural stereotypes.

Guiding Questions

- Is there anything controversial, inflammatory, or insensitive in a scenario, reading passage, or item context?
- Is the language likely to be familiar to <u>most</u> examinees regardless of socioeconomic status, region, language proficiency, cultural background, or gender?
- Is there any apparent patronizing language, stereotypical descriptions, or stereotypical actions/beliefs present?
- Would an item context or content give students of a particular group, background, or region a distinct advantage or disadvantage?

Practice Passage Review

- Read the Goldilocks passage
- Decide whether the content of the passage has any of these problems:
  - ➤ Stereotyping or negative representation of any group
  - ➤ Content that is controversial or sensitive
  - ➤ Language or context that may be unfamiliar to a student because of region, cultural background, English language proficiency, socioeconomic status, etc.

Passage Issues?

Sample Item #1

Which of the following measures could be the length of a typical Par 4 golf fairway?

- O   A. 400 inches
- O   B. 400 feet
- O   C. 400 yards
- O   D. 400 miles

Bias issue: SES and/or prior knowledge

Sample Item #2

At a carnival, Rolando sees a booth that has a prize wheel. The wheel has 20 sections. Five of the sections are labeled 'Winner.'

If Rolando decides to give the wheel a shot, what is the probability that he will win a prize?

- O   A. 0.20
- O   B. 0.25
- O   C. 0.33
- O   D. 0.75

Bias issue: Idiomatic Language ... give the wheel a shot ...

Sample Item #3

Alice, Peg, and Sharon entered their quilts in the town fair. Alice entered 3 quilts; Peg and Sharon each entered 1 quilt. The quilts are of equal quality. Who is more likely to win the contest.

- O   A. Alice
- O   B. Peg
- O   C. Sharon
- O   D. Peg and Sharon together

Stereotyping: females quilting; sensitivity: personal competition.

Practice Item Review

- Read the items in the handout
- Decide whether the content of the items have any of these problems:
  - ➢ Stereotyping or negative representation of any group
  - ➢ Context that is controversial or sensitive
  - ➢ Language or context that may be unfamiliar to a student because of region, language proficiency, socioeconomic status, etc.

Item Issues?

How to Proceed

- Read through test materials, keeping in mind the guiding questions.
- Make your own judgment. Write your judgment on the review form:
  - ☐ Accept as is (no apparent bias/sensitivity issue)
  - ☐ Accept with minor revisions
  - ☐ Reject due to potential bias or sensitivity issue

How to Proceed

- As a group, we will discuss each item or passage flagged for revision or rejected.
- The recorder will take detailed notes.
- We will try to make a group decision about each passage and item.
- We will record any dissenting position.

SAMPLE READING PASSAGE FOR BIAS
AND SENSITIVITY REVIEW TRAINING

Goldilocks and the Three Bears—Revisited

Once upon a time, there were three bears that lived in their home in the forest. You may have heard that they lived in a house, but that story isn't true. They really lived in a hollow under a huge cedar tree.

The bears were Mama Bear, Papa Bear, and Baby Bear. Papa Bear was big and old and had a bad temper, just like many old men. He spent most of his day eating.

Mama Bear did what all good Mamas do. She took good care of Baby Bear when he was too young to take care of himself. She fed him and bathed him. She taught him to come to her if there was danger nearby. She taught him how to climb trees to get away from men and other animals. As Baby Bear grew older, Mama Bear taught him how to forage for berries throughout the forest and hillsides where they lived. She also taught him how to catch salmon as they swam upstream to their spawning grounds.

Baby Bear was like many young ones. He explored dark holes. He chased smaller animals. He climbed trees and tried to get Mama Bear to play with him. But Mama Bear was too busy to play. She knew that she and Baby Bear had to eat a lot of food before winter so that they wouldn't starve when the snows came.

One day, when Papa Bear, Momma Bear, and Baby Bear were out foraging for berries and catching salmon, Goldilocks wandered into the part of the forest where they lived. She had been wandering around for many hours—completely lost. She found the hollow under the tree and crawled down into it. She thought it was a good place to sleep because it was hidden and warm.

When the three bears came back to their hollow, they smelled something new. It was the smell that Mama Bear had taught Baby Bear to run away from—the smell of a human. Mama Bear quickly took Baby Bear away from the hollow. Papa Bear squeezed into the hollow to find out who was in his den. Once Papa Bear saw Goldilocks, he was confused. He sniffed. Why was this human cub in his den? Then he roared loudly.

Goldilocks woke up to the sound of Papa Bear's roar. She screamed, "AAAAAAAAAAAAA!!!!!!!!!!" Papa Bear was startled and quickly backed out of the den. He backed away, swinging his head this way and that. Goldilocks was so scared she couldn't move.

Not far away, Goldilocks's family was searching the hillsides and forests for her. Her mother and father had told her not to go far from the camp, but she hadn't listened. Now they were frightened. They heard the roar.

Goldilocks's father shouted to her mother, "Go back to camp and get the forest ranger. Goldilocks could be in trouble!"

Goldilocks's mother ran down the hill to the camp. Before you could say "Papa Bear" the ranger was driving his Jeep up the hill toward the sound of Papa Bear's roar.

Meanwhile, Goldilocks's father ran toward the sound of the roaring bear. He grabbed a big stick and started shouting as loud as he could, banging the stick on rocks along the trail.

Papa Bear heard the big human yelling and banging. He didn't know what to do. A human cub was in his house. A big human was running toward him. He backed away from the big human. He sniffed the air and found the smell of Mama Bear and Baby Bear. He turned and began to lumber in their direction with Goldilocks's father banging and yelling, "Goldilocks! Goldilocks! Where are you?"

When Goldilocks heard her father's voice, she screamed, "Daddy! I'm here!! Come save me!!"

Goldilocks's father stopped chasing the bear. He turned back toward the muffled sound of her voice.

There she was, crawling out of the hollow under the tree. Tears streaked down her dirty cheeks. Her father grabbed her and hugged her so hard he nearly took her breath away.

Just then, the forest ranger arrived in his truck. Goldilocks and her father climbed into the truck and the ranger took them back to camp.

That afternoon, Goldilocks and her family packed their camping gear and drove away from the forest. It was a long time before Goldilocks stopped crying. It was a long time before her father stopped shaking.

The three bears moved away from their hollow under the tree. They moved deeper into the forest, higher up the mountain, and farther away from the humans. No humans ever saw them again. They found a cave in the rocky mountain side. They filled it with grasses and fur and lived happily there for a long time.

Papa Bear was glad that his family was safe even though he was still very grouchy.

SAMPLE ITEMS FOR BIAS AND SENSITIVITY REVIEW PRACTICE

1 Chevy has a collectables shop. In the shop, she has 150 trolls of different sizes and colors. Thirty-nine trolls are large, 28 trolls are medium, and 83 are small. What fraction of the trolls is medium?

☐ A $\frac{1}{28}$

☐ B $\frac{1}{122}$

☐ C $\frac{150}{28}$

☐ D $\frac{14}{75}$

2 In the story, the villagers fed fish to the cat and it stopped eating the chickens. What lesson did the author want the reader to learn?

☐ A Kind people adopt and feed stray animals.
☐ B Sometimes we should make friends with an outsider.
☐ C Most cats will eat fish before they'll eat chickens.

3 An apartment complex is building a spa and pool house. Write several paragraphs to convince the management about the equipment that should available for tenants in the spa.

Sample Bias and Sensitivity Passage and Stimulus Review Record Sheet

Use this form to record your observations about potential bias issues in the passages.

Passage or Stimulus	Potential Bias Issues				Comment	Recommendation		
	S	D	SI	Other		Accept	Revise*	Reject
Sample								
1								
2								
3								
4								
5								
6								

S—Stereotyping, D—Demeaning, SI—Sensitive issue

*Published passages cannot be revised without author's permission.

Bias and Sensitivity Item Review Record Sheet

Use this form to record your observations about potential bias issues in the passages.

Item	Potential Bias Issues						Comment	Recommendation		
	S	D	SI	L	F	Other		Accept	Revise*	Reject
Sample										
1										
2										
3										
4										
5										
6										

S—Stereotyping, D—Demeaning, SI—Sensitive issue, L—Language, F—Familiarity

*Published items cannot be revised without publishers' permission.

EVALUATION OF BIAS AND SENSITIVITY REVIEW

Do not write your name on the evaluation. Your responses are anonymous.

Read each of the following statements. Then indicate whether you strongly agree (SA), agree (A), disagree (D), or strongly disagree (SD).

1	The process used for review was appropriate.	SA	A	D	SD
2	All committee members participated in the process.	SA	A	D	SD
3	Committee members honored the group norms.	SA	A	D	SD
4	Each person had an opportunity to share ideas, issues, and concerns.	SA	A	D	SD
5	The consensus building process was managed effectively.	SA	A	D	SD
6	The facilitator kept us focused on the purpose of the review process.	SA	A	D	SD
7	The recorder kept accurate records of what individuals and the group said.	SA	A	D	SD
8	I am satisfied with the results of the review process.	SA	A	D	SD

Language Complexity Reviews

Appendix D provides several documents useful in conducting language complexity reviews. I begin with the typical protocol for the language complexity review process. The supporting documents include the following:

- Group norms that review panelists are asked to honor during the review
- A sample of slides that could be used for training PowerPoint
- Sample stimulus for training purposes
- Sample items for training purposes
- Sample record sheet for stimulus reviews
- Sample record sheet for item reviews
- Sample participant evaluation form

PROTOCOL FOR LANGUAGE COMPLEXITY REVIEW

Materials are prepared for the review ahead of time—packets of stimulus materials, packets of items, reviewer record sheets, group norms, evaluation forms, sample items, and sample stimuli. All items should be numbered consecutively. All stimulus materials should be numbered consecutively. Reviewers will record their comments on the record sheet next to the item or stimulus.

It is best to decide how to divide up passages or items into batches (5–10 passages; 20–30 items) prior to beginning so that record sheets are prepared based on batches.

The process requires a facilitator and a recorder who captures the input from reviewers.

The facilitator greets reviewers and introduces themself and the recorder. The facilitator briefly explains the purpose of the review process. It is important for the facilitator to explain that the purpose of the review is not to judge the content or measure the quality of items and tasks but rather to look for features of items and tasks that might interfere with students' performances.

The facilitator asks panelists to introduce themselves and briefly describe their backgrounds.

The facilitator goes over group norms for discussion (see example in this appendix).

The facilitator goes over a record sheet where reviewers record their observations and concerns (see example in this appendix).

The facilitator then facilitates a brief training process (about 30 minutes; see example slides for PowerPoint in this appendix).

- The facilitator describes different potential sources of language complexity.
- The facilitator explains that reviewers should identify any language complexity issues they find.
- If reviewers will be reviewing stimulus materials (tables, charts, photographs, diagrams), the facilitator asks reviewers to look at one to two stimulus examples with language complexity issues (see example in this appendix).
- If reviewers review stimuli, the facilitator asks reviewers to discuss any issues they see in the stimulus; the recorder notes reviewers' ideas on a master record sheet visible on a whiteboard or projector.
- The facilitator walks reviewers through three to four test example items that have minor issues with language complexity (see sample items in slides for PowerPoint).
- The facilitator gives reviewers three to four sample items and asks reviewers to read each item independently and note any issues on their record sheets.
- The facilitator leads a discussion of reviewers' observations. The recorder captures reviewer input on a master record sheet visible on a whiteboard or projector.
- The facilitator asks reviewers if they have any questions about the process or how to complete the review form. The facilitator clarifies, as needed.

Once training is completed, the facilitator takes reviewers through an actual review.

- The facilitator assigns batches, has reviewers review passages or items in each batch, and then leads a discussion of observations for each batch.
- Although all record sheets are retained, discussion is focused on items or passages that have raised the most concerns.
- The facilitator captures reviewers' input on a master record sheet.
- The facilitator works to ensure that all reviewers have opportunities to add ideas and that all points of view are accepted and attempts to bring the group to consensus on any items for which there is significant disagreement.

The facilitator gives reviewers periodic breaks (after one or two batches) so that reviewers can rest, eat or snack, get a drink, and so forth.

Once reviews are completed, the facilitator collects all review forms and distributes an evaluation form.

The facilitator collects evaluations, thanks all reviewers for their contributions, and adjourns the meeting.

The facilitator collates review forms and provides any remaining comments or notes on the master review sheet.

NORMS FOR LANGUAGE COMPLEXITY REVIEW

☐ Share your own ideas and experience.
☐ Listen alertly to others' ideas and contributions.
☐ Ask questions for clarification.
☐ Ask about others' ideas and thinking.
☐ Encourage others to participate.
☐ Acknowledge others' perspectives.
☐ Be prompt after breaks.
☐ Keep the discussions focused on the purpose of the meeting.
☐ Help bring others back to the task if the conversation drifts.

EXAMPLE SLIDES FOR LANGUAGE COMPLEXITY TRAINING POWERPOINT

Language Complexity Review of Items

Date
Location

What Is Language Complexity?

Language structure or vocabulary prevents students with limited English from demonstrating their knowledge and skills in a content area.

Principles of Universal Design

- Assessments should be designed to be accessible to the widest possible range of students.
- Test results should not be influenced by disability, ethnicity, culture, gender, or English language ability.

Potential Sources of Language Complexity

- Technical language unrelated to the subject area
- Idiomatic expressions or figurative language
- Multimeaning words
- Complex syntax (e.g., dependent clauses)
- Long sentences
- Formal language usages
- Unnecessary prepositional phrases
- Long noun phrases

Purpose of Language Complexity Review

Review test items for potential sources of language complexity so that simpler language can allow better access for students with limited English.

Guiding Questions

- Are there technical words or phrases that are not related to the subject area?
- Could sentences be simplified to eliminate clauses, run-on sentences, unnecessary prepositional phrases?
- Are there multimeaning terms that could cause confusion about the meaning of an item?
- Is there idiomatic language that may be unfamiliar to English learners or regionally specific?
- Are there long noun phrases that could be simplified?

Stimulus Review

Review the graph and look for any language complexity issues. Provide suggestions for improvement in the "Comments" box on the record form.

Stimulus Issues?

Sample Item #1

It is the ninth inning and Juan is at bat. For his last 10 times at bat, he had 6 hits. What is the probability that Juan will have a hit this time?

O   10%

O   30%

O   40%

O   60%

Language issue: Sports language and idiomatic phrasing

Sample Item #2

An engineer is designing a suspension bridge to span the distance between the banks of a river. The bridge must be at least 1,320 feet long. How long must the bridge be, in miles?

O $\frac{1}{4}$

O $\frac{1}{2}$

O $\frac{3}{4}$

O   1

Language issue: Unnecessary technical language

Sample Item #3

If Jamal is going to build a garden with an area of 36 square feet, which of these dimensions can he use for his garden?

O   12 feet long and 4 feet wide

O   9 feet long and 5 feet wide

O   7 feet long and 5 feet wide

O   6 feet long and 6 feet wide

Language issue: Complex syntax—dependent clause

Sample Item #4

The boy and girl who went to the park walked 2 miles to the park and back. How far did they walk in yards?

O   1,760 yards

O   3,520 yards

O   5,280 yards

O   7,040 yards

Language issue: Long noun phrase; idiomatic phrasing

Practice Item Review

- Read the items in the handout
- Decide whether the items have any of these language problems:
  - ➤ Complex syntax
  - ➤ Long noun phrases
  - ➤ Vocabulary issues (unfamiliar technical language, multimeaning words)
  - ➤ Idiomatic phrases

Item Issues?

How to Proceed

- Read through a test materials, keeping in mind the guiding questions.
- Make your own judgment. Write your judgment on the review form:
  - ☐ Accept as is—no apparent language complexity issue
  - ☐ Accept with minor revisions
  - ☐ Reject due to potential language complexity issues

How to Proceed

- As a group, we will discuss each item or stimulus flagged for revision or rejected.
- The recorder will take detailed notes.
- We will try to make a group decision about each stimulus and item.
- We will record any dissenting position.

SAMPLE SCIENCE STIMULUS FOR LANGUAGE COMPLEXITY
REVIEW PRACTICE

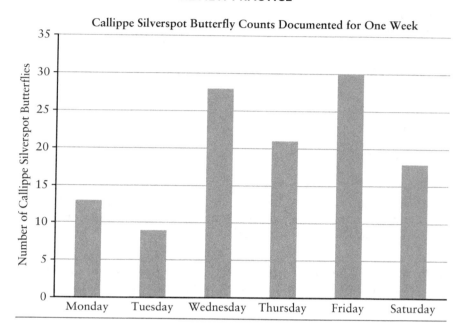

Callippe Silverspot Butterfly Counts Documented for One Week

SAMPLE ITEMS FOR LANGUAGE COMPLEXITY REVIEW PRACTICE

1 Chevy has a collectables shop. In the shop, she has 150 trolls of different sizes and colors. Thirty-nine trolls are large, 28 trolls are medium, and 83 are small. What fraction of the trolls is medium?

   ☐ A $\frac{1}{28}$

   ☐ B $\frac{1}{122}$

   ☐ C $\frac{150}{28}$

   ☐ D $\frac{14}{75}$

2 Kim needs an area of 64 square feet to build a garden in the backyard to grow vegetables. What dimensions will give Kim an area of 64 square feet for a garden? Show your work.

3 In the story, Ahmed is angry with his sister. Why is his patience running out? Use information from the story to support your thinking.

Language Complexity Item Review Record Sheet

Use this form to record your observations about language complexity issues in the stimulus materials.

Item	Language Complexity Issues						Comment	Recommendation		
	TV	M	I	CS	N	SL	Other		A	Rev*	Rej
Sample											
1											
2											
3											
4											
5											
6											

TV—Technical Vocabulary, M—Multimeaning words, I—Idiomatic phrasing, CS—Complex syntax, N—Long noun phrase, SL—Sentence length

*Published stimulus materials cannot be revised without publisher's permission.

EVALUATION OF LANGUAGE COMPLEXITY REVIEW

Do not write your name on the evaluation. Your responses are anonymous.

Read each of the following statements. Then indicate whether you strongly agree (SA), agree (A), disagree (D), or strongly disagree (SD).

1	The process used for review was appropriate.	SA	A	D	SD
2	All committee members participated in the process.	SA	A	D	SD
3	Committee members honored the group norms.	SA	A	D	SD
4	Each person had an opportunity to share ideas, issues, and concerns.	SA	A	D	SD
5	The consensus-building process was managed effectively.	SA	A	D	SD
6	The facilitator kept us focused on the purpose of the review process.	SA	A	D	SD
7	The recorder kept accurate records of what individuals and the group said.	SA	A	D	SD
8	I am satisfied with the results of the review process.	SA	A	D	SD

Questions for Accessibility Reviews

Auditory Disabilities

Is there any text in the passage (vocabulary, key ideas, descriptions) that will prevent a student with auditory disabilities from comprehending the important ideas, themes, symbols, or characters in a passage?

Is there any text in the item or task that will prevent a student with auditory disabilities from comprehending the intent of the item or task?

Is there any feature of the item or task that will prevent a student with auditory disabilities from responding correctly to the item or task?

Can an assistant complete the item or task for a student with auditory disabilities with guidance from the student without invalidating the response?

Visual Disabilities

Is there any text in the passage (vocabulary, key ideas, descriptions) that will prevent a student with visual disabilities from comprehending the important ideas, themes, symbols, or characters in a passage?

Can alternate text adequately describe a visual stimulus (e. g., graph, timeline, drawing, diagram) so that students with visual disabilities can comprehend and use the visual stimulus?

Is there any text or imagery in the item or task that will prevent a student with visual disabilities from comprehending the intent of the item or task?

Is there any feature of the item or task that will prevent a student with visual disabilities from responding correctly to the item or task?

Is there are a way to assess the same learning goal without the use of a visual stimulus?

Can an assistant complete the item or task for a student with visual disabilities with guidance from the student without invalidating the response?

Motor Disabilities

Is there any feature of the item or task that will prevent a student with
   motor disabilities from responding correctly to the item or task?
Can an assistant complete the item or task for a student with motor
   impairments with guidance from the student without invalidating the
   response?
Will an assistive device make it possible for a student with motor
   impairments to respond correctly to the task?

Academic Verbs Commonly Used in Testing

The verbs shown in the table have specific meanings in the context of testing. Learning these terms can help students understand the genre of testing. These terms are also frequently used in academic subject areas. Students need to know what they mean in the assessment context and how meaning may differ in instructional contexts.

Academic Verbs Commonly Used in Testing

Term	Meaning
Analyze	Look closely at something, at each of its parts, to make sense of the whole
Compare	Look at common characteristics and identify how things are alike or similar
Contrast	Identify the characteristics of things that make them different
Demonstrate	Show, step-by-step, how to do something or how something was done (e.g., show your work)
Describe	Present a clear picture of a person, place, thing, or idea
Explain	Provide information or evidence related to an issue, topic, idea, or action
Interpret	Make meaning and/or explain others' meaning
Infer	Finding an unstated idea in the information or clues the author provides
Persuade	State a point of view or position and use facts, statistics, beliefs, and opinions to support the position or point of view in order to urge someone to take action
Predict	Tell or describe what will happen next
Summarize	Present main ideas in a way that uses as few words as possible
Support	Provide details that help to explain an idea

Notes

Preface

1. Large-scale standardized tests include state-level accountability tests and locally selected interim or benchmark assessments.

2. Patterns in activity that are repeated over time and shared among members of group or context are called "practices"; groups that share patterns of activity in pursuit of a common goal are "communities of practice."

Chapter 1

1. When I speak of students' diverse cultural and social identities, I include students from diverse racial and cultural backgrounds, English learners, students with disabilities, new immigrants, LGBTQ+ students, low-income students, and so forth. In other words, I am referring to students who have been marginalized by an education system designed for White, middle- to upper middle-class culture.

2. We cannot assume that all students have a shared understanding of the criteria for their work or that they know what teachers expect. As an exercise to help teachers understand the importance of public expectations, we ask teachers to give a group presentation of their perspective on a controversial school issue (e.g., Should we have school uniforms? Should we eliminate grades?). Once the groups finish their presentations, we give them the scoring criteria. Inevitably, the scoring criteria include expectations teachers did not know about but could have done had they known. Teachers' experience, firsthand, how it feels to be judged based on unknown expectations.

3. See https://apnews.com/article/race-and-ethnicity-racial-injustice-business-education-government-and-politics-905c354a805cec1785160cf21f04c7ec.

4. Research suggests that, when learning goals include cultural knowledge and consciousness about social justice issues, students of color achieve at higher levels on traditional measures of achievement (e.g., Borck, 2019; National Public Radio, 2017).

5. Some may bristle at the idea of "assessment" when the aims of education go beyond state academic standards. Assessment does not equate to "testing" or "grading." It does mean gathering information and using it to make decisions—whether those decisions are about what to do next instructionally, whether an activity has helped students develop consciousness about racism, whether a project has actually benefited students and their communities, and so forth. Students know what is valued in school by what is assessed.

6. For more information about the limitations of grading machines, see Taylor and Nolen (2008).

7. Mary, a high school, student, asked her teacher why she had a B for a course grade when she had received high scores on all her assignments and tests. The teacher stated that class participation was 30% of the grade. This fact was not public. The student told her teacher, "I used to raise my hand in class but, since you never called on me, I stopped raising my hand." Not only were there hidden criteria for course grades, the teacher controlled whether students could meet all her grading expectations.

8. When teachers gather large amounts of information from homework assignments, tests and quizzes, projects, written work, and other assignments without clear goals, grades generally reflect whether students have completed their work. In a standards-driven world, grades should tell a story about whether students have achieved desired learning goals.

9. It is important to note that most of the assessment materials available through e-books, e-textbooks, and online assessment development software have the same limitations as those provided in print materials. The primary differences are in the item types that go beyond true/false, short-answer, and multiple-choice items.

10. An online search for "item writing contractors for K–12 schools" will yield a number of advertisements for item-writing jobs at item-development companies.

11. For example, a stated learning goal in one basal reading program was that students would learn "to identify the main idea and important details in a story, novel, or play." The textbook test asked students to recall main ideas and details discussed in class. Assessing students' recall of information discussed in class is not the same as assessing their ability to identify main ideas and important details on their own.

12. Most countries have also established learning goals, and national tests are designed to measure whether students have learned what they are expected to learn.

Chapter 2

1. These types of studies are no longer conducted due to the negative impact on students.

2. For example, students are more likely to analyze patterns of precipitation over the course of a year to predict the likelihood of rain, if rain will prevent them from going to an outdoor concert or if they need to decide what clothes to wear. Extraneous information could include details about the outdoor concert or the name of the designer of outdoor clothing.

3. Many gender DIF studies in reading and mathematics have been focused on tests composed entirely of multiple-choice items. These studies led to significant conclusions about differences in girls' and boys' abilities, particularly in mathematics. These conclusions about abilities have been called into question as new item formats have been incorporated in large-scale tests.

4. For example, a 4th-grade performance task asked students to give advice to a movie company about what types of movies they should make based on a bar graph showing income from different genres of movies: family, drama, comedy, horror, adventure. Per the graph, horror movies had given the movie company the greatest income. A student was asked about her reasoning for selecting family movies—the

second highest income producer. The student had a more nuanced interpretation than was expected by the task. She reasoned that the income from movies depended on the number of movies made in each category. If more horror movies were being made, the company might have greater income from horror movies. But since family movies would appeal to both children and adults, family movies might generate greater income per movie. The child's response was completely reasonable; however, nuanced answers were not represented in the teachers' guide for evaluating student responses.

5. Read-alouds for items/tasks and assessment directions do not include reading passages for reading assessments. However, it is appropriate for reading test items and directions to be read aloud. The specific language structures of test questions, task directions, and test directions are very different from the connected text in reading passages. Testing has been described by some educators as a distinct genre. If a student is unable to read a passage, they will not be able to correctly respond to items or tasks even if they are read aloud.

6. LEP (limited English proficiency) at the federal level includes both English learners from immigrant families and students who have limited English proficiency due to other factors. For example, the Alaska Department of Education and Early Development includes, in their definition of LEP students, "an American Indian, Alaska Native, or a native resident of the outlying areas (Virgin Islands, Guam, American Samoa, or Northern Mariana Islands) who comes from an environment where a language other than English has had a significant impact on the individual's level of English language proficiency" (see education.alaska.gov).

7. Most educators want their assessment practices to support students' learning rather than simply serving as vehicles for generating scores and grades for a grade book.

8. For students to share their concerns about the cultural appropriateness of assessment, they must feel safe and supported by their teachers and peers.

9. "Fair use is a legal doctrine that promotes freedom of expression by permitting the unlicensed use of copyright-protected works in certain circumstances. Section 107 of the Copyright Act provides the statutory framework for determining whether something is a fair use and identifies certain types of uses—such as criticism, comment, news reporting, teaching, scholarship, and research—as examples of activities that may qualify as fair use" (U.S. Copyright Office, 2021).

10. As part of the University of Washington teacher preparation program, teacher candidates develop lessons along with the relevant assessments. They teach the lessons, administer the assessments, collect and analyze student work, and use student work to evaluate their teaching and assessment tools. One candidate found that the density of language in his assessment tool was extreme. Over 50 science vocabulary terms were used in the lesson and the assessment. Because of his own comfort with scientific language, he did not see the burden he had created for students.

Chapter 3

1. Funds of knowledge are historically accumulated and culturally developed bodies of knowledge and skills necessary for household or individual functioning and well-being. They include how families develop social networks and how they enhance their abilities to survive and thrive (Moll, 1992, p. 133).

2. Gay (2000) states that "many teachers do not know enough about the contributions that different ethnic groups have made to their subject areas and are unfamiliar with multicultural education. They may be familiar with the achievements of select, high-profile individuals from some ethnic groups in some areas, such as African American musicians in popular culture or politicians in city, state, and national government. Teachers may know little or nothing about the contributions of Native Americans and Asian Americans in the same arenas. Nor do they know enough about the less publicly visible but very significant contributions of ethnic groups in science, technology, medicine, math, theology, ecology, peace, law, and economics" (p. 107).

3. See https://www.sextontestprep.com/blog/much-can-score-improve/.

4. One teaching strategy that has been used in mathematics is to have students write their own problems related to the concepts and skills that are the target of lessons.

Chapter 4

1. Learning academic vocabulary has been shown to improve reading comprehension and overall achievement (Nagy & Townsend, 2012; Schleppegrell, 2001; Snow & Uccelli, 2009; Uccelli et al., 2015). When teachers use disciplinary vocabulary and academic language routinely in the classroom and focus teaching on helping students make sense of academic vocabulary throughout instruction, use of disciplinary language during feedback reinforces vocabulary development while ensuring that students understand how the feedback is related to their success.

Chapter 6

1. Nonfiction texts can include both informational and persuasive texts.

2. For example, schools in the Pacific Northwest sponsor schoolwide Project Reach activities. Students investigate their cultural roots and prepare posters, as in a science fair, sharing what they have learned. Students choose what aspects of their cultural histories to share and provide written reports to support their presentations. Students might share family migrations, cultural artifacts, folk tales and legends, family trees showing multicultural roots, and so forth. See for example, https://www .pps.net/Page/9405.

3. As part of their overall assessment program, Washington State has developed classroom performance assessments in social studies that can be adapted to different instructional contexts. These assessments were developed by social studies teachers and field tested by the teachers who developed them. Completion of the performances gives students opportunities to apply reading, writing, and social studies knowledge skills. The performance assessments include student directions and scoring rules related to the Washington State social studies standards. See https://www. k12.wa.us/student-success/resources-subject-area/social-studies/ospi-developed-social-studies-assessments. The performance assessments were not developed with social justice issues in mind, but they could be adapted to be relevant to students with diverse social and cultural backgrounds and to address specific social issues. The website gives details about the state's social studies assessment program; however, the tasks have relevance beyond a specific program.

Appendix A

1. The uneven distribution of technology based on income became extremely evident during the coronavirus epidemic of 2020 when online schools and home-schooling became the norm for many students rather than the exception.

2. A middle school student was supposed to write 10 book reports by the end of the semester. The student read more than 10 books, but when all 10 book reports were due, he had not completed any reports. When asked why, the very distressed student said, "I don't know how to write a book report."

3. A preservice teacher who was told by her cooperating teacher to give students a "five-paragraph essay" was shocked to find that most students did *not* know the components of a five-paragraph essay. She took a step back, taught the structure of a five-paragraph essay, and then had students redo the assignment.

Appendix B

1. An example of a real-world, community-based project occurred in an elementary school in the Pacific Northwest. The project integrated mathematics and language arts skills and took place over a semester. The city was considering whether to "daylight" a local creek (bring the creek to the surface) to allow for salmon runs. Once daylighted, the creek would run through a nearby shopping center. Students worked in teams to interview different stakeholders—business owners, customers, and city officials—about their opinions on the project. Some students collected data on projected costs and timelines. Individual students prepared graphs and summary statistics and wrote descriptions of what their graphs and summary statistics said. Each class prepared a report for the city and invited the mayor or a city council member to hear a presentation on what they had learned.

References

Aaronson, J., Fried, C. B., & Good, C. (2002). Reducing the effects of stereotype threat on African American college students by shaping theories of intelligence. *Journal of Experimental Social Psychology, 38*(2), 113–125.

Abedi, J. (2006). Psychometric issues in the ELL assessment and special education eligibility. *Teachers College Record, 108,* 2282–2303.

Abedi, J. (2011). *Performance assessments for English language learners.* Stanford Center for Opportunity Policy in Education (SCOPE), https://edpolicy.stanford.edu/library/publications/114

Abedi, J., Courtney, M., Mirocha, J., Leon, S., & Goldbert, J. (2005). *Language accommodations for English language learners in large-scale assessments: Bilingual dictionaries and linguistic modification* [CSE Report 666]. CRESST.

Abedi, J., & Hejri, F. (2004). Accommodations for students with limited English proficiency in National Assessment of Educational Progress. *Applied Measurement in Education, 17,* 371–392.

Abedi, J., Hofstetter, C., Baker, E., & Lord, C. (2001). *NAEP math performance and test accommodations: Interactions with student language—CSE Technical Report.* National Center for Research on Evaluation, Standards, and Testing, UCLA.

Abedi, J., & Lord, C. (2001). The language factor in mathematics tests. *Applied Measurement in Education, 14,* 219–234.

Abedi, J., & Sato, E. (2008). *Linguistic modification.* National Clearinghouse for English Language Acquisition. https://ncela.ed.gov/meetings/oct08leppship

Acosta, C. (2013). Raza studies and the battle over educational reform. In N. Schniedewind & M. Sapon-Shevin (Eds.), *Educational courage: Resisting the ambush of public education.* Beacon Press. https://www.utne.com/community/raza-studies-zm0z13ndzlin

Adair, J. K. (2008). Everywhere there are numbers: Questions for social justice educators in mathematics and everywhere else. *Journal of Teacher Education, 59,* 408–415.

Adams, C., & Palmer, A. H. (2017). Toward a positive explanation of student differences in reading growth. *Teachers College Record, 119*(9), 1–30.

Alexander, K. L., Entwisle, D. R., & Rabbani, N. S. (2001). The dropout process in life course perspective: Early risk factors at home and school. *Teachers College Record, 102,* 760–822.

Alim, H. S. (2007). "The Whig Party don't exist in my hood": Knowledge, reality, and education in the hip hop nation. In H. S. Alim & J. Baugh (Eds.), *Talk in Black talk: Language, education, and social change* (pp. 15–29). Teachers College Press.

Alim, H. S., & Reyes, A. (2011). Complicating race: Articulating race across multiple social dimensions. *Discourse & Society, 22*, 379–384.

Allensworth, E. M., Gwynne, J. A., Moore, P., & de la Torre, M. (2014). *Looking forward to high school and college: Middle grade indicators of readiness in Chicago public schools.* University of Chicago Consortium on Chicago School Research.

Ansalone, G. (2000). Keeping on track: A reassessment of tracking in the schools. *Race, Gender, and Class, 7*(3), 108–132.

Ansalone, G. (2009). Tracking, schooling, and the equality of educational opportunity. *Race, Gender, and Class, 16*, 174–184.

Arbuthnot, K. (2011). *Filling in the blanks: Understanding standardized testing and the Black-White achievement gap.* Information Age.

Arnaut, K., Blommaert, J., Rampton, B., & Spotti, M. (2016). Introduction: Superdiversity and sociolinguistics. In B. Rampton & J. Blommaert (Eds.), *Language and superdiversity* (pp. 31–58). Routledge.

Assor, A. (2012). Allowing choice and nurturing an inner compass: Educational practices supporting students' need for autonomy. In S. L. Christenson, A. L. Reschly, & C. Wylie (Eds.), *Handbook of research on student engagement* (pp. 421–439). Springer.

Au, K. H., & Kawakami, A. J. (1994). Cultural congruence in instruction. In E. R. Hollins, J. E. King, & W. C. Hayman (Eds.), *Teaching diverse populations: Formulating a knowledge base* (pp. 5–23). State University of New York Press.

Au, W. (2016). Meritocracy 2.0. *Educational Policy, 30*(1), 39–62.

Babad, E. Y. (1980). Expectancy bias in scoring as a function of ability and ethnic labels. *Psychological Reports, 46*, 625–626.

Baker, E. & O'Neil, H. F. (1994). Performance assessment and equity: A view from the USA. *Assessment in Education, 1*(1), 11–26.

Baker, J. A. (2006). Contributions of teacher–child relationships to positive adjustment during elementary school. *Journal of School Psychology, 44*, 211–229.

Ball, D. L., Hill, H. C., & Bass, H. (2005). Knowing mathematics for teaching: Who knows mathematics well enough to teach third grade, and how can we decide? *American Educator, 29*(1), 14–17.

Banks, J. (2014). *Introduction to multicultural education* (5th ed.). Pearson.

Banks, J. (2016). *Cultural diversity and education: Foundations, curriculum, and teaching.* Pearson.

Banks, J. A., & McGee-Banks, C. A. (2020). *Multicultural education* (10th ed.). Routledge.

Barajas-López, F., & Ishimaru, A. M. (2020). "Darles el lugar": A place for nondominant family knowing in educational equity. *Urban Education, 55*(1), 38–65.

Baron, R., Tom, D. Y. H., & Cooper, H. M. (1985). Social class, race and teacher expectations. In J. B. Dusek (Ed.), *Teacher expectancies* (pp. 251–269). Erlbaum.

Barrington, B. L., & Hendricks, B. (1989). Differentiating characteristics of high school graduates, dropouts, and nongraduates. *Journal of Educational Research, 82*, 309–319.

Beard, K. S. (2019). Getting on track: Aligning the achievement gap conversation with ethical educational practice. *International Journal of Leadership in Education: Theory and Practice, 22*, 30–54.

Beck, M. (2009, April 14). *Confessions of a test developer.* Paper presented at the Annual Meeting of the American Educational Research Association, Denver, CO.

Beckett, K. (2011). Culturally relevant teaching and the concept of education. *Philosophical Studies in Education, 41*, 65–75.

Ben-Shakhar, G., & Sanai, Y. (1991). Gender differences in multiple-choice tests: The role of guessing tendencies. *Journal of Educational Measurement, 28,* 23–35.

Bennett, R. E., Gottesman, R. L., Rock, D. A., & Cerullo, F. (1993). Influence of behavior perceptions and gender on teachers' judgments of students' academic skill. *Journal of Educational Psychology, 85,* 347–356.

Bereby-Meyer, Y., Assor, A., & Katz, I. (2004). Children's choice strategies: The effect of age and task demands. *Cognitive Development, 19,* 127–146.

Bernal, D. D. (2010). Learning and living pedagogies of the home: The mestiza consciousness of Chicana students. *International Journal of Qualitative Studies in Education, 14*(5), 623–639.

Birenbaum, M., & Feldman, R. A. (1998). Relationships between learning patterns and attitudes towards two assessment formats. *Educational Research, 40,* 90–98.

Black, P., & Wiliam, D. (1998a). Inside the black box: Raising standards through classroom assessments. *Phi Delta Kappan, 92*(1), 81–90.

Black, P., & Wiliam, D. (1998b). Assessment and classroom learning. *Assessment in Education: Principles, Policy & Practice, 5*(1), 7–74.

Black, P., & Wiliam, D. (1999). *Assessment for learning: Beyond the black box.* University of Cambridge Press.

Black, P., & Wiliam, D. (2009). Developing a theory of formative assessment. *Educational Assessment, Evaluation, and Accountability, 21,* 5–31.

Black, P., & Wiliam, D. (2012). Developing a theory of formative assessment. In J. Gardner (Ed.), *Assessment and learning* (2nd ed., pp. 206–229). SAGE.

Blackwell, L. S., Trzesniewski, K. H., & Dweck, C. S. (2007). Implicit theories of intelligence predict achievement across an adolescent transition: A longitudinal study and an intervention. *Child Development, 78,* 246–263.

Blommaert, J. & Rampton, B. (2011). Language and superdiversity. *Diversities, 13* (2), 2–21.

Boaler, J. (2002). *Experiencing school mathematics: traditional and reform approaches to teaching and their impact on student learning.* Erlbaum.

Boaler, J., & Staples, M. (2008). Creating mathematical futures through an equitable teaching approach: The case of Railside School. *Teachers College Record, 110*(3), 608–645.

Bodovski, K., & Farkas, G. (2007). Mathematics growth in early elementary school: The roles of beginning knowledge, student engagement, and instruction. *Elementary School Journal, 108,* 115–130.

Bolt, D. M. (2000). A SIBTEST approach to testing DIF hypotheses using experimentally designed test items. *Journal of Educational Measurement, 37,* 307–327.

Bond, L. (1995). Unintended consequences of performance assessments: Issues of bias and fairness. *Educational Measurement: Issues and Practices, 14*(4), 5–8.

Boone, J. A., & Adesso, V. J. (1974). Racial differences on a black intelligence test. *Journal of Negro Education, 43,* 429–436.

Boothroyd, R. A., McMorris, R. F., & Pruzek, R. M. (1992, April). *What do teachers know about measurement and how did they find out?* Paper presented at the annual meeting of the National Council on Measurement in Education, San Francisco, CA.

Borck, C. R. (2019). "I belong here.": Culturally sustaining pedagogical praxes from an alternative high school in Brooklyn. *The Urban Review, 52,* 276–291.

Boud, D. (1995). *Enhancing learning through self-assessment.* Routledge.

Boud, D., Cohen, R., & Sampson, J. (1999). Peer learning and assessment. *Assessment and Evaluation in Higher Education*, 24(4), 413–126.

Bowers, A. J. (2011). What's in a grade? The multidimensional nature to what teacher-assigned grades assess in high school. *Educational Research and Evaluation*, 1, 141–159.

Bowers, A. J., & Sprott, R. (2012). Examining the multiple trajectories associated with dropping out of high school: A growth mixture model analysis. *Journal of Educational Research*, 105, 176–195.

Brantlinger, A. (2005). The geometry of inequality. In E. Gutstein & B. Peterson (Eds.), *Rethinking mathematics: Teaching social justice by the numbers* (pp. 97–100). Rethinking Schools.

Brennan, R. L. (2013). Commenting on "Validating the Interpretations and Uses of Test Scores." *Journal of Educational Measurement*, 50, 74–83.

Brookhart, S. M. (2008). Feedback that fits. *Educational Leadership*, 65(4), 54–59.

Brookhart, S. M. (2009). Assessment and examinations. In L. J. Saha & A. G. Dworkin (Eds.), *International handbook of research on teacher and teaching* (pp. 723–738). Springer.

Brookhart, S. M. (2011). Starting the conversation about grading. *Educational Leadership*, 60(3), 10–14.

Brookhart, S. M., Guskey, T. R., Bowers, A. J., McMillan, J. H., Smith, J. K., Smith, L. F., Stevens, M. T., & Welsh, M. E. (2016). A century of grading research: Meaning and value in the most common educational measure. *Review of Educational Research*, 86, 803–848.

Brookhart, S. M., Walsh, J. M., & Zientarski, W. A. (2006). The dynamics of motivation and effort for classroom assessments in middle school science and social studies. *Applied Measurement in Education*, 19, 151–184.

Brooks, W., & Browne, S. (2012). Toward a culturally situated reader response theory. *Children's Literature in Education*, 43, 74–85.

Bryson, C., & Hand, L. (2007). The role of engagement in inspiring teaching and learning. *Innovations in Education and Teaching International*, 44, 349–362.

Burris, C. C. (2008). Accountability, rigor, and detracking: Achievement effects of embracing a challenging curriculum as a universal good for all students. *Teachers College Record*, 110(3), 571–607.

Butler, D. L., & Winne, P. H. (1995). Feedback and self-regulated learning: A theoretical synthesis. *Review of Educational Research*, 65, 245–281.

Butler-Omololu, C., Doster, J. A., & Lahey, B. (1983). Some implications for intelligence test construction and administration with children of different racial groups. *Journal of Black Psychology*, 10(2), 63–75.

Carlson, E. D., Engebretson, J., & Chamberlain, R. M. (2006). Photovoice as a social process of critical consciousness. *Qualitative Health Research*, 16, 836–852.

Carter, D. L. (2008). Achievement as resistance: The development of a critical race achievement ideology among Black achievers. *Harvard Educational Review*, 78(3), 466–497.

Casteel, C. (1997). Attitudes of African American and Caucasian eighth grade students about praises, rewards, and punishments. *Elementary School Guidance and Counseling*, 31, 262–272.

Cawthon, S. W., Dawson, K., & Ihorn, S. (2011). Activating student engagement through drama-based instruction. *Journal for Learning through the Arts*, 7(1). http://escholarship.org/uc/item/6qc4b7pt

References

233

Chan, S., & Leijten, F. (2012). Using feedback strategies to improve peer learning in welding. *International Journal of Training Research, 10*(1), 23–29.
Chang, C., & Mao, S. (1999). Comparison of Taiwan science students' outcomes with inquiry-group versus traditional instruction. *The Journal of Educational Research, 92,* 340–346.
Chapuis, S., & Stiggins, R. J. (2002). Classroom assessment for learning. *Educational Leadership, 60*(1), 40–43.
Chapuis, S., & Stiggins, R. J. (2009). The quest for quality. *Educational Leadership, 67*(3), 14–19.
Chin, M. J., Quinn, D. M., Dhaliwal, T. K., & Lovison, V. S. (2020). Bias in the air: A nationwide exploration of teachers' implicit racial attitudes, aggregate bias, and student outcomes. *Educational Researcher, 49,* 566–578.
Chunn, E. W. (1988). Sorting Black students for success and failure: The inequity of ability grouping and tracking. *Urban League Review, 11,* 93–106.
Cifuentes, L. (2004). Visualization for middle school students' engagement in science learning. *Journal of Computers in Mathematics and Science Teaching, 23,* 109–137.
Cizek, G. J., Fitzgerald, J. M., & Rachor, R. A. (1995). Teachers' assessment practices: Preparation, isolation, and the kitchen sink. *Educational Assessment, 3,* 159–179.
Cohen, E. (1984). Talking and working together: Status, interaction and learning. In P. Peterson, L. C. Wilkinson, & M. Hallinan (Eds.), *The social context of instruction: Group organization and group processes* (pp. 171–187). Academic Press, Inc.
Cohen, E. (1994). *Designing groupwork: Strategies for the heterogeneous classroom.* Teachers College Press.
Cohen, E. (1998). Complex instruction. *European Journal of Intercultural Studies, 9,* 127–131.
Cohen, E. G., & Lotan, R. A. (1997). Raising expectations for competence: The effectiveness of status interventions. In E. G. Cohen & R. A. Lotan (Eds.), *Working for equity in heterogeneous classrooms: Sociological theory in practice* (pp. 77–91). Teachers College Press.
Common Core State Standards. (2010a). Common Core State Standards for Language Arts and Literacy. http://www.corestandards.org/ELA-Literacy/
Common Core State Standards. (2010b). Common Core State Standards for Mathematics. http://www.corestandards.org/ELA-Literacy/
Connell, J. P., Spencer, M. B., & Aber, J. L. (1994). Educational risk and resilience in African American youth: Context, self, action, and outcomes in school. *Child Development, 65,* 493–506.
Connell, J. P., & Wellborn, J. G. (1991). Competence, autonomy, and relatedness: A motivational analysis of self-system processes. In M. Gunnar & L. A. Sroufe (Eds.), *Minnesota symposium on child psychology* (Vol. 23, pp. 43–77). University of Chicago Press.
Coon, C., McLeod, L., & Thissen, D. (2002). *NCCATS update: Comparability results of paper and computer forms of the North Carolina End-of-Grade Tests (RTI project no. 08486.001).* North Carolina Department of Public Instruction.
Cooper, D. H., & Speece, D. L. (1990). Instructional correlates of students' academic responses: Comparisons between at risk and control students. *Early Education and Development, 3,* 270–300.

Copenhaver, J. F. (1999, October). *The intersections of response and ethnicity: Elementary school students respond to multicultural literature.* Paper presented at the annual meeting of the South Central Modern Language Association, Memphis, TN.

Copur-Gencturk, Y., Cimpian, J. R., Lubienski, S. T., & Thacker, I. (2019). Teachers' bias against the mathematical ability of female, black, and Hispanic students. *Educational Researcher, 49,* 30–43.

Cornelius, L., & Herrenkohl, L. R. (2004). Power in the classroom: How the classroom environment shapes students' relationships with each other and with concepts. *Cognition and Instruction, 22,* 467–498.

Croft, M., Waltman, K., Middleton, K., & Stevenson, E. (2005, April). *The impact of school level accountability on local test preparation practices.* Paper presented at the annual meeting of the National Council on Measurement in Education, Montreal, Canada.

Csapó, B., Ainley, J., Bennett, R., Latour, T., & Law, N. (2010). *Draft white paper 3: Technological issues for computer-based assessment.* Assessment and Teaching of 21st Century Skills, University of Melbourne, Australia. DOI:10.1007/978-94-007-2324-5_4

Cumming, J. (2000, May). *After DIF, what culture remains?* Paper presented at the 26th IAEA Conference, Jerusalem, Israel.

Dan, R. (2014). Assessment as learning: Blurring the boundaries of assessment and learning for theory, policy, and practice. *Assessment in Education: Principles, Policy, & Practice, 21,* 149–166.

Darling-Hammond, L., Barron, B., Pearson, D. P., Schoenfeld, A. H., Stage, E. K., Zimmerman, T. D., Cervetti, G. N., & Tilson, J. L. (2008). *Powerful learning: What we know about teaching for understanding.* Wiley.

Darling-Hammond, L., Hyler, M. E., & Gardner, M. (2017). *Effective teacher professional development.* Learning Policy Institute.

Davidson, D. (1991). Children's decision-making examined with an information-board procedure. *Cognitive Development, 6,* 77–90.

Davis, J., & Martin, D. B. (2018). Racism, assessment, and instructional practices: Implications for mathematics teachers of African American students. *Journal of Urban Mathematics Education, 11*(1–2), 45–68.

Deci, E. L., & Ryan, R. M. (1985). *Intrinsic motivation and self-determination in human behavior.* Plenum.

Deci, E. L., & Ryan, R. M. (2000). The "what" and "why" of goal pursuits: Human needs and the self-determination of behaviour. *Psychological Inquiry, 11,* 227–268.

DeMeis, D. K., & Turner, R. R. (1978). Effects of students' race, physical attractiveness, and dialect on teachers' evaluations. *Contemporary Educational Psychology, 3,* 77–86.

Depenbrock, J. (2017, August 13). *Ethnic studies: A movement born of a ban.* National Public Radio. https://www.npr.org/sections/ed/2017/08/13/541814668/ethnic-studies-a-movement-born-of-a-ban

Devine, P. G. (1989). Stereotypes and prejudice: Their automatic and controlled components. *Journal of Personality and Social Psychology, 56*(1), 5–18.

Dewey, J. (1938). *Experience and education.* Collier.

Dotterer, A. M., & Lowe, K. (2011). Classroom context, school engagement, and academic achievement in early adolescence. *Journal of Youth and Adolescence, 40,* 1649–1660.

Downey, D. B., & Pribesh, S. (2004). When race matters: Teachers' evaluations of students' classroom behavior. *Sociology of Education, 77*(4), 267–282.

Downing, S. M. (2002). Construct irrelevant variance and flawed test questions. *Academic Medicine, 77*(10), S103–S104.

Duncan, R. C., & Noonan, B. (2007). Factors affecting teachers' grading and assessment practices. *Alberta Journal of Educational Research, 53*, 1–21.

Dunst, C. J., Hamby, D. W., Howse, R. B., Wilkie, H., & Annas, K. (2020). Research synthesis of meta-analyses of preservice teacher preparation practices in higher education. *Higher Education Studies, 10*, 1, 29–47.

Dutro, E., Kazemi, E., Balf, R., & Lin, Y. S. (2008). "What are you and where are you from?" Race, identity, and the vicissitudes of cultural relevance. *Urban Education, 43*, 269–300.

Eccles, J. S., Wigfield, A., & Schiefele, U. (1998). Motivation to succeed. In W. Damon & N. Eisenberg (Eds.), *Handbook of child psychology: Vol. 3: Social, emotional, and personality development* (5th ed., pp. 1017–1095). Wiley.

Educational Testing Service. (2003). *Fairness review guidelines*. Princeton, NJ: Author.

Elliott, S. N., Kratochwill, T. R., Littlefield Cook, J., & Travers, J. (2000). *Educational psychology: Effective teaching, effective learning* (3rd ed.). McGraw-Hill.

Entwisle, D. R., & Alexander, K. L. (1988). Factors affecting achievement test scores and marks of Black and White first graders. *The Elementary School Journal, 88*(5), 449–471.

Entwisle, D. R., & Alexander, K. L. (1992). Summer setback: Race, poverty, school composition, and mathematics achievement in the first two years of school. *American Sociological Review, 57*, 72–84.

Entwisle, D. R., & Alexander, K. L. (1994). Winter setback: School racial composition and learning to read. *American Sociological Review, 59*, 446–460.

Entwisle, D. R., Alexander, K. L., & Olson, L. S. (1997). *Children, schools, and inequality*. Westview.

Esposito, J., & Swain, A. N. (2009). Pathways to social justice: Urban teachers' use of culturally relevant pedagogy as a conduit for teaching for social justice. *Perspectives on Urban Education, 6*(1), 38–48.

Farinde-Wu, A., Glover, C. P., & Williams, N. N. (2017). It's not hard work; it's heart work: Strategies of effective, award-winning culturally responsive teachers. *The Urban Review, 49*(2), 279–299.

Farkas, G. (2003). Racial disparities and discrimination in education: What do we know, how do we know it, and what do we need to know? *Teachers College Record, 105*, 1119–1146.

Feldman, J. (2018). *School grading policies are failing children: A call to action for equitable grading*. Crescendo Education Group.

Feldman, J. (2019). Why equity must be part of grading reform. *Phi Delta Kappan, 100*(8), 52–55.

Ferguson, R. F. (2003). Teachers' perceptions and expectations and the Black-White test score gap. *Urban Education, 38*, 460–507.

Finn, J. D. (1989). Withdrawing from school. *Review of Educational Research, 59*, 117–142.

Flores-Dueñas, L. (2003). Reader response, culturally familiar literature, and reading comprehension: The case of four Latina(o) students. In F. B. Boyd, C. H. Brock, & M. S. Rozendal (Eds.), *Multicultural and multilingual literacy and language: Contexts and practices* (pp. 180–206). Guilford.

Flowers, C., Kim, D., Lewis, P., & Davis, V. C. (2011). A comparison of computer-based testing and pencil-and-paper testing for students with a read-aloud accommodation. *Journal of Special Education Technology, 26,* 1–12.

Floyd, C. (1996). Achieving despite the odds: A study of resilience among a group of African American high school seniors. *The Journal of Negro Education, 65,* 181–189.

Fordham, S., & Ogbu, J. U. (1986). Black students' school success: Coping with the burden of "acting White." *Urban Review, 18,* 176–206.

Foster, D., & Poppers, A. E. (2011). How can I get them to understand? In P. E. Noyce & D. T. Hickey (Eds.), *New frontiers in formative assessment* (pp. 13–67). Harvard Education Press.

Foster, M. (1993). Educating for competence in community and culture: Exploring the views of exemplary African-American teachers, *Urban Education, 27,* 370–394.

Foster, M. (1995). African American teachers and culturally relevant pedagogy. In J. A. Banks & C. M. Banks (Eds.), *Handbook of research on multicultural education* (pp. 570–581). Macmillan.

Foster, M. (1997). *Black teachers on teaching.* The New Press.

Frankenstein, M. (1990). Incorporating race, gender, and class issues into a critical mathematical literacy curriculum. *Journal of Negro Education, 59,* 336–359.

Frary, R. B., Cross, L. H., & Weber, L. J. (1993). Testing and grading practices and opinions of secondary teachers of academic subjects: Implications for instruction in measurement. *Educational Measurement: Issues & Practice, 12*(3), 23–30.

Fredricks, J. A., Blumenfeld, P. C., & Paris, A. H. (2004). School engagement: Potential of the concept, state of the evidence. *Review of Educational Research, 74,* 59–109.

Freire, P. (2000). Pedagogy of the oppressed. *Continuum.* (Original work published in 1970)

Frey, B. B., & Schmitt, V. L. (2010). Teachers classroom assessment practices. *Middle School Journal, 5*(3), 107–117.

Frisbie, D., Miranda, D. U., & Baker, K. K. (1993). An evaluation of elementary textbook tests as classroom assessment tools. *Applied Measurement in Education, 6,* 21–36.

Furlong, M. J., & Christenson, S. L. (2008). Engaging students at school and with learning: A relevant construct for all students. *Psychology in the Schools, 45,* 365–368.

Garcia, E. (2020). Meeting the challenge of cultural diversity. *Principal Leadership, 4*(1), 50–53.

Garland, S. (2014, December 29). The man behind common core math. National Public Radio. https://www.npr.org/sections/ed/2014/12/29/371918272/the-man-behind-common-core-math

Garner, M., & Engelhard, G. (1999). Gender differences in performance on multiple-choice and constructed response mathematics items. *Applied Measurement in Education, 12,* 29–51.

Gay, G. (2000). *Culturally responsive teaching: Theory, research, and practice.* Teachers College Press.

Gay, G. (2002). Preparing for culturally responsive teaching. *Journal of Teacher Education, 53,* 106–116.

Gay, G. (2010). *Culturally responsive teaching: Theory, research, and practice.* Teachers College Press.

Gay, G., & Kirkland, K. (2003). Developing cultural critical consciousness and self-reflection in pre-service teacher education. *Theory Into Practice, 42,* 181–187.

Gee, J. P. (2003). Opportunity to learn: A language-based perspective on assessment, *Assessment in Education, 10*(1), 27–46.

Gehlbach, H., Brinkworth, M. E., and Harris, A. D. (2011). Changes in teacher–student relationships. *British Journal of Educational Psychology, 82*, 690–704.

Gershenson, S., Holt, S. B., & Papageorge, N. W. (2016). Who believes me? The effect of student-teacher demographic match on teacher expectations. *Economics of Education Review, 52*, 209–224.

Gipps, C. V. (1994). *Beyond testing: Towards a theory of educational assessment.* Falmer.

Gonzalez, N., McIntyre, E., & Rosebery, A. S. (2001). *Classroom diversity: Connecting curriculum to students' lives.* Heinemann.

Good, C., Aronson, J., & Inzlicht, M. (2003). Improving adolescents' standardized test performance: An intervention to reduce the effects of stereotype threat. *Journal of Applied Developmental Psychology, 24*, 645–662.

Gotwals, A. W., & Birmingham, D. (2015). Eliciting, identifying, interpreting, and responding to students' ideas: Teacher candidates' growth in formative assessment practices. *Research in Science Education, 46*, 365–388.

Gould, J. (1981). *The mismeasure of man.* Norton.

Grant, R. A., & Asimeng–Boahene, L. (2006). Culturally responsive pedagogy in citizenship education: Using African proverbs as tools for teaching in urban schools. *Multicultural Perspectives, 8*, 17–24.

Graves, D. (2014). Black high school students' critical racial awareness, school-based racial socialization, and academic resilience. *Berkeley Review of Education, 5*(1), 5–32.

Greeno, J. G. (1998). The situativity of knowing, learning, and research. *American Psychologist, 53*(1), 5–26.

Greeno, J. G. (2011). A situative perspective on cognition and learning in interaction. In T. Koschmann (Ed.), *Theories of learning and studies of instructional practice, Volume 1* (pp. 41–71). Springer.

Greenwald, A. G., & Krieger, L. H. (2006). Implicit bias: Scientific foundations. *California Law Review, 94*, 945–967.

Greenwood, C. R., Delquadri, J., & Hall, R. V. (1989). Longitudinal effects of peer tutoring. *Journal of Educational Psychology, 81*, 371–383.

Greenwood, C. S. (1991). A longitudinal analysis of time to learn, engagement, and academic achievement in urban versus suburban schools. *Exceptional Children, 57*, 521–535.

Greenwood, C. S. (1996). The case for performance-based instructional models. *School Psychology Quarterly, 11*, 283–296.

Gross, S. (1993). Early mathematics performance and achievement: Results of a study within a large suburban school system. *Journal of Negro Education, 62*, 269–287.

Gruenewald, D. A. (2003). The best of both worlds: A critical pedagogy of place. *Educational researcher, 32*(4), 3–12.

Guskey, T. R. (2002, April 1–5). *Perspectives on grading and reporting: Differences among teachers, students, and parents.* Paper presented at the annual meeting of the American Educational Research Association, New Orleans, LA.

Guskey, T. R. (2009, April 15). *Bound by tradition: Teachers' views of crucial grading and reporting issues.* Paper presented at the annual meeting of the American Educational Research Association, San Francisco, CA.

Guskey, T. R. (2011). Five obstacles to grade reform. *Educational Leadership, 69*(3), 16–21.

Guskey, T. R. (2020). Breaking up the grade. *Educational Leadership*, 78(1), 40–46.

Gutiérrez, K. (2008). Developing a sociocritical literacy in the third space. *Reading Research Quarterly, 43*, 148–164.

Gutiérrez, K., & Ragoff, B. (2003). Cultural ways of learning. *Educational Researcher, 35*(5), 19–25.

Gutstein, E. (2006). *Reading and writing the world with mathematics: Toward a pedagogy for social justice.* Routledge.

Gutstein, E., & Peterson, B. (Eds.). (2006). *Rethinking mathematics: Teaching social justice by the numbers.* Rethinking Schools.

Hafen, C. A., Allen, J. P., Mikami, A. Y., Gregory, A., Hamre, B., & Pianta, R. C. (2012). The pivotal role of adolescent autonomy in secondary school classrooms. *Journal of Youth and Adolescence, 41*, 245–255.

Hakuta, K., Butler, Y. G., & Witt, D. (2000). *How long does it take English learners to attain proficiency?* Spencer Foundation.

Haladyna, T. M., Nolen, S. B., & Haas, N. S. (1991). Raising standardized achievement test scores and the origins of test score pollution. *Educational Researcher, 20*(5), 2–7.

Handley, K., & Williams, L. (2011). From copying to learning: Using exemplars to engage students with assessment criteria and feedback. *Assessment & Evaluation in Higher Education, 36*, 95–108.

Hartley, B. L., & Sutton, R. M. (2013). A stereotype threat account of boys' academic underachievement. *Child Development, 84*, 1716–1733.

Hattie, J. (2009). *Visible learning: A synthesis of over 800 meta-analyses relating to achievement.* Routledge.

Hattie, J. A., Biggs, J., & Purdie, N. (1996). Effects of learning skills intervention on student learning: A meta-analysis. *Review of Research in Education, 66*, 99–136.

Hattie, J. A. C., & Timperley, H. (2007). The power of feedback. *Review of Educational Research, 77*(1), 81–112.

Hayward, L. (2012). Assessment and learning: The learner's perspective. In J. Gardner (Ed.), *Assessment and learning* (2nd ed., pp. 125–139). SAGE.

Henderson, D. (2001, April 10–14). *Prevalence of gender DIF in Mixed format high school exit examinations.* Paper presented at the annual meeting of the American Educational Research Association, Seattle, WA.

Heritage, M., & Wylie, C. (2018). Reaping the benefits of assessment for learning: Achievement, identity, and equity. *ZDM, 50*, 729–741.

Hernandez, L. E., & Darling-Hammond, L. (2019, October). *Deeper learning networks: Taking student-centered learning and equity to scale.* Learning Policy Institute.

Herrenkohl, L. R. (2006). Intellectual role taking: supporting discussion in heterogeneous elementary classrooms. *Theory into Practice, 45*, 47–54.

Herrenkohl, L. R., & Guerra, M. R. (1998). Participant structures, scientific discourse, and student engagement in fourth grade. *Cognition and Instruction, 16*, 433–475.

Herrenkohl, L. R., Palincsar, A. S., DeWater, L. S., & Kawasaki, K. (1999). Developing scientific communities in classrooms: A sociocognitive approach. *Journal of the Learning Sciences, 8*, 451–493.

Hilliard, A. (2003, April 22–24). *Assessment equity in a multicultural society: Assessment and cultural validity in a culturally plural world.* Paper presented at the annual meeting of the National Council on Measurement in Education, Chicago, IL.

Høgheim, S., & Reber, R. (2017). Eliciting mathematics interest: New directions for context personalization and example choice. *Journal of Experimental Education, 85*, 597–613.

Hollins, E. R. (1996). *Culture in school learning: Revealing the deep meaning.* Erlbaum.

Hood, S. (1998). Culturally responsive performance-based assessment: Conceptual and psychometric considerations. *Journal of Negro Education, 67*, 187–196.

Horn, I. (2012). *Strength in numbers: Collaborative learning in secondary mathematics.* National Council of Teachers of Mathematics.

Horn, I. S. (2008). Turnaround students in high school mathematics: Constructing identities of competence through mathematical worlds. *Mathematical Thinking and Learning, 10*, 201–239.

Horn, I. S., Nolen, S. B., Ward, C. J., & Campbell, S. S. (2008). Developing Practices in Multiple Worlds: The Role of Identity in Learning to Teach. *Teacher Education Quarterly, 35*(3), 61–72.

Hornof, M. (2008). Reading tests as a genre study. *Reading Teacher, 62*, 69–73.

Howard, T. C. (2010). *Why race and culture matter in schools: Closing the achievement gap in America's classrooms.* Teachers College Press.

Howard, T. C., & Rodriguez-Minkoff, A. C. (2017). Culturally relevant pedagogy 20 years later: Progress or pontificating? What have we learned, and where do we go? *Teachers College Record, 119*(1), 1–32.

Huddleston, A. P., & Rockwell, E. C. (2015). Assessment of the masses: A historical critique of high stakes testing in reading. *Texas Journal of Literacy Education, 3*, 38–49.

Inside Schools. (2018, December). Brooklyn Collegiate: A College Board School. https://insideschools.org/school/23K493

Irvine, J. J., & Armento, B. J. (2001). *Culturally responsive teaching: Lesson planning for elementary & middle grades.* McGraw-Hill.

Ishimaru, A. M. (2019). *Just schools: Building equitable collaborations with families and communities.* Teachers College Press.

Ishimaru, A. M., & Galloway, M. K. (2020, August). Hearts and minds first: Institutional logics in pursuit of educational equity. *Educational Administration Quarterly*, 1–33.

Ishimaru, A. M., & Takahashi, S. (2017). Disrupting racialized institutional scripts: Toward parent–teacher transformative agency for educational justice. *Peabody Journal of Education, 92*, 343–362.

Jackson, Y. (2011). *The pedagogy of confidence: Inspiring high intellectual performance in urban schools.* Teachers College Press.

Jemal, A. (2017). Critical consciousness: A critique and critical analysis of the literature. *The Urban Review, 49*(4), 602–626.

Jimerson, S. R., Campos, E., & Greif, J. L. (2003). Toward an understanding of definitions and measures of school engagement and related terms. *The California School Psychologist, 8*, 7–27.

Johns, M., Schmader, T., & Martens, A. (2005). Knowing is half the battle: Teaching stereotype threat as a means of improving women's math performance. *Psychological Science, 16*, 175–179.

Jussim, L., Eccles, J., & Madon, S. (1996). Social perception, social stereotypes, and teacher expectations: Accuracy and the quest for the powerful self-fulfilling prophecy. *Advances in Experimental Social Psychology, 28*, 281–387.

Kane, M. (2006). Validation. In R. Brennan (Ed.), *Educational measurement* (4th ed.). American Council on Education.

Kane, M. (2012). Validating score interpretations and uses: Messick lecture, language testing research colloquium. *Language Testing, 29*(1), 3–17.

Kane, M., Crooks, T., & Cohen, A. (1999). Validating measures of performance. *Educational Measurement: Issues and Practice, 18*(2), 5–17.

Kann, L., O'Malley Olsen, E., McManus, T., Harris, W. A., Shanklin, S. L., Flint, K. A., Queen, B., Lowry, R., Chyen, D., Whittle, L., Thornton, J., Lim, C., Yamakawa, Y., Brener, N., & Zaza, S. (2016). Sexual identity, sex of sexual contacts, and health-related behaviors among students in grades 9–12—United States and selected sites, 2015. *Morbidity and Mortality Weekly Report, 65*(SS-9), 1–202. https://www.cdc.gov/mmwr/volumes/65/ss/ss6509a1.htm

Katz, I., & Assor, A. (2007). When choice motivates and when it does not. *Educational Psychology Review, 19*(4), 429–442.

Khalifa, M., Gooden, M., & Davis, J. (2016). Culturally responsive school leadership: A synthesis of the literature. *Review of Educational Research, 86*, 1272–1311.

Kluger, A. N., & DeNisi, A. S. (1996). Performance: A historical review, a meta-analysis, and a preliminary feedback intervention theory. *Psychological Bulletin, 119*, 254–284.

Koelsch, N., Estrin, E., & Farr, B. (1995). *Guide to developing equitable performance assessments*. ERIC. https://eric.ed.gov/?id=ED397125

Kostons, D., van Gog, T., & Paas, F. (2012). Training self-assessment and task selection skills: A cognitive approach to improving self-regulated learning. *Learning and Instruction, 22*, 121–132.

Kozol, J. (2005). *The shame of a nation: Restoration of apartheid schooling in America*. Random House.

Kuh, G. D. (2001). Assessing what really matters to student learning: Inside the national survey of student engagement. *Change, 33*(3), 10–17.

Kuh, G. D. (2003). What we're learning about student engagement from NSSE. *Change, 35*(2), 24–31.

Kuh, G. D. (2004). *The national survey of student engagement: Conceptual framework and overview of psychometric properties*. Indiana University Center for Postsecondary Research and Planning.

Kuh, G. D. (2008). *High-impact educational practices: What they are, who has access to them, and why they matter*. Association of American Colleges and Universities.

Kuh, G. D. (2009). The national survey of student engagement: Conceptual and empirical foundations. *New Directions for Institutional Research, 141*, 5–21.

Kurth, L. A., Anderson, C. W., & Palincsar, A. S. (2002). The case of Carla: Dilemmas of helping all students to understand science. *Science Education, 86*(3), 287–313.

Ladd, G., & Burgess, K. B. (2001). Do relational risks and protective factors moderate linkages between childhood aggression and early psychological and school adjustment? *Child Development, 72*, 1579–1601.

Ladson-Billings, G. (1994). What can we learn from multicultural education? *Educational Leadership, 51*(8), 22–26.

Ladson-Billings, G. (1995a). Toward a theory of culturally relevant pedagogy. *American Educational Research Journal, 32*, 465–491.

Ladson-Billings, G. (1995b). But that's just good teaching! The case for culturally relevant pedagogy. *Theory Into Practice, 34*(3), 159–165.

Ladson-Billings, G. (2006). From achievement gap to the education debt: Understanding achievement in U.S. schools. *Educational Researcher, 35*(7), 3–12.

Ladson-Billings, G. (2009). *The Dreamkeepers: Successful Teachers of African American Children* (2nd ed.). Jossey-Bass.

Ladson-Billings, G. (2014). Culturally relevant pedagogy 2.0: a.k.a. the Remix. *Harvard Educational Review, 84*, 74–84.

Lake, R., & Macori, A. (2020). *The digital divide among students during COVID-19: Who has access? Who doesn't?* Center on Reinventing Public Education. https://www.crpe.org/thelens/digital-divide-among-students-during-covid-19-who-has-access-who-doesnt

Lane, S., Wang, N., & Magone, M. (1996). Gender-related differential item functioning on a middle school mathematics performance assessment. *Educational Measurement: Issues and Practices, 15*(4), 21–27, 31.

Lantham, J. D. (2016). *The home place: Memoirs of a colored man's love affair with nature*. Milkweed Editions.

Lau, S., & Roeser, R. W. (2002). Cognitive abilities and mental processes in high school students' situational engagement and achievement in science. *Educational Assessment, 8*, 139–162.

Lave, J. (1988). *Cognition in practice: Mind, mathematics and culture in everyday life*. Cambridge University Press.

Lave, J., Murtaugh, M., & de la Rocha, O. (1984). The dialectic of arithmetic in grocery shopping. In B. Rogoff & J. Lave (Eds.), *Everyday cognition: Its development in social context* (pp. 67–94). Harvard University Press.

Lave, J., & Wenger, E. (1991). *Legitimate peripheral participation in communities of practice. Learning in doing (social, cognitive, and computational perspectives)*. Cambridge University Press.

Leahy, S., & Wiliam, D. (2012). From teachers to schools: Scaling up professional development for formative assessment. In J. Gardner (Ed.), *Assessment and learning* (2nd ed., pp. 49–71). SAGE.

Lee, C. D. (1998). Culturally responsive pedagogy and performance-based assessment. *The Journal of Negro Education, 67*, 268–279.

Lee, J. (2002). Racial and achievement gap trends: Reversing the progress toward equity. *Educational Researcher, 31*(1), 3–12.

Linn, R. L. (1993). Educational assessment: Expanded expectations and challenges. *Educational Evaluation and Policy Analysis, 15*, 1–16.

Linn, R. L. (1994). Performance assessment: Policy promises and technical measurement standards. *Educational Researcher, 23*(9), 4–14.

Lipman, P. (2004). *High stakes education: Inequality, globalization, and urban school reform*. Routledge.

Liu, X. (2008, October). *Measuring teachers' perceptions of grading practices: Does school level make a difference?* Paper presented at the annual meeting of the Northeastern Educational Research Association, Rocky Hill, CT.

Llosa, L. (2008). Building and supporting a validity argument for a standards-based classroom assessment of English proficiency based on teacher judgments. *Educational Measurement: Issues & Practice, 27*(3), 32–42.

Long, P. A., & Anthony, J. J. (1974). The measurement of mental retardation by a culture specific test. *Psychology in Schools, 11*, 310–312.

Love, D. (2016, January 26). Stanford study: "Culturally relevant" teaching boosts GPA, attendance for at-risk youth, so why not make it universal? *Atlanta Blackstar*. https://atlantablackstar.com/2016/01/26/stanford-study-culturally-relevant

-teaching-boosts-gpa-attendance-for-at-risk-youth-so-why-not-make-it
   -universal/

Lubienski, S. T. (2002). A closer look at Black-White mathematics gaps: Intersections of race and SES in NAEP achievement and instructional practices data.
   Journal of Negro Education, 71(4), 269–287.

Ma, L. (1999). *Knowing and teaching elementary mathematics: Teachers' understanding of fundamental mathematics in China and the United States.* Erlbaum.

Madaus, G., & Clark, M. (2001). The adverse impact of high stakes testing on
   minority students: Evidence from 100 years of test data, 49 pp. https://eric
   .ed.gov/?id=ED450183

Madaus, G., Maxwell, M. M., Harmon, M. C., Lomax, R. G., & Viator, K. A.
   (1992). *The Influence of testing on teaching math and science in grades 4–12.*
   National Science Foundation.

Madaus, G. F. (1988). The Influence of Testing on the Curriculum. In L. N. Tanner
   (Ed.), *Critical issues in curriculum* (pp. 83–121). The National Society for the
   Study of Education.

Malouff, J. M., & Thorsteinsson, E. B. (2016). Bias in grading: A meta-analysis of
   experimental research findings. *Australian Journal of Education, 60*, 245–256.

Marso, R. N., & Pigge, F. L. (1988, April). *An analysis of teacher-made tests: Testing practices, cognitive demands, and item construction errors.* Paper presented at the annual
   meeting of the National Council on Measurement in Education, New Orleans, LA.

Martin, E. J. (2003). Critical social analysis, service learning, and urban affairs: A
   course application in public policy and administration. *New Political Science,
   25*, 407–431.

Martiniello, M. (2008). Language and the performance of English-language learners
   in math word problems. *Harvard Educational Review, 78*, 333–368.

McCarty, T. L. (2009). The impact of high-stakes accountability policies on Native
   American learners: evidence from research. *Teaching Education, 20*(1), 7–29.

McCormick, A. C., Kinzie, J., & Korkmaz, A. (2011, April 9). *Understanding evi-
   dence-based improvement in higher education: The case of student engagement.*
   Paper presented at the annual meeting of the American Educational Research
   Association, New Orleans, LA.

McFadden, A. C., Marsh II, G. E., Price, B. J., & Hwang, Y. (1992). A study of race
   and gender bias in the punishment of handicapped school children. *The Urban
   Review, 24*, 239–251.

McGraw-Hill. (1983). *Guidelines for bias free publishing.* Author.

McIntyre, E., Roseberry, A., & Gonzalez, N. (Eds.). (2001). *Classroom diversity:
   Connecting curriculum to students' lives.* Heineman.

McMillan, J., & Lawson, S. R. (2001). *Secondary science teachers' classroom assessment and grading practices.* ERIC. https://eric-ed-gov.offcampus.lib.wash-
   ington.edu/?id=ED450158

McMillan, J. H. (2001). Secondary teachers' classroom assessment and grading
   practices. *Educational Measurement: Issues and Practice, 20*(1), 20–32.

McMillan, J. H., Myran, S., & Workman, D. (2002). Elementary teachers' classroom
   assessment and grading practices. *Journal of Educational Research, 95*, 203–213.

McNiel, N. D. (1975). IQ tests and the Black culture. *Phi Delta Kappan, 51*, 209–210.

Meier, T. (2008). *Black communications and learning to read: Building on children's
   linguistic and cultural strengths.* Erlbaum.

Mendes-Barnett, S., & Ercikan, K. (2006). Examining sources of gender DIF in mathematics assessments using a confirmatory multidimensional model approach. *Applied Measurement in Education, 19*, 289–304.

Messick, S. (1989a). Meaning and values in test validation: The science and ethics of assessment. *Educational Researcher, 18*(2), 5–11.

Messick, S. (1989b). Validity. In R. Linn (Ed.), *Educational measurement* (3rd ed.). American Council on Education/Macmillan.

Messick, S. (1990). *Validity of test interpretation and use.* Educational Testing Service, 33p.

Messick, S. (1994a). The interplay of evidence and consequences in the validation of performance assessments. *Educational Researcher, 23*(2), 13–23.

Messick, S. (1994b). *Standards-based score interpretation: Establishing valid grounds for valid inferences* [Research report]. Educational Testing Service.

Messick, S. (1995). Standards of validity in performance assessments. *Educational Measurement: Issues and Practices, 14*(4), 5–8.

Mitchell, I., Nistor, N., Baltes, B., & Brown, M. (2016). Effect of vocabulary test preparation on low-income Black middle school students' reading scores. *Journal of Educational Research and Practice, 6*, 105–118.

Moll, L. C., Amanti, C., Neff, D., & Gonzalez, N. (1992). Funds of Knowledge for Teaching: Using a Qualitative Approach to Connect Homes and Classrooms. *Theory Into Practice, 31*(2), 132–141.

Montenegro, E., & Jankowski, N. A. (2017). *Equity and assessment: Toward a theory of culturally responsive assessment.* National Institute for Learning Outcomes Assessment.

Moore, M. (1989). Three types of interaction. *American Journal of Distance Education, 2*, 1–6.

Moschkovich, J. N. (2007). Beyond words to mathematical content: Assessing English learners in the mathematics classroom. In A. Schoenfeld (Ed.), *Assessing mathematical proficiency* (pp. 345–352). Cambridge University Press.

Moschkovich, J. N. (2008). "I went by twos, he went by one." Multiple interpretations of inscriptions as resources for mathematical discussions. *Journal of the Learning Sciences, 17*, 551–587.

Moschkovich, J. N., & Nelson-Barber, S. (2009). What mathematics teachers need to know about culture and language. In B. Greer, S. Mukhopadhyay, S. Nelson-Barber, & A. Powell (Eds.), *Culturally responsive mathematics education* (pp. 111–136). Routledge.

Moses, R. P., & Cobb, C. E. (2001). *Radical equations: Civil rights from Mississippi to the Algebra Project.* Beacon.

Mueller, M., & Maher, C. A. (2009). Learning to reason in an informal math after-school program. *Mathematics Education Research Journal, 21*(3), 7–35.

Mueller, M., Yankelewitz, D., & Maher, C. (2010). Promoting student reasoning through careful task design: A comparison of three studies. *International Journal for Studies in Mathematics Education, 3*(1), 135–156.

Murray, J., & Summerlee, A. J. S. (2007). The impact of problem-based learning in an interdisciplinary first-year program on student learning behaviour. *Canadian Journal of Higher Education, 37*(3), 87–107.

Nagy, W., & Townsend, D. (2012). Words as tools: Learning academic vocabulary as language acquisition. *Reading Research Quarterly, 47*(1), 91–108.

Nasir, N. S. (2011). *Racialized identities: Race and achievement among African American youth.* Stanford University Press.

Nasir, N. S., & Hand, V. M. (2008). From the court to the classroom: Opportunities for engagement, learning, and identity in basketball and classroom mathematics. *Journal of Learning Sciences, 17,* 143–179.

National Assessment of Educational Progress. (1996). *Mathematics items public release.* Author.

National Center for Educational Statistics. (2020a). *Racial/ethnic enrollment in public schools.* nces.ed.gov/programs/coe/indicator_cge.asp

National Center for Educational Statistics. (2020b). *English language learners in public schools.* https://nces.ed.gov/programs/coe/indicator/cgf

National Public Radio. (2017, July 14). *Arizona's ethnic studies ban in public schools goes to trial.* https://www.npr.org/2017/07/14/537291234/arizonas-ethnic-studies-ban-in-public-schools-goes-to-trial

National Research Council. (2000). *How people learn: Brain, mind, experience, and school* (expanded ed.). Author.

Newman, F. M. (1996). *Authentic achievement: Restructuring schools for intellectual quality.* Jossey-Bass.

Newman, F. M., Bryk, A. S., & Nagaoka, J. K. (2001). *Authentic intellectual work and standardized tests: Conflict or coexistence?* Consortium on Chicago School.

Newmann, F. M., Wehlage, G. G., & Lamborn, S. D. (1992). The significance and sources of student engagement. In F. M. Newmann (Ed.), *Student engagement and achievement in American secondary schools* (pp. 11–39). Teachers College Press.

Newton, C., Acres, K., & Bruce, C. (2013). A comparison of computerized and paper-based language tests with adults with aphasia. *American Journal of Speech-Language Pathology, 22,* 185–197.

Next Generation Science Standards. (2013a). *Development overview.* https://www.nextgenscience.org/development-overview

Next Generation Science Standards. (2013b). *Next Generation Science Standards for states by states.* https://www.nap.edu/catalog/18290/next-generation-science-standards-for-states-by-states

Nguyen, H. H. D., & Ryan, A. M. (2008). Does stereotype threat affect test performance of minorities and women? A meta-analysis of experimental evidence. *Journal of Applied Psychology, 93,* 1314.

NICHD Early Child Care Research Network. (2005). A day in third grade: A large-scale study of classroom quality and teacher and student behavior. *The Elementary School Journal, 105,* 305–323.

Nieto, S. (2002–2003). Equity and opportunity: Profoundly multicultural questions. *Educational Leadership, 60*(4), 6–10.

Nieto, S. (2004). *Affirming diversity: The sociopolitical context of multicultural education.* Allyn & Bacon.

Nitko, A. J. (2004). *Educational assessment of students* (4th ed.). Pearson.

Noble, A. C. (1992, April). *Differential item functioning in innovative-format mathematics items.* Paper presented at the annual meeting of the American Educational Research Association, San Francisco, CA.

Nolen, S. B. (2001). Constructing literacy in the kindergarten: Task structure, collaboration and motivation. *Cognition & Instruction, 19,* 95–142.

Nolen, S. B. (2011). The role of educational systems in the link between formative assessment and motivation. *Theory Into Practice, 50*(4), 319–326.

Nolen, S. B., Haladyna, T. M., & Haas, N. S. (1989). A survey of actual and perceived uses, test preparation activities, and effects of standardized achievement tests. *Educational Measurement: Issues and Practices, 9*, 15–22

Nolen, S. B., Horn, I. S., Ward, C. J., & Childers, S. A. (2011). Novice teacher learning and motivation across contexts: Assessment tools as boundary objects. *Cognition and Instruction, 29*, 88–122.

Nolen, S. B., & Nicholls, J. G. (1993). Elementary school pupils' beliefs about practices for motivating pupils in mathematics. *British Journal of Educational Psychology, 63*(3), 414–430.

Nolen, S. B., Ward, C. J., Horn, I. S., Childers, S., Campbell, S. S., & Mahna, K. (2009). Motivation development in novice teachers: The development of utility filters. In M. Wosnitza, S. A. Karabenick, A. Efklides, & P. Nenniger (Eds.), *Contemporary motivation research: From global to local perspectives* (pp. 265–278). Hogrefe & Huber.

Nolen, S. B., Wetzstein, L., & Goodell, A. (2020). Designing material tools to mediate disciplinary engagement in environmental science. *Cognition & Instruction, 38*(2), 179–223. https://doi.org/10.1080/07370008.2020.1718677

Nortvedt, G. A., Wiese, E., Brown, M., Burns, D., McNamara, G., O'Hara, J., Altrichter, H., Fellner, M., Herzog-Punzenberger, B., Nayir, F., & Taneri, P. O. (2020). Aiding culturally responsive assessment in schools in a globalizing world. *Educational Assessment, Evaluation, and Accountability, 32*, 5–27.

Nuri-Robins, K., Lindsey, R., Lindsey, D., & Terrell, R. (2006). *Culturally proficient instruction: A guide for people who teach* (2nd ed.). Corwin.

Oakes, J. (1990). *Multiplying inequalities: The effects of race, social class, and tracking on opportunities to learn mathematics and science.* RAND.

Oakes, J., & Lipton, M. (2007). *Teaching to change the world.* McGraw-Hill.

Oescher, J., & Kirby, P. C. (1990, April 17–19). *Assessing teacher-made tests in secondary math and science classrooms.* Paper presented at the annual meeting of the National Council on Measurement in Education, Boston, MA.

Olivier, E., Benoit, G., Hospel, V., & Dellise, S. (2020). Understanding behavioral engagement and achievement: The roles of teaching practices and student sense of competence and task value. *British Journal of Educational Psychology, 90*, 887–909.

Olivier, E., Galand, B., Hospel, V., & Dellisse, S. (2020). Understanding behavioural engagement and achievement: The roles of teaching practices and student sense of competence and task value. *British Journal of Educational Psychology, 90*, 887–909.

Osborne, J. W. (2001). Testing stereotype threat: Does anxiety explain race and sex differences in achievement? *Contemporary Educational Psychology, 3*, 291–310.

Osborne, J. W. (2006). Gender stereotype threat and anxiety: Psychophysiological and cognitive evidence. *Electronic Journal of Research in Educational Psychology, 4*(1), 109–138.

Osborne, J. W. (2007). Linking stereotype threat and anxiety. *Educational Psychology, 27*(1), 135–154.

Palardy, G. J., Rumberger, R., & Butler, T. (2015). The effect of high school socioeconomic, racial and linguistic segregation on academic performance and school behaviors. *Teachers College Record, 117*(12), 120303.

Palumbo, A., & Kramer-Vida, L. (2012). An academic curriculum will close the achievement gap. *The Clearinghouse, 85,* 117–121.

Paris, D. (2009). "They're in my culture, they speak the same way": African American language in multi-ethnic high schools. *Harvard Educational Review, 79,* 428–447.

Paris, D. (2012). Culturally sustaining pedagogy: A needed change in stance, terminology, and practice. *Educational Researcher, 41*(3), 93–97.

Paris, D., & Alim, H. S. (2014). What are we seeking to sustain through culturally sustaining pedagogy? A loving critique forward. *Harvard Review, 84,* 85–100.

Park, S. Y. (2005). Student engagement and classroom variables in improving mathematics achievement. *Asia Pacific Education Review, 6,* 87–97.

Patall, E. A., Cooper, H., & Robinson, J. C. (2008). The effects of choice on intrinsic motivation and related outcomes: A meta-analysis of research findings. *Psychological Bulletin, 134,* 270–300.

Patrick, H., Ryan, A. M., & Kaplan, A. (2007). Early adolescents' perceptions of the classroom social environment, motivational beliefs, and engagement. *Journal of Educational Psychology, 99,* 83–98.

Payne, C. (2004, October 21). *Still crazy after all these years: Race in Chicago schools.* Paper presented at the Consortium on Chicago School Research, Chicago, IL.

Pearman, F. A. (2020). *County-level rates of implicit bias predict black white test score gaps in US schools* [Working paper no. 20–192]. Annenberg Brown University.

Pearman, F. A., Curran, F. C., Fisher, B., & Gardella, J. (2019). Are achievement gaps related to discipline gaps? Evidence from national data. *AERA Open, 5*(4), 2332858419875440.

Pedula, J. J., Abrams, L. M., Madaus, G. F., Russell, M. K., Ramos, M. A., & Miao, J. (2003). *Perceived effects of state-mandated testing programs on teaching and learning: Findings from a national survey of teachers.* National Board on Educational Testing and Public Policy.

Pelligrino, J., Chudowsky, N., & Glaser, R. (2001). *Knowing what students know: The science and design of educational assessment.* National Research Council Committee on the Foundations of Assessment & National Academy Press.

Phippin, J. W. & The National Journal. (2015). How one law banning ethnic studies led to its rise. *The Atlantic.* https://www.theatlantic.com/education/archive/2015/07/how-one-law-banning-ethnic-studies-led-to-rise/398885/

Plunger, B., Axel, M., & Umbach, N. (2019). Beneficial for some or for everyone? Exploring the effects of an autonomy-supportive intervention in the real-life classroom. *Journal of Educational Psychology, 111,* 210–234.

Poggio, J., Glasnapp, D. R., Yang, X., & Poggio, A. J. (2005). A comparative evaluation of score results from computerized and paper and pencil mathematics testing in a large scale state assessment program. *Journal of Technology, Learning, and Assessment, 3*(6). https://ejournals.bc.edu/index.php/jtla/article/view/1659

Pollitt, A., Marriott, C., & Ahmed, A. (2000, May). *Language, contextual and cultural constraints on examination performance.* Paper presented at the 26th International Association for Educational Assessment (IAEA) conference, Jerusalem, Israel.

Poorthuis, A. M. G., Juvonen, J., Thomaes, S., Denissen, J. J. A., de Castro, B. O., & van Ake, M. A. G. (2015). Do grades shape students' school engagement? The psychological consequences of report card grades at the beginning of secondary school. *Journal of Educational Psychology, 107,* 842–854.

Pope, D. (2010). Beyond "doing school": From "stressed out" to "engaged in learning." *Canadian Education Association, 50*(1), 4–8.

Popham, J. (2005, March 23). Standardized testing fails the exam. *Edutopia.* https://www.edutopia.org/standardized-testing-evaluation-reform

Popham, J. (2008). Formative assessment: Seven stepping stones to success. *Principal Leadership, 9*(1), 16–20.

Popham, J. (2011). Farewell curriculum: Confessions of an assessment convert. *Phi Delta Kappan, 79,* 380–384.

Popham, J. (2020). *Classroom assessment: What teachers need to know* (9th ed.). Pearson.

Popham, W. J. (2005). *Classroom assessment: What teachers need to know.* Pearson.

Probst, R. (1981). Response based teaching of literature. *English Journal, 70,* 43–47.

Project Tomorrow. (2017). *How America's schools are addressing the homework gap: Speak Up 2016 findings.* Author.

Puma, M., Jones, C., Rock, D., & Fernandez, R. (1993). *Prospects: The congressionally mandated study of educational growth and opportunity.* Interim report prepared for the U.S. Department of Education, Planning and Evaluation Service. https://eric.ed.gov/?id=ED361466

Purves, A. (1975). Research in the teaching of literature. *Elementary English, 52,* 463–466.

Qualls, A. L. (1998). Culturally responsive assessment: Development strategies and validity issues. *The Journal of Negro Education, 67,* 296–301.

Quinn, D. M. (2017). Racial attitudes of preK–12 and postsecondary educators: Descriptive evidence from nationally representative data. *Educational Researcher, 46,* 397–411.

Quinn, D. M. (2020). Experimental evidence on teachers' racial bias in student evaluation: The role of grading scales. *Educational Evaluation and Policy Analysis, 42,* 375–394.

Reeves, T., & Gomm, P. (2015). Community and contribution: Factors motivating students to participate in an extra curricular online activity and implications for learning. *E-Learning and Digital Media, 12,* 391–409.

Resnick, L., Nolan, K. J., & Resnick, D. P. (1995). Benchmarking education standards. *Educational Evaluation and Policy Analysis, 17,* 438–461.

Revelle, W., Wilt, J., & Condon, D. M. (2011). Individual differences and differential psychology: A brief history and prospect. In T. Chamorro-Premuzic, S. von Stumm, & A. Furnham (Eds.), *The Wiley Blackwell handbook of individual differences* (pp. 3–38). Wiley.

Rheinberg, F. (1983). Achievement evaluation: A fundamental difference and its motivational consequences. *Studies in Education Evaluation, 9,* 185–194.

Richardson, B. C., & Dinkens, E. G. (2014). Life on the reservation: Cross cultural field experiences and student learning. *Association of Independent Liberal Arts Colleges for Teacher Education (AILACTE), 11,* 57–72.

Richardson, J., Ball, D., & Moses, B. (2009). Equity and mathematics: An interview with Deborah Ball and Bob Moses. *Phi Delta Kappan, 91,* 54–59.

Riddle, T., & Sinclair, S. (2019). Racial disparities in school-based disciplinary actions are associated with county-level rates of racial bias. *Proceedings of the National Academy of Sciences, 116*(17), 8255–8260.

Risko, V. J., & Walker–Dalhouse, D. (2007). Tapping students' cultural funds of knowledge to address the achievement gap. *The Reading Teacher, 61,* 98–100.

Rodriguez, B. A. (2014). The threat of living up to expectations: Analyzing the performance of Hispanic students on standardized exams. *Journal of Hispanic Higher Education, 13*, 191–205.

Romero, A. F. (2010). At war with the state in order to save the lives of our children: The battle of ethnic studies in Arizona. *Black Scholar, 40*(4), 7–15.

Rosenblatt, L. (1976). *Literature as exploration* (3rd ed.). Noble and Noble.

Rosenthal, R., & Jacobson L. (1968a). *Pygmalion in the classroom: Teacher expectations and student intellectual development.* Holt, Rinehart and Winston.

Rosenthal, R., & Jacobson, L. (1968b). Pygmalion in the classroom. *The Urban Review, 3*(1), 16–20.

Rothman, R. (1995). *Measuring up: Standards, assessment, and school reform.* San Francisco, CA: Jossey-Bass.

Royal, C., & Gibson, S. (2017). They schools: Culturally relevant pedagogy under siege. *Teachers College Record, 119*(1), 010306, 25 pp. http://www.tcrecord.org/Content.asp?ContentId=21719

Russell, J. A., & Austin, J. R. (2010). Assessment practices of secondary music teachers. *Journal of Research in Music Education, 58*, 37–54.

Ryan, A. M., & Patrick, H. (2001). The classroom social environment and changes in adolescents' motivation and engagement during middle school. *American Educational Research Journal, 38*, 437–460.

Ryan, R. M., & Deci, E. L. (2020). Intrinsic and extrinsic motivation from a self-determination theory perspective: Definitions, theory, practices, and future directions. *Contemporary Educational Psychology, 61*(10860). https://doi.org/10.1016/j.cedpsych.2020.101860

Ryan, T. G. (2006). Performance assessment: Critics, criticism, and controversy. *International Journal of Testing, 6*(1), 97–104.

Rychly, L., & Graves, E. (2012). Teacher characteristics for culturally responsive pedagogy. *Multicultural Perspectives, 14*, 44–49.

Sadler, D. (1989). Formative assessment and the design of instructional systems. *Instructional Science, 18*, 119–44.

Sadler, D. R., & Good, E. (2006). The impact of self- and peer-grading on student learning. *Educational Assessment, 11*(1), 1–31.

Sanders, M. (1997). Overcoming obstacles: Academic achievement as a response to racism and discrimination. *Journal of Negro Education, 66*(1), 83–93.

Saxe, G. B. (1988). The mathematics of child street vendors. *Child Development, 59*, 1415–1425.

Schaeffer, K. (2020). *As schools shift to online learning amid pandemic, here's what we know about disabled students in the U.S.* Pew Research Center. https://www.pewresearch.org/fact-tank/2020/04/23/as-schools-shift-to-online-learning-amid-pandemic-heres-what-we-know-about-disabled-students-in-the-u-s

Schleppegrell, M. J. (2001). Linguistic features of the language of schooling. *Linguistics and Education, 14*, 431–459.

Schraw, G., Flowerday, T., & Lehman, S. (2001). Increasing situational interest in the classroom. *Educational Psychology Review, 13*, 211–224.

Schwartz, R., Lederman, N., & Crawford, B. (2004). Developing views of nature of science in an authentic context: An explicit approach to bridging the gap between nature of science and scientific inquiry. *Science Education, 88*, 610–645.

Shaw, S. R., & Braden, J. P. (1990). Race and gender bias in the administration of corporal punishment. *School Psychology Review, 19*, 378–383.

Shepard, L., Hammerness, K., Darling-Hammond, L., & Rust, F. (2005). Assessment. In L. Darling-Hammond & J. Bransford (Eds.), *Preparing teachers for a changing world* (pp. 275–326). Jossey-Bass.

Shepard, L. A. (1991). Psychometricians beliefs about learning. *Educational Researcher, 20*(7) 2–16.

Shepard, L. A. (2013). Validity for what purpose? *Teachers College Record, 115*(9), 1–12.

Shepard, L. A., Penuel, W. R., & Pellegrino, J. W. (2018). Using learning and motivation theories to coherently link formative assessment, grading practices, and large-scale assessment. *Educational Measurement: Issues and Practice, 37*, 21–34.

Sherman, D. K., Hartson, K. A., Binning, K. R., Purdie-Vaughns, V., Garcia, J., Taborsky-Barba, S., Tomassetti, S., Nussbaum, A. D., & Cohen, G. L. (2013). Deflecting the trajectory and changing the narrative: How self-affirmation affects academic performance and motivation under identity threat. *Journal of Personality and Social Psychology, 104*, 591–618.

Shin, R. Q., Ezeofor, I., Smith, L. C., Welch, J. C., & Goldrich, K. M. (2016). The development and validation of the contemporary critical consciousness measure. *Journal of Counseling Psychology, 63*, 210–223.

Shohamy, E. (2000, May). *Educational assessment in a multicultural society: Issues and challenges.* Paper presented at the 26th IAEA Conference, Jerusalem, Israel.

Shores, M., & Weseley, A. J. (2007). When the A is for agreement: Factors that affect educators' evaluations of student essays. *Action in Education, 29*(3), 4–11.

Skiba, R. J., Michael, R. S., Nardo, A. C., & Peterson, R. L. (2002). The color of discipline: Sources of racial and gender disproportionality in school punishment. *The Urban Review, 34*(4), 317–342.

Skidmore, R. L., & Aagaard, L. (2004). The relationship between testing condition and student test scores. *Journal of Instructional Psychology, 31*, 304–313.

Skinner, E. A., Wellborn, J. G., Connell, J. P. (1990). What it takes to do well in school and whether I've got it: A process model of perceived control and children's engagement and achievement in school. *Journal of Educational Psychology, 82*(1), 22–32.

Sleeter, C., & Stillman, J. (2005). Standardizing knowledge in a multicultural society. *Curriculum Inquiry, 35*(1), 27–46.

Sleeter, C. E. (2012). Confronting the marginalization of culturally responsive pedagogy. *Urban Education, 47*(3), 562–584.

Sloan, G. (2002). Reader response in perspective. *Journal of Children's Literature, 28*, 22–30.

Smith, G. A. (2007). Place-based education: Breaking through the constraining regularities of public school. *Environmental Education Research, 13*, 189–207.

Smith, M. L. (1980). Teachers' expectations. *Evaluation in Education, 4*, 53–56.

Smith, M. L. (1991). Put to the test: The effects of external testing on teachers. *Educational Researcher, 20*(5), 8–11.

Smitherman, G. (1993, November 17-22). *"The blacker the berry, the sweeter the juice": African American student writers and the National Assessment of Educational Progress.* Paper presented at the annual meeting of the National Council of Teachers of English, Pittsburgh, PA.

Snow, C. E., & Uccelli, P. (2009). The challenge of academic language. In D. R. Olson & N. Torrance (Eds.), *The Cambridge handbook of literacy* (pp. 112–133). Cambridge University Press.

Solano-Flores, G. (2011). The cultural validity of assessment practices. In M. d. R. Basterra, E. Trumbull, & G. Solano-Flores (Eds.), *Cultural validity in assessment: Addressing linguistic and cultural diversity* (pp. 3–21). Routledge.

Solano-Flores, G., & Li, M. (2009). Generalizability of cognitive interview-based measures across cultural groups. *Educational Measurement: Issues and Practice, 28*(2), 9–18.

Solano-Flores, G., & Nelson Barber, S. (2001). On the cultural validity of science assessments. *Journal of Research in Science Teaching, 38*(5), 553–573.

Solano-Flores, G., & Trumbull, E. (2003). Examining language in context: The need for new research and practice paradigms in the testing of English-language learners. *Educational Researcher, 32*(2), 3–13.

Solomon, G. (1993). *Distributed cognitions: Psychological and educational considerations.* Cambridge University Press.

Spalding, E. (2000). Performance assessment and the New Standards Project: A story of serendipitous success. *Phi Delta Kappan, 81,* 758–764.

Spencer, S. J., Logel, C., & Davies, P. G. (2016). Stereotype threat. *Annual Review of Psychology, 67,* 415–437.

Spencer, S. J., Steele, C. M., & Quinn, D. M. (1999). Stereotype threat and women's math performance. *Journal of Experimental Social Psychology, 35,* 4–28.

Spiegel, D. L. (1998). Reader response approaches and the growth of readers. *Language Arts, 76,* 41–48.

Staats, C. (2014). *Implicit racial bias and school discipline disparities: Exploring the connection.* The Ohio State University, Kirwan Institute for the Study of Race and Ethnicity.

Star, S. L., & Griesemer, J. R. (1989). Institutional ecology, "translations" and boundary objects: Amateurs and professionals in Berkeley's Museum of Vertebrate Zoology, 1907–1939. *Social Studies of Science, 19,* 387–420.

Starck, J. G., Riddle, T., Sinclair, S., & Warikoo, N. (2020). Teachers are people too: Examining the racial bias of teachers compared to other American adults. *Educational Researcher, 49,* 273–284.

Steele, C. (2003). Stereotype threat and African-American student achievement. In T. Perry, C. Steele & A. G. Hilliard (Eds.), *Young, gifted, and black: Promoting high achievement among African-American students* (pp. 109–130). Beacon Press.

Steele, C. M. (2010). *Whistling Vivaldi and other clues to how stereotypes affect us.* Norton.

Steele, C. M., & Aronson, J. (1995). Stereotype threat and the intellectual test performance of African Americans. *Journal of Personality and Social Psychology, 69,* 797–811.

Steele, L. (2005). Sweatshop accounting. Rethinking Schools, https://rethinkingschools.org/articles/sweatshop-accounting/

Stiggins, R. J. (1991). Assessment literacy. *Phi Delta Kappan, 72,* 534–539.

Stiggins, R. J. (1999). Evaluating classroom assessment training in teacher education programs. *Educational Measurement: Issues and Practice, 18,* 23–27.

Stiggins, R. J. (2001a). The unfulfilled promise of classroom assessment. *Educational Measurement: Issues and Practice, 20*(3), 5–15.

Stiggins. R. J. (2001b). *Student-involved classroom assessment* (3rd ed.). Pearson.

Stiggins, R. J. (2002). Assessment crisis: The absence of assessment for learning. *Phi Delta Kappan*, 83(10), 758–765.

Stiggins, R. J. (2005). Evaluating classroom assessment training in teacher education programs. *Educational Measurement: Issues and Practice*, 18(1), 23–27.

Stiggins, R. J., & Chapuis, J. (2005). Using student-involved classroom assessment to close achievement gaps. *Theory Into Practice*, 44, 11–18.

Stiggins, R. J., & Chapuis, J. (2006). What a difference a word makes: Assessment "for" learning rather than assessment "of" learning helps students succeed. *Journal of Staff Development*, 27(1), 10–14.

Stiggins, R. J., & Chapuis, J. (2008). Enhancing student learning. *District Administration*, 44(1), 42–44.

Stiggins, R. J., & Conklin, N. F. (1992). *In teachers' hands: Investigating the practice of classroom assessment.* State University of New York Press.

Stiggins, R. J., Frisbie, D. A., & Griswold, P. A. (1989). Inside high school grading practices: Building and research agenda. *Educational Measurement: Issues and Practice*, 8, 5–14.

Stobart, G. (2005). Fairness in multicultural assessment systems. *Assessment in Education: Principles, Policy, and Practice*, 12, 275–287.

Strauss, V. (2014, January 18). Everything you need to know about Common Core—Ravitch. *Washington Post*. https://www.washingtonpost.com/news/answer-sheet/wp/2014/01/18/everything-you-need-to-know-about-common-core-ravitch/

Strauss, V. (2017a, May, 9). Can coaching truly boost SAT scores? For years, the College Board said no. Now it says yes. *The Washington Post*. https://www.washingtonpost.com/news/answer-sheet/wp/2017/05/09/can-coaching-truly-boost-sat-scores-for-years-the-college-board-said-no-now-it-says-yes/

Strauss, V. (2017b, August, 23). Arizona's ban on Mexican American studies was racist, A U.S. court rules. *The Washington Post*. https://www.washingtonpost.com/news/answer-sheet/wp/2017/08/23/arizonas-ban-on-mexican-american-studies-was-racist-u-s-court-rules

Strutchens, M. E., & Silver, E. A. (2000). NAEP findings regarding race/ethnicity: Students' performance, school experiences, and attitudes and beliefs. *Results from the seventh mathematics assessment of the National Assessment of Educational Progress*, 45–72.

Summerlee, A., & Murray, J. (2010). Impact of enquiry-based learning on academic performance and student engagement. *Canadian Journal of Higher Education*, 40, 78–94.

Sun, Y., & Cheng, L. (2013). Teachers' grading practices: Meaning and values assigned. *Assessment in Education*, 27, 326–343.

Taherbhai, H., Seo, D., & Bowman, T. (2012). Comparison of paper-pencil and online performances of students with learning disabilities. *British Educational Research Journal*, 38, 61–74.

Taylor, C. S. (1998). An investigation of scoring methods for mathematics performance assessments. *Educational Assessment*, 5, 195–224.

Taylor, C. S. (2008, April 18). *Bias and sensitivity issues for the Washington assessment of student learning.* Seminar paper presented at a University of Washington College of Education, Seattle, WA.

Taylor, C. S. (2009, April 14). *Evaluation of the quality and alignment of published classroom assignments.* Paper presented at the annual meeting of the American Educational Research Association, Classroom Assessment SIG, San Diego, CA.

Taylor, C. S. (2014). *Understanding statistics: Validity and validation*. Oxford University Press.

Taylor, C. S., & Lee, Y. (2004, December 2-3). *Is reading a dimension in the WASL mathematics test? Using differential item functioning to examine the dimensions of WASL mathematics*. Paper presented at the Washington State Assessment Conference, Seattle, WA.

Taylor, C. S., & Lee, Y. (2011). Ethnic DIF and DBF in reading tests with mixed item formats. *Educational Assessment, 16*, 35–68.

Taylor, C. S., & Lee, Y. (2012). Gender DIF in tests with mixed item formats. *Applied Measurement in Education, 25*, 246–280.

Taylor, C. S., & Nolen, S. B. (1996). A contextualized approach to teaching teachers about assessment. *Educational Psychologist, 31*, 77–88.

Taylor, C. S., & Nolen, S. B. (2008). *Classroom assessment: Supporting teaching and learning in real classrooms* (2nd ed.). Pearson.

Taylor, M. C. (1979). Race, sex, and the expression of self-fulfilling prophecies in a laboratory teaching situation. *Personality and Social Psychology, 6*, 897–912.

Taylor, S., & Sobel, D. (2011). *Culturally responsive pedagogy: Teaching like our students' lives matter*. Emerald.

Taylor, V. J., & Walton, G. M. (2011). Stereotype threat undermines academic learning. *Personality and Social Psychology Bulletin, 37*, 1055–1067.

Tenenbaum, H. R., & Ruck, M. D. (2007). Are teachers' expectations different for racial minority than for European American students? A meta-analysis. *Journal of Educational Psychology, 99*, 253–273.

Thompson, N. A., & Weiss, D. J. (2009). Computerized and adaptive testing in educational assessment. In F. Scheuermann & J. Björnsson (Eds.), *The transition to computer-based assessment: New approaches to skills assessment and implications for large-scale testing*. Office for Official Publications of the European Communities.

Tierney, G., Goodell, A., Nolen, S. B., Lee, N., Whitfield, L., & Abbott, R. D. (2018). (Re)designing for engagement in a project-based AP environmental science course. *Journal of Experimental Education, 88*(1), 72–102. https://doi.org/10.1080/00220973.2018.1535479

Uccelli, P., Galloway, E. P., Barr, C. D., Meneses, A., & Dobbs, C. L. (2015). Beyond vocabulary: Exploring cross-disciplinary academic-language proficiency and its association with reading comprehension. *Reading Research Quarterly, 50*(3), 337–356.

Uhlmann, E. L., & Cohen, G. L. (2005). Constructed criteria: Redefining merit to justify discrimination. *Psychological Science, 16*, 474–480.

U.S. Copyright Office (2021, May). More Information about Fair Use. Author. https://www.copyright.gov/fair-use/more-info.html

Varelas, M., Martin, D. B., & Kane, J. M. (2012). Content learning and identity construction: A framework to strengthen African American students' mathematics and science learning in urban elementary schools. *Human Development, 55*, 319–339. https://doi.org/10.1159/000345324

Vass, G. (2017). Preparing for culturally responsive schooling: Initial teacher educators into the fray. *Journal of Teacher Education, 68*, 451–462.

Vertovec, S. (2007). Super-diversity and its implications. *Ethnic and Racial Studies, 30*(6), 1024–1054.

Vygotsky, L. S. (1978). *Mind in society: The development of higher psychological processes*. Harvard University Press.

Wade, R. C. (2000). Service-learning for multicultural teaching competency: Insights from the literature for teacher educators. *Equity & Excellence in Education*, *33*(3), 21–29.

Walker, C. (2021, April 9). *Assessment and teacher education*. Division D vice presidential address at the virtual annual meeting of the American Educational Research Association [Virtual meeting]. https://convention2.allacademic.com/one/aera/aera21/index.php?cmd=Online+Program+View+Session&selected_session_id=1715257&PHPSESSID=r8utag2m6g5orgjf9mpmuq6c8o

Walkington, C. (2013). Using adaptive learning technologies to personalize instruction to students' interests: The impact of relevant contexts on performance and learning outcomes. *Journal of Educational Psychology*, 10, 932–945.

Walkington, C., Sherman, M., & Petrosino, A. (2012). "Playing the game" of story problems: Coordinating situation-based reasoning with algebraic representation. *The Journal of Mathematical Behavior*, *31*(2), 174–195.

Warikoo, N., Sinclair, S., Fei, J., & Jacoby-Senghor, D. (2016). Examining racial bias in education: A new approach. *Educational Researcher*, *45*, 508–514.

Wentzel, K. R. (1997). Student motivation in middle school: The role of perceived pedagogical caring. *Journal of Educational Psychology*, 89, 411–419.

Wigfield, A., & Wentzel, K. R. (2007). Introduction to motivation at school: Interventions that work. *Educational Psychologist*, 42, 191–196.

Wiggan, G., & Watson, M. J. (2016). Teaching the whole child: The importance of culturally responsiveness, community engagement, and character development in high achieving African American students. *The Urban Review*, *48*(5), 766–798.

Wiggins, G. (1989). The futility of trying to teach everything of importance. *Educational Leadership*, *49*(3), 44–59.

Wiggins, G. (1992). Creating tests worth taking. *Educational Leadership*, *49*(8), 26–33.

Wiggins, G., & McTighe, J. (2005). *Understanding by design* (2nd ed.). Association for Supervision and Curriculum Development.

Wiggins, G., & McTighe, J. (2011). *Understanding by design: Guide to creating high quality units*. Association for Supervision and Curriculum Development.

Wiliam, D. (2011). What is assessment for learning? *Studies in Educational Evaluation*, *37*(1), 3–14.

Wiliam, D., & Thompson, M. (2007). Integrating assessment with instruction: What will it take to make it work? In C. A. Dwyer (Ed.), *The future of assessment: Shaping teaching and learning* (pp. 53–82). Erlbaum.

Windschitl, M., Thompson, J., & Braaten, M. (2011). Ambitious pedagogy by novice teachers? Who benefits from tool-supported collaborative inquiry into practice and why. *Teachers College Record*, *113*(7), 1311–60.

Wormeli, R. (2006). Accountability: Teaching through assessment and feedback, not grading. *American Secondary Education*, *34*(3), 14–27.

Wright, B. J., & Isenstein, V. R. (1977). *Psychological testing and minorities*. National Institute of Mental Health, Division of Scientific and Public Information.

Yankelewitz, D. (2009). *The development of mathematical reasoning in elementary school students' exploration of fraction ideas* [Unpublished doctoral dissertation]. Rutgers University.

Yankelewitz, D., Mueller, M., & Maher, C. (2010). Tasks that elicit reasoning: A dual analysis. *Journal of Mathematical Behavior*, 29, 76–85.

Yosso, T. J. (2005). Whose culture has capital? A critical race theory discussion of community cultural wealth. *Race Ethnicity and Education, 8*(1), 69–91.

Young, E. (2010). Challenges to conceptualizing and actualizing culturally relevant pedagogy: How viable is the theory in classroom practice? *Journal of Teacher Education, 61,* 248–260.

Zacharias, J. R. (1975). Testing in the schools: A help or a hindrance? *Prospects, 5* (1), 33–43.

Zenisky, A. L., Hambleton, R. K., & Robin, F. (2004). DIF detection and interpretation in large-scale science assessments: Informing item writing practices. *Educational Assessment, 9,* 61–78.

Zimmerman, M. A, Ramirez, J., Washienko, K. M., Walter, B., & Dyer, S. (1994). Enculturation hypothesis: Exploring direct and protective effects among Native American youth. In H. I. McCubbin, E. A. Thompson, & A. I. Thompson (Eds.), *Resiliency in ethnic minority families, volume I: Native and immigrant American families* (pp. 199–220). University of Wisconsin Press.

Index

About the Authors

Catherine Taylor is professor emerita in the College of Education at the University of Washington. Taylor has spent over 40 years in teaching, research, and other work related to large-scale and classroom-based assessment. Her primary goal as an educator is to help teachers integrate instruction and assessment in ways that support all students' learning and create positive and inclusive learning environments for their students and themselves. Taylor's research is focused on teacher preparation in classroom assessment, validity issues in large-scale testing, and high-quality performance-based assessment. She and Susan Nolen developed a portfolio-based classroom assessment course for teachers, which led to involvement in national and state design teams for portfolio-based teacher assessments. In addition to her academic career, Taylor has worked for testing companies in roles ranging from psychometrician to senior leadership and provided technical support to states for their large-scale testing programs. Taylor, with Nolen, coauthored *Classroom Assessment: Supporting Teaching and Learning in Real Classrooms* and authored *Validity and Validation* as part of the Oxford University Press "Understanding Statistics" book series.

Susan Bobbitt Nolen is professor emerita in the College of Education at the University of Washington. A teacher-educator and learning scientist, her research focuses on how the motivation to learn and take up new practices develops over time in social contexts. Research projects have included creating inclusive, engaging environments in university engineering programs and studying how and why teachers take up new practices, including assessment practices. With Catherine S. Taylor, she coauthored the book *Classroom Assessment: Supporting Teaching and Learning in Real Classrooms*.